David Bowie, Enid Blyton and the sun machine

Manchester University Press

'A dazzling act of literary-critical rebellion, a portrait of pandemic family life and an intimate exploration of personal history. This book illuminates the recent cultural past, casting new light on the lives of David Bowie and Enid Blyton, and infuses the future with the brightness of its invention and wit.'

Naomi Booth, author of *Exit Management*

'This is IT: the book you couldn't possibly have been waiting for. Enid Blyton and a telepathic dog called Timmy take a bow for Bowie, who nods at COVID in a disturbing Toyland called Earth. A magical series of ghostly lectures from beyond the graves of academe, all served with lashings of lingering veer. Once again, Royle has rung my bell.'

Timothy Morton, author of *The Stuff of Life*

'A fascinating mix of the autobiographical and the scholarly, woven deftly around two of the major cultural figures of recent times. Nicholas Royle mixes family and cultural histories in typically insightful and learned fashion.'

Andrew Maunder, author of *Enid Blyton: A Literary Life*

'*David Bowie, Enid Blyton and the sun machine* is about how literature and music burrows tunnels through our lives, connecting worlds of imagination and memory, connecting us to each other, creating new spaces for light to enter. Fragile and abundant, indulgent and generous, it is about how the "peculiar goings-on" in a *Famous Five* book or a stray line from a David Bowie song can change the way you see the world.'

Leah Kardos, author of *Blackstar Theory: The Last Works of David Bowie*

'Hugely pleasurable. An adventure in life-writing and a highly original celebration of the life-forces of art and song.'

Alison Light, author of *A Radical Romance*

'This is a fascinating book. Harassed academics will immediately relate to it, and so will all Enid Blyton and David Bowie fans, but it is about much more than any of those topics. It is an evocation of a time and a place, south London in the mid-twentieth century, the world that produced two such disparate figures as Blyton and Bowie, but also the author himself. I read it with great pleasure and interest.'

Gabriel Josipovici, author of *Forgetting*

'Words, sounds and silences are explored closely as Nicholas Royle explains the intertextuality between two writers we had never thought were linked so intimately.'

Nick Smart, editor of *David Bowie: Glamour* magazine

'The book's appeal and strength is the very unusual melding of Royle's own story, Enid Blyton, Beckenham, David Bowie (including "Memory of a Free Festival"), which all coalesce by pivoting time and geography.'

Stephen Finer, painter

'Written with a poet's playful ear and a sometimes fierce polemical rage. Nicholas Royle's book has moments that will make you gasp with wonder. Turns of thought, passion and story feel as if they come from a master film director or a virtuoso storyteller. Linking Blyton with Bowie in ways we never dreamt imaginable, Royle illumines the solar wonder of both figures – and reminds us of the glories that both inhabit and surround us all.'

Denis Flannery, editor of *The Cambridge Companion to David Bowie*

Other books by Nicholas Royle

Telepathy and Literature: Essays on the Reading Mind
Elizabeth Bowen and the Dissolution of the Novel (with Andrew Bennett)
After Derrida
E. M. Forster
The Uncanny
Jacques Derrida
How to Read Shakespeare
In Memory of Jacques Derrida
Quilt: A Novel
Veering: A Theory of Literature
An English Guide to Birdwatching: A Novel
Mother: A Memoir
Hélène Cixous: Dreamer, Realist, Analyst, Writing
An Introduction to Literature, Criticism and Theory, 6th edn (with Andrew Bennett)
This Thing Called Literature, 2nd edn (with Andrew Bennett)

David Bowie, Enid Blyton and the sun machine

Nicholas Royle

Manchester University Press

Published by Manchester University Press
Oxford Road, Manchester M13 9PL
www.manchesteruniversitypress.co.uk

British Library Cataloguing-in-Publication Data
A catalogue record for this book is available from the British Library

ISBN 978 1 5261 7365 2 hardback
ISBN 978 1 5261 7363 8 paperback

First published 2023

Typeset
by Cheshire Typesetting Ltd, Cuddington, Cheshire

For Matthew
On this short day of frost and sun

Contents

Contents

Illustrations

Photographs of David Bowie by Stephen Finer (courtesy of the artist) appear between pages 114 and 115

Will you come? Will you walk among the people of the Golden Years?

H. G. Wells

For if the exaltation lasted we should be blown like foam into the air. The stars would shine through us.

Virginia Woolf

The sun machine is coming down and we're gonna have a party.

David Bowie

Preface

Last night I saw Brett Morgen's *Moonage Daydream* with my friend Ben. It is a compelling visual and auditory blast that concludes with a mashup of the *Blackstar* video, with people gyrating and circling around to the chorus of 'Memory of a Free Festival' (*The sun machine is coming down* ...) and David Bowie dazzled by the light as he looks up, holding a book in his hand.

That juxtaposition – the book and the song of the sun machine – has uncanny affinities with the pages in front of you. It's about zeitgeist, chance and coincidence, the weird jammings of time, and what's about to be writ again. Like Morgen's film, this is a book about the sun machine, though in very different ways.

Other works that deal directly or indirectly with the sun machine appeared as I was writing. These also seemed like cases of what Mark Twain calls *mental telegraphy* – at once funny and spooky. In particular, there was Jeff Hilson's wonderful essay, 'The God-Awful Small Affair of the Invisible Organist', and Leah Kardos's brilliant book, *Blackstar Theory*. Along with Morgen's documentary and a proliferation of new books (from John O'Connell's *Bowie's Books* to *The Cambridge Companion to David Bowie*, ed. Denis Flannery), these works testify to a new appreciation of Bowie's importance – both culturally and intellectually – as a musician, artist and thinker.

Preface

David Bowie, Enid Blyton and the sun machine came, for me at least, out of nowhere, and I hope that it retains strong traces of its mysterious irruption. It is a book about how my life has been bound up with the music of David Bowie, especially in ways I hadn't realised. I never met Bowie in person, although I had the good fortune to see him in concert. The first time, at the Wembley Empire Pool in May 1976, was the greatest music event I ever experienced.

Bowie (David Jones) was born in 1947, a full ten years my senior. He was way ahead of me in so many respects. He was somewhere else. But then, like so many thousands of other people, I watched him singing 'Starman' on Top of the Pops in July 1972 and noted his way of pointing – at you, me, the listener, the watcher, the one 'picked on'. It is also the case that we both grew up in suburban South London; and we shared (as becomes evident in the pages ahead) a special relationship with Croydon, a town that lay geographically between us.

The age difference between me and Bowie was the same as between himself and his half-brother Terry Burns. My brother Simon (two years younger than me) loved Bowie's music too and my relationship to the songs is inextricably linked to him. This book is anchored in the countless hours we spent listening to Bowie's music, especially the earlier albums, from the two called *David Bowie* (the second of these now more familiarly known as *Space Oddity*) through to *Low*. Terry died in 1985. Simon died in 1986. Bowie's music is, for me, pervaded by this shared but absolutely incommensurable experience of a lost brother.

When Bowie died on 10 January 2016, I felt, like many others who never knew him, a sense of shock and intimate loss. Some major presence had gone out of the world. That week I was busy trying to write a lecture called 'Shakespeare's Foreplay', due to be delivered at Kingston University on 21 January. All the time I was writing about the playfulness of desire in *Romeo and Juliet* I was thinking about David Bowie. I couldn't see how to articulate this, but then right at the end of the lecture I found a connection.

Preface

It had to do with kissing. The kiss is something that Bowie – in 'Memory of a Free Festival', 'Five Years', 'Young Americans', 'Wild is the Wind', 'Heroes', 'Blackout' and elsewhere – makes sensuous, thrilling, even life-changing, like no one else in English history since Shakespeare.

Foreplay, I argued in my lecture, goes hand in hand with the kiss. I discussed the challenge of writing about how words touch, haunt our lips and play together in Shakespeare. I concluded by suggesting (my own voice now trembling) that this entails a sense of danger akin to what David Bowie calls *putting out fire with gasoline.* It's like playing with fire and gunpowder at the same time. As Shakespeare's Friar Laurence says:

> These violent delights have violent ends
> And in their triumph die, like fire and powder,
> Which as they kiss consume.

This is a book about love and memory, desire and loss. It's about listening, once again, to 'Five Years': *I kiss you, you're beautiful* … It's a book about today, and about Bowie as a singer and thinker of the now.

It is also a book about Enid Blyton. Putting Bowie and Blyton together was not my idea. The sense of a fundamental disjunction between them was, indeed, what started me off. But connections emerge.

David Bowie, Enid Blyton and the sun machine is not a work of fiction: I ask the reader not to be fooled by the fact that Part I takes the form of a third-person narrative. It's real life or what I call reality literature. Any fictional dimension is confined solely to the concluding section (Part IV), and even that is based on historical documents: my grandmother's journal of a trip to Paris and Switzerland in 1911, and a book published by my great-grandmother in 1920.

Most of all, I am interested in art and song, voice and storytelling. This is not an *academic* book – at least not, I hope, in any dry sense of that word. But it is about the question: What is education for? And, especially perhaps, what is a university for? Do we need universities, especially the contemporary, marketised, monetised, corporate institutions that seem in so many respects to embody what Bill Readings, in the mid-1990s, was already calling (in his powerful book of that title) *the university in ruins*? The sun machine, as I see it, offers an alternative to university education.

When Ben and I left the cinema at the end of *Moonage Daydream* and stood outside on the street, growing shivery in the late twilight, we were in accord that it was a fascinating film about the idea that art (both Bowie's and Morgen's) is about affirming chaos and *doing something with it*. We also agreed that our thoughts about the film – itself a stunning 'vortex of fragments' (in Bowie's phrase) – were in chaos too: we'd need a few days to sort things out. Alone on the short drive home over the South Downs, I found myself listening, twice, to two very different Bowie songs: the marvellous reworking of Pink Floyd's 'See Emily Play' on *Pin Ups*, and the spooky and mesmeric 'Sunday' on *Heathen*. (It was a Sunday, after all.)

And I also found myself reflecting on two seemingly unrelated words that come out of David Bowie's mouth during Morgen's documentary. The first word is *exhilaration*. Bowie's pronunciation brings out the hilarity lurking within. It is exhilaration 'at actually being alive'. It's the beating heart of life in the now, focusing especially on the intense pleasures and provocations of literature, painting and music. The second word is *extracurricular*. This has to do with what is outside the system, not part of the programme, not 'core' or 'central' to one's educational or to one's otherwise usual activities. Bowie uses the word in the context of painting, acting and mime, referring to things in his life that remain mysterious. *David Bowie, Enid Blyton and the sun machine* is a book about exhilaration and extracurricular thinking.

Part I

Living in the M times

When the virus came Daddy called it the Metamorphosis.

It was not yet spring. Everything stopped. The sun was shining. Then it was spring. The sun was still shining. Then it was summer.

Mummy and Daddy had two little boys and they all lived together in Sussex by the sea. They felt lucky. They lived in their own house. It had a garden. Also there was an outbuilding that was good to play in. It had weights and mats and an exercise bike and mirrors because it was Mummy's place to work out. Mummy was starting a new business. She was going to be a fitness coach.

Daddy worked in the university. He was older than Mummy.

Everything stopped. No one went anywhere. Planes were grounded. Roads were empty. Wildlife crept back. The air cleared. It was a time to think.

When a Black man was murdered trying to say *I can't breathe* it was obvious that the world was crying something huge.

Mummy and Daddy didn't tell the little boys about the Black man. They talked about it when they thought the children weren't listening. It was difficult to talk when they were all together in the same space practically the whole time. It was very difficult.

No one knew that Daddy called it the Metamorphosis. Not even Mummy. If she had known she would have scoffed *Pretentious!* But Daddy would say he only called it that so that he could tell her that they were living through the M times and then Mummy would laugh and it would be OK. But Mummy didn't laugh because Daddy never told her.

It wasn't necessary to wake up as a gigantic insect. All that was required was to wake up. It was a time to think.

The World Health Organisation declared: *The world is moving into uncharted waters.*

The university campus was closed. Daddy had to teach at home on his computer. He taught courses about literature. He had to give lectures to nobody. He had to record a lecture, press a button, then it was gone. It was called *asynchronous*. Daddy told Mummy it was like perching on the edge of an abyss and speaking into it. Mummy didn't seem impressed. Why would she be?

Mummy was upset about the outbuilding. It used to be called the workshop, but now it was called the studio. She was just about to begin her career, then everything stopped. Mummy was sad. Daddy was sad for Mummy.

Daddy gave several lectures over a short period. Each lecture was about a classic novel or a dead poet. But he kept straying to the topic of the virus. It was all anyone could do. Term ended and the students submitted their essays. Some of the essays were about books with no obvious connection to epidemics, pandemics, plagues or poxes of any description. Others discussed Defoe's *Journal of the Plague Year*, Camus's *The Plague*, Ballard's *The Drowned World* or Márquez's *Love in the Time of Cholera*. But all of the essays reflected on what was happening, even when they didn't mention it. The shadow of the M times fell across every page.

Everyone was in the same boat. Uncharted waters. The fear. The disappearance of painkillers and toilet paper and flour and pasta from the shops. The dread at what was coming.

Mummy and Daddy had to 'make it fun' for the children. They had to do this day after day after day after week after week after week. Daddy said it was like being catapulted back into the Second World War. Mummy couldn't relate to this.

Mummy was American. She didn't grow up with catapults or stories of the Blitz.

Another time Daddy said it was like the *Protect and Survive* programme: how to look after your loved ones in the event of nuclear holocaust. This was after Mummy had dug out a pamphlet in Daddy's study called *Sussex After the Bomb*. It had chapters called 'The Next War in Sussex', 'A Nuclear Explosion Over Newhaven' and 'What If We Survive?' This pamphlet was one of the things they'd found in a cupboard when they moved into the house more than ten years ago. Daddy had insisted on keeping it for historical interest. Mummy said Daddy's study already looked like Sussex After the Bomb. Mummy and Daddy laughed. This had been a long conversation by their standards. The children were downstairs on their iPads.

The iPads were a problem. Daddy knew that 'problem' was from the ancient Greek word for 'shield', but he didn't explain to Mummy that a computer screen was a form of shield that worked in two opposing ways – on the one hand, as a defence against the difficulty of living in the M times and, on the other, as an exacerbation of the difficulty of living in the M times. Daddy didn't tell Mummy this, not just because it would have required him to speak of the M times but because Mummy had a screen problem of her own. She was on her phone a lot, reading the news and searching for things and texting with her friends and even watching Netflix, and if Daddy said that the children's screens were a problem Mummy would take that as a veiled or not so veiled criticism of her own screen-dependency.

In any case Daddy had a screen-dependency too. *People in glass houses shouldn't throw stones*, Mummy would have said.

Mummy and Daddy were supposed to *home-school*. Zeph and Monty were supposed to be doing *online learning*. But Mummy and Daddy could no more have home-schooled their two little boys than psychoanalysed monkeys.

Sometimes Daddy tried to say things which were positive to the point of being, Mummy thought, utopian and stupid. Once he said: *The very ease with which 'furlough' has slipped into everyday speech shows that finance and economy, timeframes of work and expectations of remuneration, can be altered for good.* Mummy looked at him and said they should get a cat.

Monty was five. He was too young to have any clear grasp of what was happening. Not that anyone else had either. But for Monty the pandemic was very good. He hadn't been much enjoying his first full year at school and now he got to be with Mummy and Daddy, especially Mummy, *all the time.*

Zeph was eight. For him the pandemic was very bad. He missed school, he missed his teachers and friends, and he missed football as well. He used to play four times a week. He also watched it on TV. He was an avid reader of his weekly 'Match of the Day' magazine. He regarded the sport as his future.

Zeph wasn't his real name any more than Monty was his little brother's. Trying to *make it fun*, Mummy and Daddy encouraged the children to come up with different names for themselves. Daddy liked making up names, Mummy not so much.

Mummy was the daughter of a refugee. She had grown up bearing the scars of her father's losing his home and country and was still trying to process all of that and coming to see that she never would, because how can you, and she didn't particularly welcome suggestions or requests about switching names and identities: it was hard enough sticking with the one she had, the name and only thing her father had salvaged from the irreparable crime of having lost his home and country.

Daddy had some hand-puppets who had proper names and talked. There was a badger who was called Badger and he talked in a West Country accent. He sounded like another person that Daddy sometimes was, called Captain Lagoon. Daddy knew that Captain Lagoon and Badger could never meet because they had the same voice. Captain Lagoon appeared at the children's bathtime. He was a pirate. He travelled widely, especially around South America and Australasia. He had many encounters with crocodiles. He regularly lost an arm or leg. Captain Lagoon liked to drink rum. It helped him deal with the amputations.

There was an owl who was called Owl and he was Scottish. His accent was more West coast than East, but he also liked to mix things up, veer into clear Aberdeen or swoop into gruffest Glaswegian.

Then there was a mole who was called Mole. Mole had an English accent which was high and deep at the same time. Mole was a class-crosser and class-breaker, sometimes working class, sometimes middle, but also capable of high-end swank when the mood presented itself. Mole appeared to be 'he' and 'him', but these were not his preferred pronouns. Mole was feminine and mixed and multiple and wished people would appreciate that.

There were also two soft toys called Camel and Goat. Mummy called them stuffed animals, but Daddy said they were soft toys or possibly stuffed toys. They weren't *mounted taxidermy*. Mummy didn't care either way. If you were an American living in England you had to put up with all sorts of crap, obviously, and it seemed only to be getting worse and she *could care less*, she said. This was a deliberately funny thing that Mummy said, because Mummy knew that Daddy wouldn't say *could care less*. Daddy would say *couldn't care less*.

Camel was a camel, of course, and Goat was a goat. Goat had an upper-class English accent, and a pompous self-regard for the suppleness and dexterity of his vocabulary. He regularly vied with Mole over issues of lexicology and philology, orthography and etymology. Goat had a predilection for words like *desultory* and *capricious*, especially with a view to elevating his own importance.

Mole participated in these discussions, partly for his own amusement, partly with the thought of catching Goat out, but by and large Mole couldn't care less if he cared less or didn't care less. Just as he could care less if he ended a sentence with a preposition. There were so many more intriguing things to delve into.

Camel, on the other hand, wasn't on any hand, Daddy would remind his sons. Camel wasn't a puppet – he was a freely wandering soft toy animal spirit – very dreamy, pensive, and laid-back. He had a US accent but it wasn't always clear where he hailed from. Sometimes he was West coast, other times East, mid-East or Southern.

Camel liked to talk about the desert and the pleasures of having a hump and beautiful eyes and very long eyelashes and lying down and resting. He was very prone to lying down because he was so soft and floppy he couldn't in fact stand up. So he was most always or soon as possible laying hisself down in the ribbed sand of the bedcovers or sofa cushions and discoursing drowsily on the delights of warm sand and sleep and starlit dreams.

Every night Zeph listened to current or old football podcasts on the BBC. It was anodyne footie banter, transfer news, short interviews with players and other commentators. It was Zeph's way of getting to sleep. The football pundit equivalent of the Goldberg Variations.

Breakfast time was chaotic. So were other times. It was a very uneasy situation. This very uneasy situation had only been going on for a couple of weeks when, one morning at breakfast, Zeph concluded a sentence with the words: *multiple organ failure and coma.* He delivered it in an eerie, singsong fashion. Abrupt. Out of the blue.

Daddy quickly grasped what must have happened. The previous night he had tucked Zeph up in bed and said goodnight with a new podcast just starting up. As he was leaving the room, he heard the words: *So tell us: What* is *a virus?* And then some other voice began: *Okay, well, a virus is very, very small …*

Daddy hadn't given it any further thought at the time. It must have been some special programme about the pandemic. What Mummy and Daddy assumed was a bland podcast about footie had instilled in their son a vivid terror of *multiple organ failure and coma.*

From that moment on, Zeph lost all interest in football podcasts or magazines or even watching football on TV.

Within a week the young boy found a replacement. He became deeply knowledgeable and enthusiastic about motorbike racing. There was a TV channel that showed it practically the whole time. He watched MotoGP races over and over and over. He knew all the track locations and the dates of championships. He had the names of all the stars. All the stats. Stretching back decades.

Mummy recalled her Florida uncle's phrase for motorbike riders: *organ donors*. Mummy's uncle should know. He was a surgeon. Mummy and Daddy thought that, when it came to activities incurring ghastly injuries, motorbike-racing at 220 mph had the edge on playing football. But none of that seemed to matter to Zeph. He was just watching TV.

Zeph was clever. He acquired encyclopaedic knowledge just like that. At the age of four he could recite the whole of Hamlet's most famous soliloquy without a prompt. *To be or not to be* ... The whole speech, all the way until Ophelia comes in.

The early weeks of the M times were uncanny. Other people said *weird*. The media said *weird*. The world was living through *weird times*. But Daddy said *uncanny* was more apt. Daddy said it to Mummy in one of those oases when they had five minutes to themselves and it wasn't necessary for him to be Camel even if there was an oasis. It was in the bedroom.

– Is *oases* a word? Mummy wondered.

Daddy was unsure. Mummy compounded the uncertainty:

– When did anyone see a bunch of oases?

Mummy and Daddy loved one another very much. They agreed that they needed more oases. Longer, bigger ones. Without Camel or anyone else.

Daddy used up the oasis by telling Mummy stuff she knew already. He said that what *uncanny* has that *weird* doesn't have is a feeling of the strangely familiar. He told her that in his lectures he'd encouraged his students to think about the meaning of 'uncanny' in terms of *creepily uncomfortable recognition.* The familiar becoming unfamiliar, but also the unfamiliar itself as spookily *already known.*

He told her how he put it to the students: *We already knew about viruses – about SARS and AIDS and the Spanish flu, the bubonic plague and the Black Death. We knew about the wet markets of the Far East. About the gruesome inappropriateness of factory farming across the world, and about the decades-long mistreatment of animals of all kinds. The whole thing is –*

– *Un*-fucking-*canny*. That's what Mummy said, in a quiet voice, as Monty's steps sounded on the stairs.

Daddy thought even the weather was uncanny, but he wasn't going to tell Mummy that. He selected his adjectives with care. He said: *Freaky*. And then: *Gorgeous though.* To all the family he said, as if they really were on holiday:

– It's another lovely day, guys!

The weather wasn't like a flood or a hurricane. There was just non-stop glorious weather. Continuous sunshine without a break from early March onwards. England wasn't like this. It felt 'arranged'. Everybody had been dipped in the same fatal wash and the sun was compensation.

Mummy and Daddy agreed it was important to have routines. Twice a day they all went out together. In the morning they went to the seafront. Very soon Monty learned to ride a bike. He was so pleased with this new ability that he clucked like a chicken.

Mummy and Daddy walked while the boys cycled in the unremitting sunshine, a mile down to the end of the esplanade and then back again. In the afternoon they went to the park. Sometimes it was with Mummy and Daddy together. Other times it was with just Mummy or just Daddy.

Sometimes Daddy walked with one of the boys up the cliff path and over the now out-of-use golf course. Daddy recalled from reading a book of local history how, in the early 1940s, the whole area had been allotments for growing vegetables. It was part of the 'war effort'. Now the only visible sign of the war was a concrete pillbox some distance away, across the golf course in the Downs.

One day Daddy and Zeph went up the cliff path with a picnic. Picnics were not really allowed, but it was just a sandwich and some crisps and a drink for Zeph. A fillip for the outing. Suddenly as they were ascending the cliff, Zeph flew off, literally like the wind, like a horse racing before the wind. Not off the cliff, but in the other direction. He raced up and down and up again, over the sward, without warning, and didn't stop till he reached the pillbox. The boy quickly climbed on top and sat there like the caterpillar in *Alice in Wonderland.*

Zeph was too far off for his expression to be seen. But Daddy envisaged his son triumphant and delighted. Daddy started to cry. No one saw him. It was very sunny.

Other times Daddy played with Zeph and Monty in the studio. They built dens with mats and blankets and clambered about from bench to climbing frame to bench. Daddy glanced awkwardly at his ageing, bulky reflection in the wall of mirrors.

Mummy liked to have an hour or so by herself each day in the studio, doing her fitness exercises, and that was one of the periods when Daddy was in charge. Daddy needed time each day to do his university work and then Mummy was in charge. Often it was easiest at these times for them to let Zeph and Monty play on their iPads. But they also tried to encourage other activities: drawing, painting, Lego, Play-Doh, wooden building blocks.

Sometimes Daddy fetched up Mole and other creatures. Sometimes Mummy baked cookies. Sometimes the children watched something on TV, such as Story Bots or a nature documentary, but Mummy and Daddy knew this wasn't easing the problem of screen-dependency.

Every day was frazzling. At last dusk came and the children were in bed unconscious. Mummy and Daddy would talk for a few minutes about how exhausted they were, and about some practicality or other regarding the day just gone or the day to come.

Then Mummy went to bed and Daddy tried to switch off. He retreated to the kitchen. He turned down the lights, poured a drink and listened to David Bowie. The kitchen was built as an extension separate from the rest of the house, so the music could be loud without disturbing anyone. Daddy listened to David Bowie night after night after night.

Minutes, weeks, days, months seemed to pack up in a tiny tinder box, because time was now M time. All words for time became strange. Mummy and Daddy knew that all words for time had always been strange, but now they were having a new kind of relationship with it. Like an animal that had gone to sleep. You couldn't wake it up. You could no longer pretend you knew what you were talking about when you referred to days of the week or hours of the day or months of the year.

But still the sun was shining and still there was the virus. The virus was little and little was known. It was so little that, according to one mathematician, all the specimens of it in the whole world could be fitted into the space of a single Coke can. It was so little that some people just couldn't get their heads around the thing at all and didn't believe it existed. Mummy and Daddy knew that it was real and scary.

The routine Mummy and Daddy developed included shopping and cooking. Mummy did both. Before the M times, Daddy often shopped and cooked as well. Mummy and Daddy did not talk about this new division of responsibilities. This was because Mummy was sad that she couldn't start her new business as a fitness coach and Daddy had to work to make money and he believed that she felt, to justify her existence, she had to do the shopping and the cooking.

Daddy would like to have told Mummy that she didn't need to justify her existence because Daddy loved Mummy very much and it wouldn't matter if she sat down in a ditch all day and did nothing he would still love her.

When Mummy came home from shopping and Daddy called out *Hello!* he knew straightaway how she was. If she called back

Hello or *Hiya* she was OK, but if she called back *Hola!* in Spanish, with a silent 'h', Daddy knew Mummy was sad.

Occasionally Zeph and Monty played alone together. But it never lasted long. The endless bickering of young brothers. Flaring up at the smallest thing.

Zeph would put his hands round Monty's neck. Or he would come up unannounced and kick Monty vigorously. Then he would walk back to his own seat, calm as you like, and start playing again on his iPad. Monty was built like a miniature ox. He would wait. A few seconds. Or several minutes. Then he would wander over and thump his older brother repeatedly on the back.

It made Mummy and Daddy sad. They told the children that hitting and kicking were not OK. They had to tell them this sometimes several times a day. It was a very difficult situation.

Zeph was remarkably loquacious from a very young age. Monty was always stumbling along behind. But what Monty lacked in linguistic know-how, he made up for with emotional articulacy. He was besotted with his older brother. But for Zeph, as Mummy and Daddy's firstborn, the arrival of a baby brother had been and remained a source of resentment. Zeph wanted someone to *put him in the garbage*. Or *back in the sewer*. Anywhere but *sharing our house*.

One day Monty asked his brother as directly as his words allowed: *Why do you don't love me?* To Mummy and Daddy it felt as if the hardest question in the history of humanity had been formulated anew. Why do you don't? Why do you don't like Black people? Why do you don't like Jews? Why do you don't like Palestinians? *Why do you don't?*

Mummy and Daddy slept in separate rooms because Monty slept with Mummy and anyway Daddy snored and would have kept everyone awake. Mummy was sleep-deprived. She could scarcely get an hour straight without being woken up by Monty. Sometimes he would wake Mummy and ask in the middle of the night: *Did you have any good dreams yet, Mummy?*

Monty always slept naked. He was elementally beautiful, like a dark sweet goblin. Zeph was paler-skinned and perfect as an elf. He slept in his own bed, marvellously motionless. But Monty never kept still. He always needed to occupy the centre of the bed and kicked and clambered and slid over his bed-fellow, sometimes a laborious lobster, at other times a dream-speeding octopus.

Mummy put a mattress on the floor and tried to fool him into sleeping on that. For the first two nights Monty's body failed to register that he hadn't spent the night in the same bed as Mummy. *Did I kick you in the night, Mummy?* he asked for the second day running. After that he realised the trick and Mummy had to give up.

Monty was a dreamer. He liked to sit or stand somewhere and *have a dream.* There would be a certain place on the beach or corner of the park, a tree he'd stand under, or a bush he'd go into. He'd go there and have a dream, sometimes for twenty minutes or more at a time.

No one in the family became ill with the virus. The plague that fell on their house had no name. It was an interior quietness. Every day the kitchen was full of sunlight and the boys sat bolted to their screens. Hour after hour after hour. Mummy and Daddy thought about the report a social worker gazing on this domestic scene might compile. They drew a blank.

What are we doing? Mummy and Daddy opened and closed their mouths without actually saying these words. Like goldfish going round and round and round in a sunlit bowl.

In the wake of a career-launch resembling a private Space Shuttle *Columbia*, Mummy wasn't coping well. Interrupted sleep also took its toll. She was spending more and more time reading books about psychotherapy. Some of the titles were more hopeful than others: *Childhood Disrupted*, *The Meaning of Pain*, *Good Reasons for Bad Feelings*, *I'm OK – You're OK* … Daddy felt worried that Mummy wasn't getting the kind of help from him that she needed and deserved.

Daddy wasn't doing a great deal better. His teaching and examining duties had ended for the year. He was supposed to be pursuing his research. He had a contract with an academic press to write a book about 'novel theory'. But he couldn't lift a finger.

Then the university announced a voluntary severance scheme. Daddy was invited to talk to his head of department. He told Mummy about it in a jokey, dismissive way. But he found himself seriously contemplating it.

The way Daddy went about this was weird. That was the word Mummy used when they found him upstairs in his study, one afternoon, sitting alone but talking ten to the dozen.

Daddy thought Mummy and the boys were still at the park. He was so immersed in his contemplating that he didn't hear the key in the front door.

– Who is Daddy talking to upstairs?

Daddy was chairing a symposium. It was not an online university event. He was alone in his armchair with the Mob (Mole, Owl, Badger and the others). He was being questioned about his job and the 'hostile environment' of his workplace. He was asking each of the creatures in turn what they thought of VS (voluntary severance). Should Daddy accept the invitation to end his career?

Goat kept referring to VS as VH: he had somehow misconstrued the acronym as 'voluntary halal'. Mole took pleasure in putting him right.

At any rate Goat was vociferous in propounding the case for carrying on, regardless of the rocky terrain. There were always new peaks and vistas to encounter. All kinds of fresh challenges to chew on.

Mole took a dim view of that, as alas he had to do of everything, and argued that Daddy should join him in his burrow. Daddy was welcome to come and take a subterranean vacation with Mole for as long as he wished. An underground cruise.

– Oh aye? As long as a piece of string? wondered Owl.

– As long as Ariadne's thread, replied Mole.

Badger pushed a boisterous but persuasive vision of the life-changing opportunities of VS. It would be like living in a world where culls were no more. *Just consider all the rooting and rummaging! Imagine the sheer mental freedom days VS would offer!* Badger liked calling it by this acronym, as if voluntary severance were some Very Strong cider full of bits of Cornish straw, to be sampled with pleasure before a jolly lolloping back in the after-hours, along a gurgling stream lit up by glow-worms, to the undisturbed peace of his woodland sett.

Daddy heard Mummy and the boys coming upstairs but he didn't see the point of stopping.

– What are you doing? the boys asked eagerly.

– Weird, said Mummy.

Mummy and Daddy needed to take hold of the situation. This is what Mummy thought and she told Daddy and Daddy agreed. Mummy could see that Daddy was struggling with this question of voluntary severance, but she didn't say anything.

*

That's when Enid Blyton showed up.

She descended on the house in the form of a box-set: all twenty-two of the *Famous Five* books. Mummy brought it into the kitchen one morning. She told Daddy it had been upstairs for months. Mummy did this with things. She ordered stuff online and when it came she hid it away somewhere like a squirrel. *Just waiting for the right moment* (she smiled).

Zeph was old enough to read by himself, but he still liked being read to. Monty struggled to write his own name, but he loved listening.

So began the reign of Enid Blyton.

Mummy and Daddy would each read a couple of chapters of a *Famous Five* book aloud each morning. Then they would read more in the afternoon. The boys were captivated. It became their bedtime reading too. Mummy and Daddy would take turns, reading two or three chapters to one or other of the boys last thing in the evening. They would go to sleep with Blyton and wake up with Blyton.

Zeph and Monty loved every book. Mummy could feel their excitement as she read from one paragraph to the next. The sheer pull of the storytelling. The way Blyton drew them into the sensuous fearful pleasure of a face at the window or a peculiar noise in the dark. Mummy was impressed. Growing up in America, she had never even heard of Enid Blyton.

Daddy knew the *Famous Five* books from his boyhood, but what exactly did 'knowing' them mean? He could hardly remember anything about them. If asked, he couldn't even have listed the names of the Five. It came as a complete surprise to him that one of them was a dog.

At first a complete surprise. But all of that changed too. It was part of the M times.

The reign of Blyton trumped the iPads. Mummy and Daddy felt relief and even amazement. But then began a new form of blur. They would read the opening chapters of one *Famous Five* book to one child, and then might read it again later the same day to the other. Or Daddy would have to pick up where Mummy had got to, or Mummy, Daddy, having missed the preceding chapters. Before very long they were no longer reading them in order and lost track of which ones they hadn't read. Mummy and Daddy would finish reading one volume and start another they'd already completed.

The sense of disarray deepened when the audiobooks by Jan Francis arrived. In the sun-filled kitchen, her rendition of one or other of the books became an ongoing daily service. But having Jan Francis in the house did not release Mummy and Daddy from their *Famous Five* reading duties. They were still required to read before bed and at other times of the day.

In some ways the presence of Jan Francis merely intensified the feeling of chaos, for Jan Francis had no sense whatever of whether she was reading them in order or which one she had read before. She read the books very well, but she couldn't for a moment be trusted to remember and get things straight. So now there might be several *Famous Five* books being read aloud on any given day. The house was crazy with the sound of Blyton.

Throughout these weeks, Daddy was weighed down with the question of voluntary severance. It felt like a new version of some ancient torture, like the wooden horse or Judas cradle. The weights being placed on Daddy's body were imaginary, but it reminded him of the historical phenomenon of being 'pressed to death'.

But then Daddy had a moment. He was in the studio with his sons. He'd helped build them a den with tunnels. Foam mats and blankets draped across benches. The boys were in seventh heaven. Crawling about and shouting and hiding from one another. Adjusting and rearranging the den.

Daddy sat in a deckchair. He saw himself in the wall of mirrors that ran down one side of the studio. Black hoodie and black joggers. He looked himself in the eye. He remembered David Bowie at the Wembley Empire Pool in May 1976. The introduction to 'Station to Station' underway. An engulfment of sound. Stage smoke rising and swirling in the air.

Then Bowie appeared. His presence sparking delirium. But the performer was detached from all of that. He reposed. Smoking a Gitane. Resting on one elbow on the floor. Dragging modishly on his cigarette until it was time to sing. The return of the thin white duke.

Now Bowie had been dead for several years, and Daddy himself was growing old. Life was not realistic. Daddy gazed into the mirror. He saw an ancient ship being readied for departure. He saw the sunlight on the weathered sails, the glittering but battered prow. And then he saw the boy. Himself. Back in the hall of mirrors at Madame Tussaud's with his little brother. In a den of childhood. Crystalline. Transparent.

Daddy had pulled his hoodie down over his face. One of his children was calling. Daddy's pale white knuckles clutched the hood and kept it held down over his face. Zeph exclaimed: *Your bony hands are no match for the modern technology of* mine!

Under the hood in tears in the dark as his young sons were laughing and trying to prise their way in to see, Daddy's future came clear. Quick as a pole-position MotoGP rider out of the bend into the final straight he saw what he had to do. He must voluntarily sever himself. To preserve his own sanity and the rest of the family's.

Now the hood was off, like the back ripped from a crab. A triumph of modern technology. The young boys were still laughing. They were excited. Monty was struggling to tell Daddy about how they *builded* the den again and Zeph was giving his own report, loquacious, grammatical, at three times the speed.

When Daddy told Mummy about his decision, the tears shot out of her eyes, as if they'd all been hiding in cupboards and under tables and now could come out. But as Daddy went on talking, she saw how it could be right. Daddy would be able to spend more time with the children and, once a vaccine was discovered and the world returned to some semblance of what it used to be, Mummy would get her career as a fitness coach off the ground. With her earnings, and his severance package and modest pension, they could make ends meet.

– There'll still be mountains to climb, she said, thinking this suddenly funny, as if they were seasoned alpinists who'd just heard that Mount Everest had been blown up.

– You sound like Goat, Daddy said, and Mummy laughed.

Daddy went through the appropriate hoops and virtual meetings on Zoom. He signed the relevant documents. He would leave the university just before the start of autumn term. He would never give another class or lecture again in his life.

After Daddy's decision, Mummy didn't feel so sad any more. But Daddy began to be sad in a way Mummy had never witnessed. It was not like him. He seemed very down. Mummy was worried.

But then an idea wafted in, like a strange bird. Mummy had taken the boys for a bike ride along the seafront. Daddy was standing alone in the warm late summer sunshine, in the courtyard at the back of the house, admiring the young olive trees in big old pots and the wild array of red and pink roses that festooned one end of the garden.

That afternoon in the kitchen the creatures made Daddy's idea public. To get everyone's attention, Goat cleared his throat at some length. Mummy managed only to half-listen, as she was making chocolate chip cookies. Zeph and Monty enjoyed the animals' press conference, without really following what it was about.

Goat explained, in a rather grave but authoritative tone, that Daddy was *planning to deliver a series of virtual or electronic lectures … Amounting*, he added with all possible gravity, *to a single, extended valedictory speech*.

– It'll be his final statement, Mole enthused.

– He'll be blethering till the cows come home! cried Owl.

Monty wanted to know what Badger and Camel had to say.

– Let there be worms! exclaimed Mole.

– We should have ourselves a party, Badger now exclaimed. I'm for some of that excellent VS cider!

Then Camel floppily interjected that he too was *up – or down – for a party*, as he hadn't *touched a drop* – of water, that is – *in donkey's years*.

Goat queried Camel's *asinine lingo* but concurred that refreshments were in order.

Then Owl called for *a pint of heavy* and something about *palling at a hootenanny*.

– Hoot what? asked Goat, indignantly.

Daddy poured lemonade for the boys, and a Distillers Edition Glenkinchie with a little water for himself. Even Mummy had a sip. Zeph and Monty tucked into delicious oven-warm cookies, oblivious, while Mole sought to hammer out, really for Mummy's ears only, details of how quickly the lectures could be put together and what time of day would be most practical for Daddy to deliver them.

The university campus was closed and out of bounds, but there was nothing to stop a lecturer entering the premises remotely. It was perfectly possible to sit in the peace and quiet of one's own home and record some talks using the university's Panopto technology and publish them to students. There was no reason why Daddy should prepare any lectures for anyone at all. But that was precisely the appeal.

Part II

A sense of the ending

Memory of a free festival (first lecture)

Hello everyone. I don't know if it's Good morning or Good night. No matter. I'd like to warmly welcome you to 'Memory of a free festival', the first in this farewell lecture series. Farewell lectures indeed!

You are all familiar with trigger and content warnings. I hereby issue as many as you care to imagine. You may think I'm joking, but please note the possibility of being offended, disturbed, reduced to tears or terrified at any time. What did you want to study literature for otherwise? Literature is indissociable from madness. Surely you knew at least vaguely what you were letting yourself in for? Why else come to this institution, at which I have had the honour of spending most of my teaching life, a university with what it calls a 'distinguished tradition' of 'disruptive and experimental interventions'? If I had to give out trigger or content warnings in a rigorous and considered manner, I'd never get the lecture underway.

I therefore dispense with all of that, except to add just one personal caveat. Assume I have departed. Yes, folks, consider me well and truly gone. It's not important whether my initial resting place was the special mortuary facility lately installed on campus for strictly non-academic pandemic purposes, or my final the lovely churchyard at Bishopstone, Widworthy, Honiton or other venue of passionate interest to me. I think you can safely ignore any difference between initial and final in this context.

I would just say, however, that *location* is going to be a focal point for our concerns. Among other things, this question: Do people follow people around, or do places follow people?

Another focus has to do with voice – my voice, your voice, the voice or voices one hears or thinks one hears in a piece of literature. This means dealing with *prosopopoeia* (some of you, I suspect, may have heard me use that term before), the rhetorical figure for the 'voice from beyond the grave'. Literature and prosopopoeia are inseparable bed-fellows. Queer or straight as you wish. Prosopopoeia is an ancient Greek word that literally means 'giving or making a face or mask', 'forming or making a person'.

Is this some tasteless joke about masking up and pandemic reality, you may be wondering. But I'm not just messing about. A classic form of prosopopoeia would be an epitaph, such as the words that appear on the gravestone of the comedian and writer Spike Milligan (1918–2002) in St Thomas Churchyard at Winchelsea, in East Sussex: 'I *told* you I was ill.'

In fact the inscription is in Irish, which presumably made it more acceptable to the church authorities who permitted it to appear on his tombstone. Some of you may also have come across Milligan's remark upon hearing of the death of his friend and former fellow Goon Show member, the celebrated Welsh comedian and singer Harry Secombe (1921–2001): 'I'm glad he died before me, because I didn't want him to sing at my funeral.'

These quips are comical, because recognisably fictive. You don't get to make a snippy post-mortem remark about your prior state of ill-health, any more than you get to oversee the ceremonial proceedings (or lack thereof) after you've popped your clogs. You can rate your professor, but you can't rate your own funeral. Milligan's witticisms are resonant in another way: they invite us to think about the idea that literature – whether fiction, poetry or autobiography – is prosopopoeia. Literature is about the resurrection of the dead. It's about the way the voice or voices of the dead return. Or keep talking.

And so there should be no cause for any agitation if you're supposing that the voice addressing you at this moment is that of a dead person. As my father said to me on the eve of his death: *These things happen from time to time.*

Such is the nature of the asynchronous lecture. Think of me as a teacher *condamné*, a virtual interlocutory device, a ghost academic. If I'm not actually, I might as well be, in the next dimension. On the plus side, with an asynchronous session like this, we're not constrained by space. We don't have to vacate the lecture theatre after fifty minutes to enable the next lecturer and next group of students to come in. We can slow down, for example, and listen to some music.

So my thought is to play a song or piece of music occasionally. In each case, obviously, you can click and skip if you want. As you may be aware, especially in the context of the pandemic, senior management – here and elsewhere across the UK – has been encouraging lecturers to trial much shorter sessions – mini-lectures of fifteen or twenty minutes. University managers seem to think that your attention span is a threatened species, in rapid decline.

I'm not convinced by this. I suspect that there is a reason why lectures tend to be fifty minutes long, just like sessions with a psychotherapist. But if you want to arrest me, so to speak, of course you can do it, at any moment, at the flick of a switch. In any case I'll do my best not to bore you. Indeed, I hope to stimulate, entertain and even at moments amuse you.

These lectures are about the love of reading and about that peculiar, slippery thing called literature. They are about what E. M. Forster called, in his remarkable eponymous book of 1927, *aspects of the novel.* I want to dig down and explore further something that also fascinated Forster, namely the relationship between literature and music, the musicality of language, rhythm and refrain, the lyrical and enchanting dimensions of voice and writing. In this chthonic space, distinctions between the novel, children's books, autobiography and memoir dissolve.

I will be looking, in particular, at one writer and one musician. The writer is Enid Blyton. The musician is David Bowie. And then there'll also be a third, mystery guest, later on.

The title of this lecture series is *A Sense of the Ending*. The phrase is in playful homage to Frank Kermode's celebrated book of 1967, *The Sense of an Ending: Studies in the Theory of Fiction*. Obviously I have already given away a sense of the ending in divulging the title, but, as David Bowie sang, at the end of his life, *I can't give everything away*.

The homage to Kermode is playful, as I said. I've got his phrase slightly askew: 'a sense of the ending' is not the same as 'the sense of an ending'. It's meant as an affectionate riposte. It's an RIP riposte, unfortunately, since Sir Frank (as he came to be known) passed away in 2010. He was the examiner of my PhD, back in 1984, and practically the only thing he wrote in the margins of its 400-plus pages – admittedly it was a long and dreary opus, about imagination, war and apocalypse in the later poetry of Wallace Stevens – was to wrongly correct the spelling of 'unnamable' to 'unnameable' (with an 'e' before the 'able'), with regard to Samuel Beckett's very funny book of that title.

I hope that these lectures might provide you with some useful threads or guide-ropes to hold on to. *It's confusing these days*. Then again, I hope they won't make you feel like mere rock-climbers, clambering slowly upward, pitching and scrambling and gronking, where each new lecture in the series feels like another ascent, and the whole experience becomes just a continual struggle for ascents of the ending. In fact, I am at least equally interested in the joy of falling, in the descent or descents of an ending.

Certain Bowie songs stick in my mind with diamond needle sharpness. Certain turns in sound and vision. Melodic shifts. Lyrical veerings. Solitude lifting. There's the line, for example, that engulfs 'Memory of a Free Festival' – which I'm going to play to you in a moment. It's about *feel*. As Bruce Robb says: Bowie is 'all about feel'. 'Feel' is about the present, but also the future – about what Timothy Morton calls 'future feel'.

A sense of the ending

I began with prosopopoeia, the idea of the voice-from-beyond. Everyone is, in a way – not to put it too gravely (ha ha) – already posthumous, but some people are more attuned to this than others. Bowie's preoccupation with the idea that 'we are the dead' runs all through his work, right up to *Blackstar*, the album whose release coincided with his death and which has been too hastily and crudely categorised as 'death art'.

If you want to explore this topic in greater detail, I recommend Leah Kardos's *Blackstar Theory: The Last Works of David Bowie*. Her book began as a study of 'death art' – but then she came to realise it was really about *life art*. Bowie was, by his own account, 'always aware [of] death' and this gave him a 'feeling of buoyancy' that led to a lifetime of 'colossal, obsessive activity'. We are dead a lot longer than we are alive. *Moondust will cover you*. All art of any interest is death art, impelled by the passions of life. When the absurd Russell Harty asked him who or what he worshipped, Bowie said simply: 'Life. I worship life.'

'Memory of a Free Festival' was recorded in September 1969, a few weeks after a festival that Bowie co-organised in his hometown in Kent on 16 August. The recording I'm going to play is the 2019 remix by Tony Visconti. Bowie is playing the harmonium at the start. Apparently he sang and played the whole thing in one take. Flawless – right down to the playful, slightly John Lennonish rhetorical question at the beginning about whether to announce the title. The crowd of forty or so people at the end, including Marc Bolan (then of Tyrannosaurus Rex), had also attended the actual festival the previous month.

'Memory of a Free Festival' is upbeat – 'bliss', 'ecstasy' and 'heaven' all feature here. Bowie does something richly interesting, at once fuzzy and profound, in suggesting that the machines that start appearing in the sky and anticipate the descent of the sun machine in the second half of the song emerge out of a sense of joy and love that can be compared to *satori*. *Satori must be something just the same*: it's *not* satori, it's different from satori, but it is something *just the same.* This line offers a fine illustration of Bowie's singularity: he is a singer-thinker not of identity or identifications, but of uncanny resemblances. 'Satori', as Jack Kerouac comments in his book *Satori in Paris* (published three years earlier, in 1966), is the Japanese word for 'sudden illumination', 'sudden awakening' or simply 'kick in the eye'. The sun machine is Bowie's figure of illumination or enlightenment, strangely like – but different from – satori.

'Memory of a Free Festival' is also, at the same time, an extraordinary song of mourning. It is *in memory* – not only of the festival the preceding month, but more particularly of Bowie's beloved father, John Jones, whose funeral took place five days before the festival. 'Memory of a Free Festival' is a love song and a song of grief. There is a lot of kissing in it. It is a song about the tenderness and longing of the kiss.

Dear as remember'd kisses after death, as Tennyson says in his stunning little poem 'Tears, Idle Tears'.

And it's a song about becoming 'unchained': the association with slavery is clear. Likewise, because it's the end of the sixties – literally, heading into its final months – it's difficult not to sense also in this song the end of an era, the end of something more than a summer festival or summer of festivals. This Bowie festival happened, in fact, the same weekend as another free festival, the biggest of all time, namely Woodstock, in upstate New York.

'Memory of a Free Festival' is a song about music as coming, as event. There is a sun machine. And it is coming down. It's like the planetary collision at the end of Lars von Trier's film *Melancholia*, but without the lugubriosity. Bowie's song gives us a quite different sense of the ending. Something big is ending – but something new is coming.

[Play David Bowie, 'Memory of a Free Festival']

The song is *about* a sun machine, but it also aspires to *be* the sun machine that it is about. It recalls Walter Pater's contention (in his book *The Renaissance*, first published in 1873) that *All art constantly aspires towards the condition of music.* 'Memory of a Free Festival' is about the eerie beauty of what Beethoven called *hearing in heaven.* You know that Beethoven was quite deaf at the end of his life and his last words were 'I shall hear in heaven.' (In German, obviously: he wouldn't have said this in English.) In any case, even if you've never really listened to Beethoven's music, I expect you've heard that one: 'I shall hear in heaven.'

Not that we need construe heaven in terms of 24/7 music. As Lawrence Ferlinghetti explains in *A Coney Island of the Mind*:

> because even in heaven
> they don't sing
> all the time

Silence might be heavenly too. At any rate, attunement to silence will be a recurring focus in these lectures, especially in the context of Bowie's music.

There is something demonic about the repetition of the line about the sun machine in the second half of 'Memory of a Free Festival'. We might suppose that it's also a son machine. It's spelt 's-u-n', but the homophone of 's-o-n' is there to be heard. Some listeners feel a close connection between the second part of the song and the chant in the Beatles' 'Hey Jude', which came out a year earlier, but Bowie's song is foreboding in a quite different way. It's closer to the hypnotic, haunting quality of Pink Floyd's 'Set the Controls for the Heart of the Sun' (1968). But with Bowie there is a kind of *activated* thinking and feeling that *performs* the premonitory, forecasting and conjecturing. Roger Waters' song is about getting ready, setting the controls, but Bowie's is about the event, in its emergence.

The sun machine is cryptic. We are not really told what it is. It has to do with coming, with a movement of descent. But it's also about the conjunction and the party. There's something delirious in the promise – of a party that is going to happen. In this respect it seems to prefigure a haunting Talking Heads song that appeared about ten years later, called 'Heaven' – the idea of a song that would be ecstatically shared, at a kind of dream party. A party to come.

There's another intriguing contemporary correspondence. This is with the Beatles album, *Abbey Road*, released in the same month that Bowie first recorded his song. 'Here Comes the Sun' and 'Sun King', on *Abbey Road*, are also concerned with the idea of the sun coming. I don't know if this is just coincidental or not.

What is coincidence? That is a question at the heart of art and song, even if it's very little discussed. Songwriters of course quote other songs in a more or less obvious or deliberate way – and Bowie, as everyone knows, was a great nicker. He was constantly assimilating and adapting stuff from others. This is what makes him such 'a sponge for the zeitgeist'. But there is also, I think, the idea of something less certain, more dreamy, less identity-driven. This is the idea that music reverberates, songs sing to each other, like ghostly birds, over alien acoustic territories, unknowing.

In this opening lecture, I want to explore the idea of a sun machine as a way of approaching literature. I have in mind Pater's idea of 'the condition of music' – that is to say, the experience of voice, the sound effects of language, the musicality of poetry and fiction. This is about the words, but also the pauses and interludes, rhythm and repetition. When it comes to writing, it's all a matter of rhythm, as Virginia Woolf says in one of her essays. Or perhaps it's in one of her diaries – I can't remember. And I'm afraid I don't have the relevant book to hand.

But if you can home in on it, if you can pick up this rhythm or let this rhythm pick you up – because that's the thing, in a sense it's really not about *you*, at all …

What is a sun machine? It's something at once visual and auditory, even – I'm tempted to suggest – a kind of *phantasmagoric synaesthesia* – but let's not get bogged down in that for now. I want to invite you to consider the proposition that a novel can be a sun machine. I'm not talking about reading on a sun-drenched beach or lounging in a comfy chair on a bright patio, although that kind of pleasure is certainly part of it.

Let me put it this way. You know sometimes when you read a novel …

Oh but hang on – do you? I mean: *do you*, just, sometimes, *read a novel*? You're studying English literature here at the university, so sometimes you read novels, right?

It's not certain. I accept that. Some people come and study for three years and only ever read – well, not even the novels they're 'required' to read. I mean, for instance, when Michael Gove studied English Literature at university, do you think he read any books? If he did, they appear to have left no impression. How otherwise to explain his determination to turn English Literature, as a subject at GCSE and A level, into a box-ticking dead-end? How to construe his public service as Secretary of State for Education, if not as a rejection of the virtues of reading, imagination and free-ranging critical thinking that go with the serious study of literature? I think we have to give Mr Gove the benefit of the doubt and accept that he *never really read a work of literature in his life*. Or alternatively, perhaps he did, he read a novel and was so triggered and traumatised that he could never read anything literary again. Either way, we can reasonably suppose that the Right Honourable gentleman wouldn't know the difference between a sun machine and a hole in the ground.

Let me just emphasise that this is not a party-political remark. Every UK government over the past twenty years or more has grotesquely mishandled the matter of education, especially in the field of what is called the humanities. I have written very few letters to national newspaper editors. But there was a time when the hollowness and hypocrisy of the Labourite mantra 'Education, education, education' led me to submit the following one-liner: 'Education, er, education, maybe, education, not.' This was possibly the highest point of my publishing career, as the letter appeared not only in *The Guardian* but was also taken up and quoted in *The Times*. And all I'd contributed to the debate was *er, maybe, not.* Anyhow, enough!

And then there are people who simply *can't* read a novel by Charles Dickens, say, or George Eliot. Not to mention some more obscure and challenging, experimental 'modernist' production by James Joyce or Jean Rhys. It's just beyond them. This lamentable affliction may apply to you. If so, I'm sorry.

But don't fret. You're not alone. Perhaps you feel bad about it, but that's OK. You should feel bad. Sometimes it's important to feel bad. You'll get there. I freely admit that I was the same. When I was an undergraduate, I read virtually nothing. It was ridiculous. Indeed it was so ridiculous, it was so bad that, literally the day after I'd finished my final year exams as an undergraduate, I decided it was time to start reading.

But this didn't mean I carried out my decision. Alas, no. On the contrary. It was mere subterfuge. A way of tricking myself into taking myself seriously. I made the decision and then went inter-railing. On what in the hifalutin' terminology of the eighteenth century would have been called a European Tour. But this was the summer of 1979, not 1799. I travelled by train with a backpack, a couple of friends and very little money to France, then Switzerland and Italy, through Yugoslavia (as it was then called) to Greece, ending up for a week on the island of Naxos before meandering back to England via West Germany (as it was then called) and France again, then to my parents' house in Surrey.

In all that time I do not recall reading anything whatsoever. The only book I remember was the one my companion, Richard, had with him when we were in Greece: Carl Jung's *Memories, Dreams, Reflections*. I didn't read it. Indeed, it would be a good while before I really started reading anything.

But by the time I began teaching, I'd come to see that reading is more or less the most vital thing a person can do. Unfortunately,

British governments have long taken a different view of the matter and as a result they have facilitated a major, ongoing disaster. It's called the education system.

But that's not my subject here. Or rather it *is*, obviously. How could it not be? For a start, how could I pretend, at the conclusion of several decades of university teaching, not to be concerned that you might – quite mistakenly – consider everything I am saying here to be somehow in league with, or even in defence of, this 'education system'?

One of the drawbacks with the asynchronous online lecture is that I can see my words but I can't see you and you can listen to me but you can't *see* my words, and therefore you are perhaps more liable to miss those moments (which in truth are going on all the time) when I insert – not scare quotes, because, as I hope I've already made clear, I don't wish gratuitously to scare anyone at all – but 'quote unquote' marks in order to signal not only critical caution but often also, I confess, derision, as was the case a couple of minutes ago when I used the word 'modernist', and as I do with my voice, if you're willing to tune into this, when I suffer to cross my lips the phrase 'education system'.

No one should be able to say 'education system' without wanting to throw up, or without feeling compelled to do penance in some Ancient-Mariner-like solitary confinement with icebergs high as tower-blocks floating by and collapsing in their face. 'Education system' is a criminal phrase. There are plenty of sick locutions in day-to-day English. Just at this moment I think, for example, of my local fish and chip shop's 'veggie options' (as if eating the dead bodies of other animals was the natural default position), or capitalist schemers' talk of 'carbon offsetting', or my employer's term with respect to my own rapidly approaching joblessness, 'voluntary severance'.

But as a form of linguistic poison, 'education system', in its very dryness, takes the biscuit. Whoever thought they could get away with putting these two words next to one another? I tell you that my whole life as a teacher and researcher has been spent in resistance to anyone and anything that promulgates some natural meaning to 'education system', to anyone or anything that upholds any belief in education as a system, or indeed, I would go so far as to say, any belief in the purity and integrity of *any system whatsoever*.

But let's not get unduly carried away. If I appear to go *off piste*, as I did just now to criticise that abject phrase which I hope I never again have to utter in public, it is also in the spirit of wanting you to contemplate the possibility that digression itself is at the heart of thinking and life. For the upside of the business about trigger or content warnings with which I initiated today's proceedings has to do with those moments when, in the course of a digression, we discover something of which we had little or no idea. Unanticipated, in a word, and of a perhaps beautiful, transporting, even life-changing kind.

My concern is with *reading*, therefore – after all, that is where the word *lecture* comes from: it's the Latin *lectūra*, from the verb *legĕre*, 'to read' – and more particularly with the idea that reading a book can be akin to having a sun machine descend on us.

Usually when people use the word 'Bowiesque', they are referring to his music, hairstyle or clothes; but we might also make space for a notion of Bowiesque *reading*, a passion for reading that has nothing to do with any programme, institution or curriculum, and a good deal to do with chance, experiment and adventure. As you perhaps are aware, David Bowie was very into *reading*. He was constantly at it. He never went anywhere without books. When he was asked 'What is your idea of perfect happiness?', he replied without hesitation: 'Reading.' Very Bowiesque.

You know sometimes – I was saying – when you read a novel, you come across an image or idea that chimes with your own life. Of course, we might say, that is why people read in the first place. And this would be true whether we're talking about reading a work of fiction, a memoir, a biography or even a history book. It's all about identification or, better perhaps, resemblance. It's about encountering someone, a narrator or character who reminds you of yourself, or someone you know or would like to know (perhaps even in a biblical sense), or someone you would like to be, and so on, and it's about encountering a situation or event that reminds you of something you yourself experienced, or something you know someone you know experienced, or something you yourself would like to experience or definitely *not* like to experience, and so on.

Everything depends on the example. I'm trying here to follow the kind of advice about essay-writing that I've been giving in seminars and lectures for many years. The example is what counts. There's no strong critical thinking or writing without it. And in providing this example, if it's any good, something happens. You take the reader from something specific and singular to somewhere beyond. Beyond yourself and beyond the example.

So, here's the example. It's in a Japanese novel I read recently called *Sanshirō* by Natsume Sōseki. I was reading it in English. Alas, I have next to no knowledge of Japanese. In any case it's a lovely book. I recommend it to you without reservation. It was first published in 1908. It's set in the wake of the Russo-Japanese war (1904–05). But it is not a novel about war, except insofar as it affirms something altogether foreign to war. It's a very gentle kind of *Bildungsroman*. You know that German term for a novel that deals with the formative years or spiritual development of a particular individual, usually a man.

Sōseki's novel is about a young man called Sanshirō Ogawa who grew up in Kyushu, the most southerly of the principal four islands of Japan, about three days' journey by boat and train from Tokyo. He moves to Tokyo to begin his university studies. It's really a novel about student life in the early twentieth century and about student friendships and about the relationship between students and professors. And then there's a love thing – Sanshirō becomes infatuated, in his shy, awkward way, with this sort of liberated 'new woman' called Mineko, but it doesn't come to anything. It's a novel in which nothing much happens and there are lots of disappointments – it's all about disappointment – and yet it is a very beautiful, haunting and curiously uplifting book.

What really chimed for me was when the narrator describes Sanshirō's experience of attending university lectures:

> He found it strangely pleasant that he could not understand the lecture. As he listened, cheek in hand, his senses became dulled, and he began to drift off. This was the very thing, he felt, that made lectures worthwhile.

When I read these sentences for the first time they practically took the roof of my head off. It was as if I had been transported in time – suddenly I was deposited back in the autumn of 1976 when I was first attending lectures at university and I found myself remembering, as I hadn't for literally decades, what it was like, how I felt, how intoxicating and (as Sōseki puts it) how 'strangely pleasant' it was, not because the lecture was intellectually exciting or because it delivered 'learning outcomes' (in the ludicrous terminology of current university bureaucracy), but on the contrary because it was really rather dull and unappealing and I began to drift off and that was the point. That somnolent, semi-dreaming, dislocated drifting and submission to incomprehension was what made the whole thing important.

Are you still with me?

A book would be a sun machine. A work of light. Its darkness is created in the penumbra of that light. The book generates, reflects and carries its own sun. In a sense, any and every title of a novel bears a trace of Ernest Hemingway's *The Sun Also Rises*. There is a sun that rises in a book as well as in the world. It rises and also of course comes down. Hemingway takes his title-phrase from the Book of Ecclesiastes: 'The sun also ariseth, and the sun goeth down, and hasteth to his place where he arose' (1:5). The Bible of course works on a pre-Anthropocene basis:

generations come and go, but the sun still shines and the earth doesn't change, it 'abideth for ever' (1:4).

Of course, the sun has no 'place' of this kind. It doesn't sneakily hasten back, under cover of darkness, to where it came up. Nor is the sun male, though the links between the sun and the father and thus the s-u-n and the s-o-n are to be found throughout human history and still mark many languages today. In French it's *le soleil* (masculine), in Spanish *el sol*, in Italian *il sole*, and so on. In English we say the sun has got his hat on: if only unconsciously, the sun, in English, is male. This childlike conception of the sun as male, and implicitly as father-figure, is a controlling motif of Kazuo Ishiguro's recent novel *Klara and the Sun*, a book centred on the sun and 'his nourishment', 'his pattern', 'his special help'.

Nor does the earth abide forever. That's why, right now, it seems to me, we have *a sense of the ending* as never before. What are we doing with this profound and palpable precarity? If this sense of the ending is true, what is becoming clear now, in new and unprecedented ways?

The sun is conceptual art. It appears to 'come up' in the east and 'go down' in the west. Reverse the come and go and things already seem odd: we don't ordinarily speak of the sun going up and coming down. What makes a book a sun machine is in part its capacity to show, to bring to light, the artificial nature of this sun, of how we think of the sun. Every book of fiction invites us to read it for its own sun and therefore its own moon and its own darkness. The moon, after all, is only visible to us thanks to the sun.

What about clouds? I must simply note here that they come and go in these lectures. It's intriguing and apt, I think, that David Bowie played the role of Cloud in Lindsay Kemp's *Pierrot in Turquoise* in 1967. Kemp himself thought of Bowie as cloudlike, always floating in and out. 'Memory of a Free Festival' is all about the cloudy London sky. That's one of the most striking images in the song, I think – going up through 'the ivory vibrant cloud'. It's a song as much about clouds as about crowds. At the end of *Romeo and Juliet* we are told that 'The sun, for sorrow, will not show his head'. Shakespeare's formulation is beautiful, but also (as we would say today) gender-biased, and curiously heliocentric (it's the clouds, stupid). One of the wonderful things about the novel *Sanshirō* is its preoccupation with looking at the sky and especially at clouds.

There I go again, like Sanshirō, drifting off …

A novel is a study in light, a study *of* light. It's a photology. The sun machine is, if you like, a theory of the love of reading. I'm thinking here in the first instance of what, for the past few centuries, we have called novels, but the sun machine is also a figure for thinking about books in which the distinctions between fiction, poetry, drama and memoir melt.

I suppose you have come across the phrase 'creative non-fiction'? If so, perhaps you're OK with it. Personally it makes me sad. It seems to me a kind of desperate marketisation-speak. I'd like to suggest that one attraction of the idea of books as sun machines is that it offers a way of by-passing such rather nasty-sounding categories. Falling in love with a book, the book is falling too, it descends on us, it impacts, it lights us up. It invites us to think sun and earth afresh.

We might think for a moment of books whose opening words figure the sun. Samuel Beckett's *Murphy*, for instance, begins: 'The sun shone, having no alternative, on the nothing new.' Elizabeth Bowen's *A World of Love* starts with the sun rising on a 'landscape still pale with the heat of the day before'. Zadie Smith's *NW* opens with the sticky sentence: 'The fat sun stalls by the phone masts.' But every book – even one as literally and figuratively dark as Jose Saramago's *Blindness* – has to situate itself in the context of light. Every novel has its own way of letting there be light.

One of the first novels I ever remember reading was John Masefield's *Sard Harker*. We had to read it at school, now more than half a century ago. I recall nothing about it, except a sense of light. Somewhere close to the beginning. Morning sunlight on the sails of a ship heading out to sea.

The sun doesn't have to appear in a dramatic or ostentatious manner, however, and of course it is never simply literal. That's the point – there is no literal for the sun. If the novel is, in D. H. Lawrence's celebrated phrase, the 'bright book of life', it is different every time. To be an author, to put together a sun machine, is about closing your eyes. It's as much about listening and rhythm as it is about vision. In any case, a book engineers its own special solar character and lighting effects. And the books that have the greatest impact are perhaps those that let us appreciate that the sun itself, the sun as we think and talk about it in everyday language, is a fictional thing.

How does one start to think about the sun? As Wallace Stevens suggests at the beginning of his great long poem *Notes Toward a Supreme Fiction*, it is an 'inconceivable idea'. You can't look at it. As the Victorians said of masturbation, it makes you go blind. It's the source of life but it burns you up.

It has to do with the memory of earlier years. That's the fuel for a sun machine. Memory of childhood, if you are lucky, is like the memory of a free festival. Memory is or can be a free festival. That's what Bowie's song gives us to think.

My earliest sense of a sun machine came in an English lesson at school with Mr Curtis (Ken, as we were later allowed to call him) when we read Ray Bradbury's 'The Golden Apples of the Sun', a short story from the early 1950s. It's a bizarre piece of writing – absurdly melodramatic, deeply unrealistic and yet strangely captivating. It's about a spaceship whose captain wants to obtain a cupful of the sun, or as Bradbury puts it, 'a bit of the flesh of God, the blood of the universe, the blazing thought, the blinding philosophy that set out and mothered a galaxy'. Bowie no doubt knew Bradbury's story. Indeed, he knew Bradbury: Alice Cooper (he of the 'School's Out', no more 'education system' song) recalls them all having dinner together on one occasion in Los Angeles.

I didn't know at the time, but Bradbury's title-phrase takes on further alien resonance because it goes back to W. B. Yeats's early poem, 'The Song of Wandering Aengus', first published in 1897 under the title 'A Mad Song'. Yeats's poem ends with the end of time and times, with the speaker saying that he will

> walk among long dappled grass,
> And pluck till time and times are done,
> The silver apples of the moon,
> The golden apples of the sun.

A literary work is a sun machine insofar as it makes the sun other, lets us feel the otherness of the sun. We speak of a powerful book as dazzling, blazing, shimmering, illuminating, brilliant, luminous, enlightening – so many adjectives to do with light and seeing. But at the same time, as I've also been trying to suggest, the sun machine comes through the voice: it's about tone and rhythm, being borne away in the voice or voices of others. A sun machine is made of words and the sounds of words. A mad song, as Yeats might say.

Is this making you sleepy? That's OK, don't worry, go with the flow. As David Bowie liked to say: 'Let go, or be dragged.'

If the sun also rises, it drifts off too. You must be careful of course, but there's nothing nicer, in a way, than having a doze in the sunshine.

Next time I'm going to introduce you to something called the undermind. I leave you for now with another early David Bowie song, also dating from 1969, about 'protein pills' and getting seriously disorientated. This was why the BBC originally resisted playing it on public radio: they weren't sure, but they worried that it might be a song endorsing *drug culture*. Here is 'Space Oddity', a fitting song, I think, for floating away, leading us out into whatever or wherever there is, between now and next time.

[Play David Bowie, 'Space Oddity']

The undermind (second lecture)

[Play the second movement of Bach's Concerto for Two Violins in D minor]

Hello. I hope people are somewhat awake. I'm not sure that I am, but that's maybe not such a drawback. It's all to do with *the undermind*, which is the subject of this second lecture. I just played you the second movement of Johann Sebastian Bach's Concerto for Two Violins in D minor. This is one of the pieces of music my father used to play to me and my brother on a regular basis on Sunday evenings, when we were in bed and supposed to be going to sleep. It quite possibly does nothing for you, and you may wonder whether it's not a bit unfortunate that a famous composer should have a name that suggests the noise made by a dog, but I wanted to play it not just because, for me at least, it's sublimely beautiful, but also because it's an example of the way that music is about memory and the dissolution of place. I warmly recommend listening not just to that second movement but to the whole thing. It's so stunning, uplifting, tranquillising. It always has me *floating in a most peculiar way*.

In the previous lecture I used the word *chime*. I don't suppose you noticed, but I felt faintly embarrassed. I was talking about how, when you read a novel, it can *chime* with something in your own life. 'Chime' is an old word. In the sixteenth century it was spelled 'cheyme' or 'cheime'. I blushed, privately, because it *sounded like the name of where I grew up*. A place called Cheam. Cheam, Cheyham, Chime. I spent the first five years of my life in Fulham. Bowie spent his in Brixton. Then we both moved to somewhere quieter, away from the centre. The burbs.

When I lived in Cheam, I could hardly pronounce, indeed I could hardly *think* the name in my head. It sounded so awful to me. So posh and excruciating. I'm mostly reconciled to it now. It's one of the ways David Bowie helped me, or it's one of the affinities I've always felt with him. The sheer embarrassment of the suburbs. The cut-glass English pronunciation of 'Cheam'. And then 'Cheam' in cockney. The absurdity of an accent. Voice and class. The ridiculousness of where you supposedly come from. And the deep need to be elsewhere.

We often think of music in terms of remembering where we heard it – this house, that festival, this car ride, that pub and so on – but music explodes its place. I listen to this second movement of the Double Violin Concerto and I am transported. I'm taken back to Cheam. Then lost in space. Lost in time. Hallo Spaceboy.

My father had no musical sense. He never sang, except one song. I won't talk about that today. Perhaps I'll get to it by the end of these lectures. He played no instrument and showed no interest in going to concerts or even listening to music on the radio. He was a silent type, a self-styled Buddhist, very quiet, very reserved. But certain pieces of music, of which this Bach was most prominent, he had as vinyl records – with that label called His Master's Voice; perhaps you've seen it, funnily enough with a dog on it, though it was a listening dog, it didn't bark – and he had a record player, and he put this Bach record on every Sunday evening and he showed no real emotion, no obvious sadness, no joy either, but I know now how much it must have meant, how intensely he must have felt, his almost unbearable loneliness.

Last time I began talking about the idea of a sun machine as a way of thinking about a book. It's a poetic and musical thing.

A sense of the ending

A book that stays with you, a book that you love, or once loved, is a sun machine.

My focus in these lectures will be on an author whose work no one, so far as I know, has ever described as 'obscure' or 'challenging' – let alone designated as a 'modernist' author. I am referring to the children's writer Enid Blyton (1897–1968). If you don't know them or don't remember them, it's the *Famous Five* books I'll primarily be talking about. There are twenty-two of them altogether, the last being a collection of short stories. Have a look, if you can, at one or two of these before we next meet. It doesn't greatly matter which volume, though I'm sure it wouldn't do any harm to start with the first in the series, *Five on a Treasure Island*. Reading a 'Five book' can change your sense of the world.

That's what happened to me. That's the subject of this lecture series – it's the story of what happened to me when, after a gap of more than fifty years, I started re-reading or re-hearing the *Famous Five* books. It's where I stumbled into the realisation that a book can be a sun machine.

It's risky talking about Enid Blyton. I mean talking about any writer is risky. It's always – or always should be – dangerous, anguishing, unnerving. But even before beginning, it seems to me, there are two major and obvious risks in talking about Blyton.

The first concerns seriousness. Usually when academics come to the end of their teaching careers they are in a state that might be termed, if not vegetative, at least utterly exhausted. Gardening is indeed a common option. They have grown weary in mind and body. They have toiled and had sufficient. I am talking about when people retire or feel compelled, as in my own case, to take 'voluntary severance' – a phrase I am unable to utter without derision, a phrase apparently designed to make you feel that, as a long-serving representative of your distinguished institution, you are actively choosing the gas chamber, you're not volunteering to sever one of your limbs, it's not voluntary castration or other major limb amputation they're talking about, it's voluntary severance of your entire body and being.

At this point, in any event, the last thought in the minds of such academics is of devoting further time and energy to a new research project that might in due course lead to the publication of yet another academic monograph. Has the world not already more than enough of academic monographs? Is it not more sensible for these worn-out folk just to disappear into the undergrowth, into the garden as I was saying, and the less said the better?

For a small number of these creatures, however, the desire to write has not been thoroughly extinguished, and these seemingly incorrigible individuals turn their attention to an author whose *oeuvre* they might quietly and admiringly have been reading over the decades and only now at the end of their careers feel at liberty to write about. It might be Shakespeare, for example, or Dostoevsky. It might be Jane Austen, or Toni Morrison.

It's not going to be Enid Blyton.

It was certainly not what I envisaged, in the wake of agreeing to take voluntary severance. But that's how it turned out. It was a question of how, as severee, I was to proceed. What to do with 'the fire in me now', as Samuel Beckett calls it in *Krapp's Last Tape*? Like Charles Darwin at the beginning of his autobiography, I felt 'as if I were a dead man in another world looking back at my own life'. What to say, what to talk about, in the event of my vocation being abruptly and for all time lopped off?

In all my years as a teacher only once did anyone come to me expressing a wish to pursue research on Enid Blyton. I don't recall the student's name. She had long red hair. I discouraged her. I told her what I assumed she already knew. Blyton's books lack intellectual complexity. There is nothing philosophically interesting about them. Blyton just isn't a serious writer.

Not serious? That now seems to me a miserably patronising judgement. Blyton began (like most serious writers) as a poet and after receiving (like most poets) many rejections, some of her early poetry was published in a special *Poetry and Song* issue of *Teacher's World*, alongside such notable contemporaries as Rudyard Kipling and Walter de la Mare. Her poetry, however, did not develop. In 1932 she wrote a 90,000-word adult novel called *The Caravan Goes On*, but she couldn't secure a publisher. Her novel-writing for adults ended there.

But she was seriously gifted as a writer of children's stories. My concern in these lectures is to try to do justice to this writing. Which also means – I must just add – trying to do justice to the *comical* dimensions of her work. Blyton, after all, can also be seriously funny. I know this, because when I read her books out loud to my children they laugh. At times they positively throw themselves around with laughter. Their comic pleasure is uncontrollable.

The second set of risks has to do with how her work is open to charges of – to name a cluster of unpleasantries – ethnocentrism, xenophobia, class-prejudice, racism, sexism, misogyny and sadism. These aspects of her writing have given rise to criticism, even to condemnation and outright dismissal. Indeed, they have also led to modified editions. As you may know, recent printings of her books bear witness to attempts at cleaning up and, as far as is at least superficially possible, eliminating these troubling and offensive elements.

I have no interest in offering any kind of apologia in this context. My reckoning with these aspects of her work will emerge here or there, I hope, as I go on – if sometimes in rather oblique fashion. Candour is indispensable, but I believe that obliquity can also be effective.

A *Famous Five* as a sun machine? Blyton doesn't see her world as a machine world. But there are machines in any case. There are bicycles that might remind us of Chinua Achebe's metaphor of the 'iron horse'. There are cars, including the occasional big American one, as if turning up out of the pages of *The Great Gatsby*. There are trains and planes and motorboats, radios and telephones. All of these, however, appear secondary. Everything in Blyton is first and foremost about the sentient body. The amazing pleasure of being alive. Vigorously in life. Being able to walk or run or climb. To see and hear. To eat and sleep. To lie in bed so excited at the fact that it's the holidays you clench your legs in joy.

My concern is with this quickness – with how Blyton provides a kind of matrix for thinking about the joy of books, the excitement of reading or listening to a story, the mysteries of being a child and its relation to what David Bowie calls – in the lovely instrumental at the start of *Low* – 'speed of life'. And then, too, this quickness in Blyton loops back to the question of the machine, above all to the sense of writing as a machine.

Every *Famous Five* book is sunlit – pleasingly bright and reliable, reassuring and happy. They are all such sunny stories. 'Sunny stories' was a sort of signature phrase for Blyton. It was the title of a magazine she edited from 1926 to 1952. Fit for a Sunbeam Society, we might say. This was the name of a charity for blind children with which she was involved; and she wrote various 'sunbeam' books, including *The Sunbeam Annual* (1937) and *The Sunbeam Book for Children* (1953). But in a more general fashion, I suspect, Blyton thought of all her readers as a kind of 'sunbeam society'. Each *Famous Five* book enacts a heliotropic logic, turning itself and its readers sunward. It's all about sunny days, about the synonymity or *sunny-nymity* of sunny days as holidays.

I'd always associated the *Famous Five* books with summer holidays, but I have more recently discovered that this is not a consistent factor. Still the sun shines. Not just the summer, but the Easter holidays are also beautifully sunny. Even an October half-term – in *Five on a Hike Together* (Book 10), for example – takes place in 'warm sunshine'. Consistently, in book after book, the first day of the holidays is sunny as if by decree, like the 'sunny pleasure-dome' in Samuel Taylor Coleridge's 'Kubla Khan'.

But if every *Famous Five* begins and ends in the sun, it has shadowy innards.

Like Iceland. I don't know if you've ever been to Iceland. For all I know, you may actually be Icelandic (in which case: *Hæ hæ!*). I spent just three days there. I stayed in a very nice hotel close to the seafront in Reykjavik, in October 2014. The city was small, and the people were warm and welcoming. The first morning was bright sunshine. So bright I wondered if I was in my right mind.

I walked out of the hotel and stopped in my tracks. I looked about me. I was discombobulated. It was absolutely huge. Not the hotel. The sun. I mean, the sun *is* huge, I know, but this sun, the sun that morning was manifestly – how can I say? – *extra-large.* Extra-extra-large. Super-size. I retreated back into my accommodation and queried it with the young woman at reception.

– Oh yes, she said, that's the volcanoes. The eruptions at the moment make the sun look much bigger.

A surrealistically large sun is one thing, but then next day I took a bus into the Icelandic interior. I'd never in my life been or seen anywhere so dark and otherworldly.

It's the same with a *Famous Five* book. It starts off sunny – even improbably, overwhelmingly sunny – but it's all about going into the dark. With or without the moon. With or without stars. With or without torches. It's about going down into the caves and tunnels. Into the subterranean and submarine passageways of the night. There's no sun machine without going into the dark. An immeasurable, unplumbable, thrilling, vertiginous darkness.

Undermind: that is the word that Enid Blyton proposes in response to the professor of psychology in New Zealand who writes to her in the 1950s asking where she gets her ideas from. It is her undermind. She proffers this word. Or she disinters it. She doesn't say: *My books come from my unconscious.* 'Unconscious' is not in her lexicon. As always, she is on the side of the child, in the quick, ever-verging-on-supernatural world of childhood. With 'undermind' she makes a territorial gesture. She is not having any truck with the Freudians. Or the Jungians. She is cutting herself off from all those types.

'Undermind' may not sound particularly original, but it is distinctive. It goes with her name: the letters of 'Enid' are scattered in it, almost twice over. It's possible that she picked the word up from Virginia Woolf, who picked it up, unnoticed, in Charles Dickens. In 'The Leaning Tower', a talk given in Brighton in 1940, Woolf argues for the importance of 'unconsciousness' in Dickens and, by extension, for writers in general. Unconsciousness is the state in which, she says, 'the under-mind works at top speed while the upper-mind drowses'. It seems as if Woolf is tossing the word off in passing. She gives it a hyphen and thus renders it as a compound noun.

But the word does not appear in the *Oxford English Dictionary* in either form. There is no established critical or philosophical *Guide to the Undermind.* It doesn't place Blyton in any school or camp of thought. People might decide it's synonymous with 'unconscious' or 'subconscious' or 'intuition', but it's none of these things. *Undermind* involves a separate Blytonic domain, with landscapes and seascapes of its own. A singular topography, with other kinds of maps. It is more suggestive of a location than 'unconscious' or 'subconscious'. As in *undercliff* or *underpass* or *underground.* And it is duplicitous in a way that would have greatly irritated Freud: it is at once under a mind and a mind that is under.

'Under' works quite differently from 'un' or 'sub'. It's more physical, but also secretive. More redolent of concealment. It has connotations of the *underhand.* The *underside.* The eeriness of *undertaking* and *undercurrents.* And one perhaps also hears 'undermined'. The feeling of being undermined, of having one's world undermined. *Undermind* makes 'understanding' different.

Mind out. Mind how you go. Never mind.

Mind the gap. Stand back from the edge of the platform.

Enid Blyton goes under. Into the dark. She goes somewhere underneath that is not her. She is down in the undermind. From one phrase or filament to another. She doesn't really see where she's going. You can feel her feel her way in the sense of surprise that flickers and slides through the syntax from one clause to the next. It's something audible. Best heard in the dark.

For me it started early on in the pandemic – listening to David Bowie alone in the evenings, after days spent reading Enid Blyton to my children. I got drawn back into my youth. Day after day, week after week, I was reading the *Famous Five* books to my children. I was reading these books aloud and hearing the writing as I imagined they might be hearing it. My wife would read too, and when both of us were just too exhausted we resorted to audio versions. Every day there was more Enid Blyton than anyone could realistically be expected to cope with. By early evening I felt completely done in. Blighted and blitzed, buried and blytoned alive.

Finally everyone, including my wife, would go to bed, and I would stagger downstairs and sit alone in the kitchen with a beer or glass of wine or whisky and Bowie. Every night I would listen to David Bowie. And because our kitchen is like a sort of soundproof pod, a fairly new extension to the house, I could turn up the volume as loud as I liked. Sometimes it would be just one album. Sometimes it would be a certain song over and over. In no particular order, I listened to 'In the Heat of the Morning', 'Space Oddity', 'Letter to Hermione', 'Memory of a Free Festival', 'All the Madmen', 'The Man Who Sold the World', 'Life on Mars', 'Quicksand', 'The Bewlay Brothers', 'Five Years', 'Starman', 'The Jean Genie', 'Time', 'The Prettiest Star', 'Drive-In Saturday', 'Lady Grinning Soul', 'See Emily Play', 'Sorrow', 'I Can't Explain', 'Diamond Dogs', 'Sweet Thing', 'Win', 'Fascination', 'Across the Universe', 'Somebody Up There Likes Me', 'Station to Station', 'Golden Years', 'Word on a Wing', 'Stay', 'Wild is the Wind', 'Cat People (Putting out Fire)', 'Speed of Life', 'Sound and Vision', 'Always Crashing in the Same Car', 'Be My Wife', 'Subterraneans', 'Heroes', 'Blackout', 'Sense of Doubt', 'Moss Garden', 'The Secret Life of Arabia', 'Let's Dance', 'Modern Love', 'China Girl', 'Absolute Beginners', 'I Can't Read', 'Jump They Say', 'Thursday's Child', 'Seven', 'Outside', 'Hallo

Spaceboy', 'The Motel', 'I'm Deranged', 'Thru These Architects Eyes', 'Strangers When We Meet', 'Nite Flights', 'Imagine', 'America', 'My Death', 'Shadow Man', 'Sunday', 'Slip Away', 'Everyone Says Hi', 'New Killer Star', 'Where Are We Now?', 'Love is Lost', 'I'd Rather Be High', 'Blackstar', ''Tis a Pity She Was a Whore', 'Dollar Days', 'I Can't Give Everything Away' … I'd shut my eyes. The day had been simply too much.

To listen to Bowie was to switch off from Blyton. But then one night, listening to 'Memory of a Free Festival', something happened. I think it must have had to do with the odd mix of innocent and demonic in that song. I started thinking about the idea that a sun machine could be a book.

I had never previously gone out of my way to read anything about the life of Bowie or about the life of Blyton. I quickly discovered that, by critical consensus, 'Memory of a Free Festival' was when Bowie started coming into his own. What does it mean, I wondered, 'coming into one's own'? More or less overnight I became a makeshift scholar, doing research on David Bowie and Enid Blyton.

The festival of 16 August 1969 took place at a park in Beckenham, Kent. At that time Bowie was living in Beckenham with Mary Finnigan. They used to hang out at the Three Tuns, the pub on the High Street where he would also perform on Sunday evenings. It was here that Bowie set up the Beckenham Arts Lab.

Enid Blyton was born in 1897, in East Dulwich, but moved a few months later to Beckenham. In those late Victorian days Beckenham was just a little village in the Kent countryside. It is now – and for a long time has been – part of the London borough of Bromley. Crucial early memories for Enid were walking in and around this rural environment with her beloved father, Thomas, observing and learning about nature. David Bowie (David Jones) was born in 1947 and moved to Bromley in 1953.

It was just a coincidence, this Blyton–Bowie–Beckenham thing. But then, as I tried to suggest in my first lecture, there's no art or song without coincidence. That's life – exposed to chance, the quick, the speed, the paths it lights.

Blyton and Bowie: born fifty years apart. They have nothing in common, surely?

Three years before his death, Bowie published a list of the 100 books that most influenced him. Angela Carter's *Nights at the Circus* and Jack Kerouac's *On the Road* are included. Spike Milligan's *Puckoon* is there. Even comics such as the *Beano* and *Viz* are listed. But there's no book by Enid Blyton. Why should there be? In any case, you wouldn't expect someone to specify a particular title by her, even if Blyton were acknowledged as important. It's not like she produced two or three stand-out masterpieces.

Another book in Bowie's top 100 is Colin Wilson's *The Outsider*. Bowie and Blyton are both outsiders. In terms of a recognised canon of writers, Blyton is so much of an outsider that, for many people, she seems literally unmentionable. It amounts to a kind of prohibition, a taboo against taking her seriously. I mean this not just in an academic context but in a more general public way. For many years, for example, the BBC would have nothing to do with her. Blyton herself evidently took this resistance as a sign of 'snobbery or jealousy'. And in other respects, too, she is an outsider – in terms of the intensity and relentlessness of her identification with children, for example, or, in a different and perhaps subtler vein, her imaginative attachment to the life and culture of 'travellers'.

In part, it seems to me, we don't take Blyton seriously because her books are not addressed to us. This is the strong, even disturbing sense of the phrase 'children's writer'. Her books are addressed *to children*. This is true even of her autobiography, *The Story of My Life* (1952). I warmly recommend reading it. But it's weird, first and foremost because of that pervasive idea: it's a life-story written *for children*. *Bildungsroman* as arrested development. It's like a kind of autobiography in a coma. It's totally open and forthcoming and totally closed and cryptic at the same time. In a sense it doesn't let you in at all. It makes *you*, as a 'grown-up' reader, an outsider.

This impression of autobiography as a sort of paralysis formed very rapidly, as I was reading the opening pages of *The Story of My Life*. I should say that it's a pretty short book. I read it at a single sitting. You might be able to appreciate the eerie feeling that came over me when I reached the final pages in which Blyton refers to an experience of *infantile paralysis*.

It's the strangest moment in the book, when the author recalls that her horse-loving daughter Imogen couldn't go riding because she was suffering from infantile paralysis 'at the time'. In the 1940s and 1950s, 'infantile paralysis' was a common idiom for the polio virus. But the phrase sends out strange ripples right across the book. You don't talk about 'infantile paralysis' like that to children. The remark is itself an outsider. It doesn't belong to the tone and register of the rest of the book. It says more and other than what it seems or wants to say.

In any case, with this idea of the outsider I began to consider certain resemblances between these creatures of Beckenham. Above all I thought how, in both Blyton's books and Bowie's music, we encounter a spirit of generosity and imaginative otherness, a sense of desire as danger, an attraction to what is queer, fantastical and surreal, an affirmation of non-belonging, and also a kind of irony and humour – all of which collectively embody, perhaps, the nearest thing to an idea of Englishness, or being 'English', that is meaningful and even worth celebrating.

Blyton and Bowie have much in common. They are extollers of the undermind and the possibilities of transformation. They are voracious readers. They are both obsessive about their work. They share a comic fascination with Englishness itself, especially in terms of doing funny things with their voices. They are brilliant mimics. They share a love of music, circus and theatricality, acting and disguise, cross-dressing and class-crossing. They are both bisexual. They have a profound attraction to the otherworldly, whether in the form of fairies and magic or in the form of loving the alien. They are both, if I can put it like this, education system escape artists.

And then of course they are also light years apart. Their paths don't cross. While he was growing up as an extraterrestrial in Bromley, she was already long established at Green Hedges in Beaconsfield, far away in Buckinghamshire to the west of London. She died a year before the Beckenham free festival.

It's hard to picture them meeting in, say, the spring of 1967 and hitting it off. Enid would perhaps have been quite puzzled by David's appearance and disturbed by his music. He would perhaps have rather despised her moralistic and Christian preciosity, her good old British Empire values. Of course she was suffering from Alzheimer's by this point. That spring he was working on the first *David Bowie* album, which featured a variety of strikingly childlike songs that I'm tempted to describe as Blytonic Demonic or Demonic Blytonic, whichever sounds less of a tongue-teaser or perhaps tongue-tweezer.

In the spring of 1967, afflicted with dementia, Enid insisted on being driven back to Beckenham in her Rolls Royce to be once again in the place she was as a girl. I'd like to imagine David supping a pint in the Three Tuns gazing out on the High Street as the Rolls rolls past with her off her rocker in the backseat. But actually he doesn't get to the Three Tuns till a year or so later. In any case she would be one of the mad people, like his schizophrenic half-brother Terry. David might have felt sorry for her. Meeting him might have been just what Enid needed, lifting her, if only momentarily, out of the abyss of memory loss and anguishing disorientation. The odd couple, alone together, in a Beckenham of the undermind.

Blyton and Bowie were perfectly capable of producing very mediocre work, but then they also made things that swept the world away. Both were, in their different ways, stardust creatures.

The undermind is not safe. It's unknown. It's where there's no Ground Control. All trigger warnings gone. You only get there by letting go, submitting to the unforeseeable, sinking in quicksand, flying into the blue, loosening the ropes, veering out from the shore in the dark. Wandering off into the labyrinth of the underworld.

'Undermind' is not Bowie's word. But Blyton's undermind corresponds, it seems to me, with Bowie's interest in losing identity, giving way to otherness, *waiting for the gift of sound and vision*; his fascination with dreams and alien, magical, otherworldly spaces; his affirmations of madness or being (to recall an image from the early song 'All the Madmen') one of 'the sane' who choose to be 'underground'. Bowie had a lifelong commitment to the idea of *having no head. On Having No Head* is, by the way, another title on his top-100 reading list: it's an appropriately brief book about Zen Buddhism by Douglas Harding, with (as Hamlet might say) no shriving time allowed.

The undermind is not about the 'I' or ego. It's more about voluntary severance of self, if I may rework that nasty business-speak phrase with a certain derision. Comedy is a key in all of this. Blyton's undermind speaks to Bowie's laughing gnome, with *no direction 'ome*. The undermind is not about the self but others. It's a place of strange resemblances, doubles and imperfect copies, mimicry and disguise. It's unnerving. It's a way of disappearing into others or letting others come through. Next time, I'll talk more about all this in relation to telepathy.

I thought it might be interesting to end today with a couple of short early Bowie songs – as evocations of that Blytonic Demonic or Demonic Blytonic I just mentioned. Both songs are notably zany and childlike. The first is 'There is a Happy Land', from the first *David Bowie* album. The second comes from the *'Mercury' Demos with John 'Hutch' Hutchinson* and it's called 'When I'm Five'.

[Play David Bowie, 'There is a Happy Land' and 'When I'm Five']

Telepathy (third lecture)

Hello and welcome once again from your ghost academic! I'd like to start off today, if I may, with the melancholy, rather hypnotic Bowie song I referred to last time, 'All the Madmen', from the 1970 album *The Man Who Sold the World*. As I said, it's a song about the undermind. Listen out for the refrain that closes the song, in the intimate second-person form in French: *ouvre le chien*. Open up, open sesame, we might say, but more literally: *open the dog!*

[Play David Bowie, 'All the Madmen']

This lecture is called 'Telepathy'. At the end of the previous session, I proposed that thinking about the undermind leads us to the question of telepathy. Some of you may be wondering what on earth ... There's a kind of knee-jerk response that associates telepathy with the supernatural, but I'm inclined to turn this back to front and say that telepathy in the context of works of fiction is, in many respects, normality itself. It's natural in the sense of naturalised. In other words, readers take it for granted.

A work of fiction is a work of mind-reading: the book takes you inside the thoughts and feelings of another or others – inside the world of a narrator, inside the minds and bodies of characters, and so on. Readers are mind-readers in turn. This is a role that they accept without really thinking about it. Readers are in fact quietly rather pleased to be telepathic. It's an opportunity to indulge in magical thinking. They take it in their stride. Like breathing clear, country air. The most natural thing in the world. We all do this.

But telepathy is also freaky. It provokes uneasy questions: Is my mind my own? Where does one person's thought or feeling begin or another's end? Is there even such a thing as personhood or subjectivity in the first place?

Naturalisation involves the artificial. It's like the sun, as I was saying in the first lecture. A sun machine is the kind of book that invites reflection on the natural and unnatural, the unnatural natural, nature become fantastical. A sun machine takes us down into the undermind. It leads, as if by old, perhaps strangely intimate or familiar paths, to the uncanny. An uncanny feeling arises when we experience a situation, an event, a place, a piece of writing or music as *suggestive* of the supernatural without, however, *being* supernatural.

A typewriter can be uncanny. It is a rather ordinary, familiar, old-fashioned kind of machine, but you can perhaps recall movies in which the typewriter comes to play a creepy, even frightening role. The typewriter evokes something spooky, without actually being supernatural. We might think of Stanley Kubrick's *The Shining*, for instance, in which Jack Torrance (played by Jack Nicholson) has a relationship with his typewriter that sets a particularly bad example to anybody interested in creative writing. He's trying to write a novel and he can't get started. He has the mother of all writer's blocks. It's enough to turn him into an axe-wielding madman.

Enid Blyton's first husband Hugh gave her a typewriter in 1927. It took her a while to get attached. To the typewriter, I mean. Hugh was a Scottish, military, older man on whom she seemed to get hooked in a trice. In any case, before long she was writing on her typewriter every day. She had it on a cushion in her lap. She couldn't do it otherwise. A relationship was forged, a dependency developed, between the typewriter and Enid's hands. There is strangeness in the phrase 'manual typewriter'. That was what she did for much of the day every day. She never learned to touch-type. She just plonked away with her two forefingers.

When you type everything has to come out in a straight line. One line under another. It must all be in order. You see how a man like Jack Torrance, left to his own devices, might get stuck. How do you go on if there's nowhere to start? How do you make a start when you are feeling overlooked, when you're holed up in a huge empty hotel called the Overlook?

There is something that happens as Blyton is typing and typing on her lap every day, from first thing in the morning until late in the afternoon. She goes into another world. She loses herself in a rhythm that belongs to that world and sounds in the turns of the sentences and the brightness of the simple sun machine, a completely new and strange machine that is coming out under her fingers.

I used to assume – insofar as I'd ever given the matter any consideration – that Blyton mapped out a bold and simple synopsis and proceeded according to plan. That everything had been sketched out on the back of an envelope. But now I see that is not the case. It's a sun machine that is descending in the typing. She doesn't – she can't – look at the sun.

Let's quickly recap on how a *Famous Five* goes. There's Julian, Dick, George and Anne, plus the dog. And they have an adventure. You pick a number, any volume in the series, and it's the same. The children are never at school, it's always the holidays: escaping, breaking out from some educational institution, getting away, is Blyton's starting point. The Five are always *going* somewhere – of the twenty-one full-length Famous Five books, eight have 'go' in the title. And they are always going *to* somewhere or else they are *in* it, *on* it or *into* it. All these little prepositions – 'to', 'in', 'on', 'into' – give us a sense of *happening*, an intimation of the *Famous Five* books as, in Nicholas Tucker's striking phrase, an 'ecstasy of action'. *Five Go Adventuring Again*, *Five Go to Smuggler's Top*, *Five Go Off in a Caravan*, *Five Go to Demon Rocks* …

Blyton rocks like a demon, the writing seeps like sunlight out of her typewriter. She has no definite idea what she's doing. She's putting her fingers to the keys with a half-dreamy apprehension of the length of the book and the fact that it will break up into about twenty chapters, and she always begins in a recognisable way and always comes with happiness to 'the end of the day'; but as for what happens in between – she is blind. She gives herself up to the Five and follows what they have to say. Or growl or woof. She is led by forces other than herself. She is not in control. She hands herself over to the typewriter. The manual of the *undermind.*

When Blyton starts typing the first book, *Five on a Treasure Island*, in war-torn 1942, she's aware of the luxury and preciousness of paper. But there are no paper shortages in the undermind. She types away and away and on and on and it comes out as it comes. There's no going back. It's an adventure in typing. You only need look at the opening pages of the first chapter. She is clear about the children. She knows all about Julian and Anne and Dick. They talk to her as autonomous beings from the beginning. Their speech is so much their own, not hers, that they make her laugh out loud as she goes.

The sun's up, it's breakfast time and the question is: What's planned for the summer holidays? In the past they've gone to Polseath. (A place-name that resembles, but isn't, Polzeath, in Cornwall.) They need to become the Famous Five. Which means that their parents need to sneak off on holiday by themselves to Scotland and the children can go – the father spontaneously suggests – to stay with his brother Quentin and his family by the sea. Why did this never occur to him before? Because Blyton is making it all up as she goes along.

The children will be going to stay with their Uncle Quentin and their Aunt Fanny and their cousin Georgina *whom they have never met.* The author tells us that Georgina and Dick are about eleven and Julian is twelve and Anne is ten and none of them has *ever* met their cousin. Why not? Then Anne asks her father what this place by the sea is like, and he tells her he doesn't remember. It's called Kirrin Bay. He can say that much. But otherwise he just draws a blank on the place. Like a character in a Hitchcock film. Drifting into psychopathic reverie. The Blytonic Demonic …

Until he snaps out of it. Brought to his senses by the children's enthusiasm, he gets up and goes to phone Fanny to see if this holiday idea can be realised. There's a bit of Freudian kettle logic thrown in at this point – in other words, more explanations than are logically necessary. We learn that the father just happens to have met up with Fanny in London a few days earlier and discovered that she and Quentin could do with a bit of extra money. If blood isn't thick enough, they're going to buy their way into this holiday.

It's not called 'phoning' of course. It's *telephoning*. And you don't *telephone someone*, you telephone *to* them. You *go* to telephone *to*. The telephone is in the hall. When I was small it was in the hall, too. In a space or room of its own. It was a bit like going up to the altar or a strangely open confession box. To be overheard, if not overlooked. It may seem tangential here, but the first book I ever wrote (back in the 1980s) was all about telepathy and literature but also telephones: the telephone keeps getting in the way, the telephone *is* the way of getting in the way. Tangentially. Strange word. Don't mock me, it's one of those words I can't help stumbling over: gentians in the sun, picking up a tan, secret agent in the word, a special tang, to be enunciated *gently*. Spoken like a gentleman. Tangential.

In the end, whether critical or creative, writing is a matter of how you get your telephone fitted.

The telephone is in the hall. The telephone call is the manual thing the father does. Blyton is typing and the children can hear – the author can hear – the man in the hall dialling. She is very good on the details of such sound effects. The telephoning *to* launches the narrative. The 'to' is blind. Secret. It's a question of getting through to. Does he speak to his brother or only to Aunt

Fanny? It's not clear. A voice here. A voice there. The father telephoning to Kirrin Cottage is also a figure of the book telephoning to us. A *Famous Five* book is a sort of magical telephone call, with multiple voices in play, a *party line* as people used to say.

Like the time as a teenager when I went out into the hall, picked up the telephone to make a call and heard the sound of typewriters and a voice said 'Sutton Police …'

So much oddity has already been smuggled into the opening pages of *Five on a Treasure Island.* Two adult brothers – with offspring of the same age – who do not see or communicate with each other. A married couple who – as soon as all the children are back from boarding school – cannot wait to send them away again for several weeks. A man who warmly recommends staying in a place by the sea which he's visited but simply cannot remember. And then the 11-year-old girl none of them has ever met. The strange cousin who is simply referred to as *unknown.*

'Strange happenings': that is Blyton's phrase. 'Peculiar goings-on': that's another.

Such phrases prompt thoughts of the supernatural – for the children in the *Famous Five* books and for readers. But nothing ever transpires to be supernatural. There are plenty of *suggestions* of the otherworldly, but we are always brought back to the everyday.

The books are full of improbable things that consistently, in one way or another, fall to earth. A girl who has her own private island. Complete with ruined castle. A group of children who get into mortally dangerous difficulties every time the school holidays come around. Always crashing in the same car. A mass of burglars and kidnappers and smugglers and spies and circus folk and travellers constantly invading their lives. Children who can be heroes, at the end of the day. Children who can be themselves, children who have got to win, and as if grin every time: 'We can be us!'

Strange happenings are *mysterious* or *spooky* or *eerie* or *funny*. They make the children and indeed the dog feel *uneasy*. Blyton does not speak of the uncanny. In all the *Famous Five* books the word occurs, I believe, only once. It is in the penultimate volume – *Five Have a Mystery to Solve* – when she describes a boy called Wilfrid and the *uncanny way* he has with animals. This is late Blyton, writing in 1962. 'Uncanny' is a bit discordant. It interferes with the childlike register. It makes her sound like D. H. Lawrence. It recalls the rather quirky Lawrence of 'The Man Who Loved Islands', which itself sounds, at least in its opening paragraphs, oddly like a story by Enid Blyton.

Children don't find things uncanny. Adults find things uncanny because they are not children. But adults can be uncanny in their ability to remain childlike or their apparent inability to move out of the world of the child. This is what Sigmund Freud noted about Leonardo da Vinci: 'the great Leonardo remained like a child for the whole of his life … Even as an adult he continued to play, and this was […] why he often appeared uncanny and incomprehensible to his contemporaries.' In extraordinarily creative but singularly different ways, Enid Blyton and David Bowie were also childlike. They were both, we might say, radically childminded.

An uncanny feeling only lasts a moment. It's a surprise. Like a shiver. A brief subsidence. You might think: Whoa! that's strange!

You experience a fleeting sense that something out of this world is occurring. But this quickly goes away. You may feel you've tapped into something, but it doesn't last. At any rate that's how it's always been for me.

You don't really want to hold on to an uncanny feeling. You might think you do, but your better judgement tells you otherwise. It's a King Lear thing: *that way madness lies*. There's the flickering realisation that madness is not a separate building. It's not offshore. There are always tunnels. Surprise doors. A sudden cavernousness …

Like *déjà vu*. It's a funny feeling. It can even be titillating. But you wouldn't want to hold on to it.

Like *déjà vu*. It's a funny feeling. It can even be titillating. But you wouldn't want to hold on to it. (Sorry, I couldn't resist that.)

In her autobiography Blyton recalls how, in her imagination, the characters make their way forward, as if to the footlights of the Undermind Theatre stage, and then they start talking. They say things she would never have expected. She simply becomes their secretary.

The telling of a *Famous Five* book is a telepathic arrangement with strings. Telepathy – literally distant (*tele*) feeling or mind (*pathos*) – is everywhere. The narrator doesn't impose, she hardly seems to say anything, she is so busy reporting who everyone else is, and what they say, and where, this time, they are going on holiday, and how, or already gone. She disappears in the sunlight, with just an occasional flutter or flicker.

Blyton lets us know what a certain character is thinking or feeling, as and when necessary, so that we always sense that she knows, but we don't pay much attention to that, as there's so much already underway in the broad brushstrokes of sunshine and someone else saying something and characters arriving or not yet, and an ongoing difference of opinion or light-hearted altercation, or something involving the dog, and the fact that it is the holidays and the excitement of what they are going to do and where and how and food, always, yes, the delectable cataloguing of eating as a shared experience, filling the day, and going to bed and waking up, walking or riding bicycles, rowing a boat, taking a tent, scrambling up or down cliffs, and all of it reaching out beyond the human to the sentient lives of other animals, especially the dog.

The Blyton narrator is so camouflaged in the sunlight, like a parrot, so blended into the voices of the characters that she scarcely seems to show herself at all. There are moments of breaking the fourth wall, when she addresses us directly with an 'And we will leave them there' kind of remark (as she does, for instance, in *Five Run Away Together*), but this is only at the end, by which point she has had her way with us and we don't hold it against her, in fact we are with her, she is one of us, we are one of her, we who leave them there. For it's time to move on to the next volume – that's finally Blyton's point, the Demonic Blytonic, to have been taken, to have been a party, and to be told that there's more, always, another book, another sun machine.

The narrator has a telepathic connection with her people and lets us know. We acquiesce without a murmur. It is inherent in the pleasure of listening to the voice as it starts up in the opening sentences of the book and abducts us. Child abduction occurs in a literal sense in *Five Get Into Trouble* (Book 8), *Five Have Plenty of Fun* (Book 14), and also in the story called 'Good Old Timmy!' (in Book 22); but really it is underway from the start, and all along, in every book, at the level of the narrative voice. We don't mind. It's fine. Kidnap us, please! What an adventure!

And then, also, the narrator has a telepathic connection with her people and *doesn't* let us know, but that's also fine, we like that too. This is about reading or listening to a book as an experience of mind-reading. It's why detective fiction (not just in the *Find-Outers*, but in the *Secret Seven*, the *Adventure* series, *Malory Towers* and the *Famous Five*) is an integral dimension of Blyton's storytelling.

The Blyton narrator doesn't let us know. She withholds knowledge, so that we, along with the children in the book, can't tell at first if someone is a villain (like the young Jo in *Five Fall Into Adventure*) or when a bad man transpires to be good (like the burly Morgan in *Five Get Into a Fix*). The narrator doesn't make a great conceptual song and dance about it. This is not Henry James after all. It's more the fleet-foot of Lewis Carroll's *Alice in Wonderland* and *Through the Looking-Glass*, two of the books that, by Blyton's own account, had a particularly strong influence on her.

There are many correspondences between the *Alice* and *Famous Five* books, especially in the way both authors evoke the immediacy of thinking and feeling, looking and other physical gestures. But what the *Famous Five* narrator does that the *Alice* narrator avoids, is to draw readers into the 'feel' and 'atmosphere' of telepathic collusion. 'Feel' and 'atmosphere' are the words Blyton uses and puts in quotes when, in *The Story of My Life*, she is reminiscing about the power of another book that deeply affected her as a child, George MacDonald's *The Princess and the Goblin.*

The *Famous Five* books are like a party or group outing that includes the reader. The *Alice* books work quite differently. The Lewis Carroll narrator constantly, bountifully exposes what Alice is thinking and feeling: the *Alice* books are major nineteenth-century telepathy texts. But, at the same time, the narrator watches – and invites the reader to watch – from a certain twisted exteriority. The *Alice* books are knowingly addressed to a double readership – the child and the not-child. Enid Blyton isn't really concerned with the not-child, except from the child's perspective. There is none of Carroll's somewhat sinisterly manicured dual-focus and telephoto-lens work.

The sun machine of a *Famous Five* book entails a shared experience of listening, responding, having a sentient body that enables you to hear, laugh, eat, see the island in the sunlit sea and scramble up cliffs, and scowl and smile and say things that parrot or anticipate the Five themselves. You feel the same. You think the same. The narrator has tuned telepathically into her characters: she is recording their thoughts and feelings. But it's also how the narrator involves the reader: you are participating in this telepathy.

Call it collusion, even if it's delusion. As you perhaps know, the verbs to *collude* and *delude* are both versions of the ludic – they come from the Latin *lūdere*, to play. You feel the same. You think the same. Blyton never says these words in the *Famous Five* books. But they operate as guiding threads that run through every chapter and paragraph. Her autobiography, *The Story of My Life*, is more explicit: there she confides the telepathic logic without hesitation. You children *feel* this, she tells them. You *think* this too.

Most narrative fiction makes consistent use of words such as 'thought' and 'felt': *she thought that* such and such, *he felt* such and such. It's telepathic naturalism. It's the basis of literary realism. Blyton weaves her braid differently. She generally avoids the explicitness of 'he thought' or 'she felt' or their many variations ('she decided', 'he wondered' and so on). Instead, her telepathic tapestry is hung on dialogue and woven in adjectives and adverbs. The more or less constant use of simple adjectives provides telepathic knowledge of the mood or manner of a character or situation – a telepathy shared between character, narrator and reader, or just between narrator and reader.

And adverbs dangle loosely, strung through the sentences like creepers in the forest. Open any one of the *Famous Five* books and see for yourself. The most common adverb is *suddenly*, but there are countless other examples: *certainly*, *possibly*, *obviously*, *quickly*, *awfully*, *tremendously*, *properly*, *eagerly*, *urgently*, *generously*, *steadily*, *absurdly*, *unexpectedly*, *safely*, *brightly* and so on and on and on.

Such adverbs tell us, knowingly but discreetly, how characters are feeling or what they are thinking. They are one of Blyton's signature-effects. They are like ticker tape signed 'Blyton'. Literally, she plies and supplies the 'ly' of her surname across the page. This preponderance of *-ly* is a lovely feather in her cap, a *fleur-de-lys* in her forest, a remarkably consistent if also largely unnoticed element in the great Blyton Parrot Show.

Suddenly! Early! Ghostly! Absolutely lovely! And rightly so!

The Five have such a strong sense of what is right. Including the dog. The *Famous Five* books are about being right. In Bowie's words, doing it right. Taking and making things right. Writing the right. Righting the night. Outside the *Famous Five* books Blyton speaks of the importance of Christianity, but the books themselves don't conform to this. No one prays. There's not a lot of churchgoing. There's right and wrong, but Jesus and God and the immortality of heaven and hell are not relevant. It's more about childhood as a Wordsworthian state of immortality, and about making order out of the chaos of the undermind. Some of the people the Five encounter seem dodgy but turn out to be fine.

Or vice versa. But everything is clear in the end. Good and bad. Right and wrong. In her autobiography Blyton assures us that she is 'a storyteller, not a preacher'. Christian morality may inform her narratives, but the energy of what I have been calling the Blytonic Demonic is always in play.

Julian is the oldest. The most sensible and responsible. His brother Dick looks up to him and in turn teases their little sister Anne. Anne is the sweetest and most prudent. The least inclined to adventure-for-the-sake-of-adventure. George is their cousin, a tomboy of about Dick's age. She dresses as a boy but she's a girl. She's a girl who would like to be a boy. Her full name is Georgina but she can't stand that. She's the one who, Blyton intimates, is most closely based on the author herself. George is an only child who lives by the sea at Kirrin Cottage with her curmudgeonly scientist father and downtrodden mother. 'Uncle Quentin' and 'Aunt Fanny' to her cousins. George can be bad-tempered, just like her father. She has anger issues. She has more of the demonic than her cousins.

And then there is the telepathic dog. George's dog is called Timothy in the first book, but gradually comes to be known as just Timmy or Tim. Timmy barks or growls or whimpers or finds his hackles rising or his unusually long tail swinging from side to side for this or that reason. The reason can only be communicated in writing, but it is nonetheless attributed to him as a sentient being without words. Writing what's right. Doing it write. Right on right on. Timmy's telepathy is in the bodies of the beholders, but it is also in the telling.

The famous four never doubt the intelligibility of a Timmy woof. Its meaning is transparent. A single phrase or sentence is usually sufficient. But sometimes Blyton transcribes the dog's thoughts and feelings at greater length. She translates into English, as if each book could also have been written in Timmy tongue. Written by Timmy in the form of woofs and growls and other canine flourishes. Timmy understands what the children are talking about.

He follows conversations as well as any of them. Sometimes the children are unsure of why Timmy is troubled or unhappy, but there is never any doubt that he has feelings and memories and is capable of analysing a situation and making decisions as sharp-nosed as the rest of them. The *Famous Five* books are singular works of child-and-dog telepathic realism.

Forgive all this talk of telepathy. I have been banging on about this topic for more than forty years. Now at the terminal point of my professional life, I can look back and see that no one was really listening. I'm like that lecturer in *Sanshirō* more than a hundred years ago.

I used to worry that people thought I was wacko. After all, telepathy is a branch of parapsychology (fit for nutcases) or it's a branch of psychiatric disorder (fit for nutcases), isn't it? But I have now come to a different view of the matter. I suspect that readers are disinclined to acknowledge telepathy in literature because it interferes with their 'imaginative immersion' in what they consider comfortable and familiar. To attend to the workings of telepathy is to engage with turbulent and uncertain dimensions of reading. It requires readers to register that what appears natural is not natural, like thinking about anthropogenic climate change and mass extinction. Indeed, I am now inclined to think that the unwillingness to acknowledge and think critically about telepathy in literature is not simply *analogous* to the unwillingness to acknowledge climate emergency. They go together. They belong to the same *structure of feeling*, as Raymond Williams might say.

Telepathy was a big thing in the decades following its coinage as a word in 1882. Novelists and playwrights and poets were deeply attuned to its literary ramifications. It is a significant and explicit focus in the writings of Rider Haggard, Thomas Hardy, H. G. Wells, Rudyard Kipling, Franz Kafka, August Strindberg and many others. But, in part due to the magisterial influence of Henry James, what came to dominate the language of literary criticism was a quite different term: *omniscience*. The omniscient author and the omniscient narrator. You can read about this in Percy Lubbock's *The Craft of Fiction* (1921), as well as in Forster's *Aspects of the Novel*.

It's easy to see the attraction of the omniscient. Literally, the all-knowing. It's very much in keeping with the reassurance of a Christian God or some other monotheistic being. Someone is in control, folks. Everything is fine here. We have an omniscient narrator in the driving seat.

But there is no driving seat.

It might be illuminating to think of a novel as a *drive-in*, but not on the basis that you're the driver or owner of a vehicle, any more than the author is. You're sat comfortably in front of a book, that's all.

Talking in terms of omniscience shores up a religious fantasy – the author or narrator as God-figure, and the reader or critic as a quietly gratifying reflection of that. You may recall that Milton, in *Paradise Lost*, more than once refers to God as our Author – the omniscient one, 'Author of all being', 'Author of this universe'. To shrug one's shoulders and carry on regardless, talking the 'omniscient narrator' talk, is disingenuous and falsifying. It is also a way of trying to close off the undermind.

This is one of the things that seems to me compelling and appealing about Blyton. She gives us the workings and surprises of the undermind – not the know-all, calculating aloofness of the omniscient. Mimicry and disguise keep knowledge shifting and unfixed. The closest we get to an embodiment of omniscience in the *Famous Five* books is Timmy the dog. But Timmy is no God. He is just a god backwards, a form of comic divinity in reverse thrust.

Omniscience says: 'I am King, I am Master.' Because of course, Omniscience is also a male fantasy. It's patriarchal and phallogocentric. Whereas Telepathy is about sharing and mixing it up. It's about mastery relinquished. Telepathy is all over the place, strictly non-binary, easy come, easy go. Telepathy says: 'Come and join, not sure what's happening here but – *we're gonna have a party!*' Telepathy offers us a different opening, a different way of thinking about literature.

Telepathy is at odds with those dry and fusty types who assemble around the feet of Omniscience in jittery obeisance to sovereign knowledge and mastery. I'm thinking here of figures such as 'Point of View', 'Focalisation', 'Focaliser' and 'Free Indirect Discourse'. They're all a kind of nonsense – fake-scientific fabrications of precision. These terms lose all sense of purpose and reality at the telepathic picnic. Let's move on from all that desiccated old vocabulary of pseudo-control, all that deadly godlike self-importance and scientistic earnestness. Let's talk picnics and new places!

'Picnics' happen out of doors. A picnic is a pleasure-oriented, holiday kind of thing. It makes me think of Wittgenstein's idea about 'when language *goes on holiday*'. He wasn't talking about telepathy, or at least that's not how he's normally read in this context. And a picnic is also a meal, and so it recalls not only the emphasis on eating and sharing food that is a mark of so much of Blyton's writing, but also her conception of a good book, as she describes it in her autobiography: it's 'like a very good dinner, sound and satisfying'. Let's not forget that 'Enid' is 'dine' backwards.

Blyton invites us to join in. I'm saying 'picnic' here, also, just *because* it's fanciful. There's something funny, I think, about a telepathic picnic. Blyton's writing calls for stranger, rangier, more imaginative critical responses than it has so far received. I'm not trying to lay down regulations, but rather free things up. We could equally talk about a telepathic circus or fair or indeed about going on holiday to Telepathy Island. I leave you to think about it.

In the next lecture I promise to talk about sex – and time.

I'd like to conclude today's lecture, however, with a few words about telepathy and David Bowie. In a sense Bowie has been singing and playing here all along. *Ouvre le chien*, for example: doesn't that resonate in what I was saying about child-and-dog realism? There is an *Open sesame!* in the voice, giving admission to the past and what is hidden.

'All the Madmen' is one of a handful of Bowie songs – along with 'In the Heat of the Morning', 'Memory of a Free Festival', 'The Man Who Sold the World' and a couple of others I'll try to touch on in a later lecture – it's one of the songs, I was saying, that I cannot hear without my brother Simon, without his listening with me, letting me hear in memory being with him, Si, the sound, where some part of me would rather stay, locked away. And listening is admission not only to this split-libido ghost-world, but also to the opening of the future – because of how in music we are (as the philosopher Jean-Luc Nancy puts it) 'propelled into an expectation, urged towards a presentiment'.

David Bowie seems deeply interested in this – in music's propelling and urging, the feel and promise of what is coming. It is integral to his fascination with stories and storytelling. Bowie's narratives tend to be fragmentary, cut up, left in suspense: he likes to, as he says, 'fracture everything' (and I'll return to this in a later lecture). The storytelling is occasionally third-person ('he', 'she', 'they'), but more usually in 'I', 'we' or 'you' form. These forms are, in any case, consistently unstable and shifting.

Let's briefly consider the classic 'Starman' on *Ziggy Stardust*. 'There's a starman waiting in the sky': this is third-person narrative. The singer knows what this starman feels and thinks – it's telepathic narration as I've been sketching it here – but then the moment in the telling when the singer picks on *you* is a telepathic clinch of another kind: *so you heard him too*. 'I' and 'you' become the 'we' who might tune into him on the same channel. *We may pick him up on channel two*. 'Starman' is notably, also, a song that comes down to the child, to the enigma of something children share by losing (*let the children lose it*).

Telepathy in Bowie's music is invariably linked, it seems to me, with some force of interruption. There is telepathic rapport as erotic fusion: his songs are in the tradition of the Romantic sublime, the voice of the lover, like Catherine in *Wuthering Heights* or Rochester in *Jane Eyre*, in the wildness of the wind, and that is a fact, flying over mountains. But they are also knowing songs of the impossible, singing the impossible, which is what gives them their wonderfully melodramatic character. And at the same time their highest fidelity is to interruption: they are songs of losing, cutting, veering off, becoming other, like birds, like dolphins, like aliens. The interruptions acquire a ghostly character, in which expectancy and presentiment *trail* the listener.

What is going on in the desire to *become* music? If, as Pater suggests, music is what all art aspires to, how is it *shared*? What does it mean to suppose that all and anyone can be a party to this, in the party to this?

Bowie's music is about letting go of identity, admitting oddity, becoming stranger. Contrary to what some commentators seem to imply, it's not about fixed, steady-state *personae* (called 'Ziggy' or 'the Thin White Duke'): it's about flight and becoming other – an unfinished becoming, veering and disappearing. David Bowie is, if I may put it like this, more a major veerer than a Major Tom.

We're gonna have a party: this desire to share in music (the sun machine) is indissociable from the desire to *become* music ('I am a DJ, I am what I play'). If Shakespeare is, in John Keats's phrase, the chameleon poet, Bowie is *chameleonic disappearance.* Shakespeare, for Keats, 'has no Identity'; but what Bowie gives us, rather differently, is a disappearing without original. He disappears into the environment of the music. This is 'chameleon' only as a shifting embodiment of dissolves. It's about proliferating layers and multiple stops and transitions. Becoming others, polyphony in and of the voice, but also becoming – losing oneself in – the instruments. And this is becoming on the run, it's otherness in flight. It's what David Wills calls, in a phrase that I suspect you may find difficult to get your mouth around, 'polyphonico-rhythmic otherness'. You can try this at home, saying it to yourself or perhaps to your dog or to the childhood dog in you: *polyphonico-rhythmic otherness.*

Not now but some time before the next lecture, you may care to have a listen to 'Sunday', the first track on the album *Heathen* (2002). The song title itself resounds, to my ear at least, with the sun machine of 'Memory of a Free Festival'. Alongside Tony Visconti's eerily synth-sounding backing vocals, Bowie's voice on 'Sunday' is superbly rich and precise, full of 'ambient menace' (in Nicholas Pegg's fine phrase). But the song is finally about rising 'as on wings' (as a bird or some other alien flying object) and – through the very singing of the word 'changed' ('everything has *changed*') – voice itself veering, disappearing into drums.

In this domain of instrumentalised becoming, which is both erotic and mournful, 'in memory' and 'to come', the saxophone has a unique place. The saxophone is David Bowie's telepathic instrument *par excellence.* He translates and transforms thought and feeling through this wind-instrument. It is the sound-machine of longing and loss, bliss and fusion, notes on a wing, voice's makeover. This ghostly saxophonic force, lingering and longing *after* the voice, is perhaps most uncanny on the final album *Blackstar* – on ''Tis a Pity She Was a Whore', 'Dollar Days' and 'I Can't Give Everything Away' in particular.

Rather than play one of those songs here, however, I thought I'd finish with Charles Mingus. David Bowie's love of jazz was a lifelong thing, and Mingus was a crucial figure for him. I want to play you 'Goodbye Pork Pie Hat' from the 1959 album *Mingus Ah Um*, with John Handy and Booker Ervin on tenor saxophone, Horace Parlan on piano, Dannie Richmond on drums and Mingus on bass. 'Goodbye Pork Pie Hat' is an elegy for the saxophonist Lester Young. The saxophone is perhaps the instrument that most hearkens towards the thought that mourning is originary ('I mourn therefore I am'): there is a sort of telepathic communing in the very sounding. I hope, in any case, you might pick up some connections here.

[Play Charles Mingus, 'Goodbye Pork Pie Hat']

The time machine (fourth lecture)

[Play Chopin's Nocturne in E flat, Op. 9, No. 2]

Hello and welcome to Lecture no. 4. This lecture is called 'The Time Machine'. One of the nice things about a lecture series is that the speaker can, as I did last time, leave off in a somewhat unexpected place, because it's OK, it's a series, and we can always come back to something later. Enid Blyton loved a certain seriality: the reassurance of return, the recurrence of the same-but-different. One *Famous Five* book after another, more or less every year, for more than twenty years. This is how she wrote (the *Famous Five*, the *Secret Seven*, *Malory Towers*, the *Adventure* series, the *Find-Outers* and numerous others): she was no serial killer but in her own imaginative manner she was, as a writer, a serial child-abductor.

She talks in *The Story of My Life* about her love of annuals, too, books that come back year after year – like flowers, but texts – with illustrations as well. You'll probably already have noticed that the *Famous Five* books are all illustrated by Eileen A. Soper. 'What is the use of a book,' as Lewis Carroll's Alice asks before she goes down the rabbit-hole, 'without pictures or conversations?' As I suggested last time, conversation bulks large in a *Famous Five* book: it's the canopy in which the narrator-parrot conceals herself.

What about the pictures? you may be wondering. I'll come to pictures later, I promise.

In any case, as I was saying, a lecture series can have a comfortable kind of ruggedness: it goes with the flow, it's OK to have spur-of-the-moment jiggles and digressions. That's something I love about E. M. Forster's *Aspects of the Novel*, a book based on a series of lectures – the extempore nature of where and how a lecture ends, a looseness given at least some degree of coherence by the fact that there will be a next time. It goes along with Forster's chatty tone – always deceptive because of the sharpness of his perceptions and his way of drawing us down into a singular underworld. As Virginia Woolf once described it: 'Mr Forster has the art of saying things which sink airily enough into the mind to stay there and unfurl like those Japanese flowers which open up in the depths of the water.'

The music I played for you a moment ago is by Chopin. It's his Nocturne in E flat, opus 9, no. 2. Enid Blyton loved Chopin's nocturnes. She had indelible childhood memories of listening to her father playing the piano in the evening as she was falling asleep. When she recalls this in her autobiography, she remarks on the power of the music to transport her right back to being in bed as a child listening. It gives her 'a queer feeling', she says – the power of music and memory, the capacity for a piece of music to take you down memory lane and dump you there. This is another deep link between Blyton and Bowie – she was brought up with the idea that she was going to be a musician. Her love of music doesn't disappear, it merely discandies into the voices of her writing.

So, I have irons in the fire – not Jeremy Irons, though I used to contemplate that, back in the day when he once tried to take my girlfriend off me. I promised to talk about sex, before getting on to the subject of time. Or the other way round. Of course I've already started, in my references to *seriality*, the *extempore*, and the *queer feeling* of music in the memory or memory in music.

And so to the question of sex … The most obvious route to thinking about sex in the *Famous Five* books is Timmy the dog. I don't mean to sound obscene. It's just that the physicality of the

Famous Five books, the feeling of the books as a kind of constant bodily movement, circles around Timmy. And it's good to talk about him first, also, as a way of restating a sense of Blyton's world as, in profound respects, neither confined nor reducible to the human.

Timmy tongue: I noted this earlier. Timmy loves to lick. He licks you all over your face and you love it. He licks your legs. Anywhere that's bare. And he loves to get his teeth into something. He is a figure of the author with the bone of a book. (There's nothing vegetarian about Blyton: in the undermind she's always quite ready to eat little bunnies, like Jack in *The Secret Island*.) And then Timmy is also military. A dog of war. Timmy does your bidding. He is your prosthetic fighter armed to the teeth. Instruct him to do something and he goes to it, all guns blazing. He is like George or her father or mother, finally released into their rage. The fantasy of having power and control over Timmy is what allows George to manage her aggression: he is her thing, she is his. Timmy vanquishes the enemy. Especially in the early books, and more clearly than any of the children, he embodies the spirit of England at war. Undaunted and unfazed.

Timmy is a big dog. He is a big-tongued dog. He must have had a huge donger too. But this is never mentioned. No dongers appear in any of the *Famous Five* books. Likewise, through all their multifarious outings and escapades, none of the children ever needs a pee or a number two. There are no toilets. And there is no sex. We are a long way here from the sexual explicitness of David Bowie, whether it's the guitar fellatio with Mick Ronson during a Ziggy concert at Oxford Town Hall in June 1972, the wanking in 'Time' (on *Aladdin Sane*), the relentless 'sex' in 'Sex and the Church' (on *The Buddha of Suburbia*), Johnny's fondness for 'pussy in cars' in 'I'm Afraid of Americans' (on *Earthling*), the asshole of 'Pablo Picasso' (on *Reality*), the cock in ''Tis a Pity She Was a Whore' (on *Blackstar*), or even the Nabokovian sun that 'licked me all over with its big, smooth tongue' (recalled in 'I'd Rather Be High').

There is no sex in the *Famous Five* books. That's obvious.

Or is it?

I'm not just thinking of the kind of intensity that lurks suggestively, for example, in the portrayal of young Georgina and Henrietta (or rather, George and Henry) in *Five Go to Mystery Moor* (Book 13). What I mean is that everything in the *Famous Five* books has erotic frisson. The light. The air. The weather. Landscape and seascape. Every meal and snack. Every cupping of hands for water from a spring. Every going to bed and getting up in the morning. Every morsel of conversation and every silence. Every parent and child and servant and bad man and bad woman. Every animal sound and movement and act of listening. Every setting off on a bicycle or in a boat. Every smile. Every swim. Every sunbathe.

Every lick.

If I had time – there, now I've put my foot in it, I've dropped the hideous clanger, the phrase I promised myself I'd avoid, 'if I had time'! *Had we but world enough and time*, as Andrew Marvell starts 'To His Coy Mistress', his poem about the erotic desire of and for language as a lovely palaver of lips and slips. If I had time, I was going to say, I'd say more about this love of licking, about writing and song as a kind of *lingophilia* – but that would require a separate lecture. In poetry and storytelling, as in singing, tongues never cease.

Anyhow it's no use, the words just trickled out of my mouth. *If I had time.* The point is, I don't. I'm out of time here, guys. That's why this lecture series is called *A Sense of the Ending.* All I'm trying to say is that a book of fiction is where we get to experience this *out of time* head-on, or rather head-off, in a calm and gathered way, in the experience of the unforeseeable, in the erotic folds and projections, the longing and licking, the loss and the 'having', the teasing and appeal, in the slides and newly invented orifices of telepathic writing.

I don't know if Maud Ellmann is thinking about gasoline or more specifically the original soundtrack album recording of Bowie and Giorgio Moroder's 'Cat People (Putting Out Fire)', but it's there, for me, in her lapidary remark: 'Novels run on sex, their plot lines driven by desire.' It may sound far-fetched to speak of the erotic dimensions of Enid Blyton, but it's the very form of her storytelling. Such is the child-and-dog telepathic realism in which everything in the *Famous Five* books is related. It's all in the seductive 'far-fetched' and 'related'.

To recall Bowie's Starman: *Hey that's far out.* You'll suppose I'm overstating matters, but I could talk till the far-flung cows come home about how fetching *far-fetched* is, about the 'far' and what the 'fetch' might fetch, cause to come, like pails of water fetched from a well in the underworld. Or the word 'related': in a sense this is all I want to relate – a story of this innocent-looking little word that brings family and storytelling together in a single, strangely familiar beating heart. Are we related? What does it mean to be related?

A book of fiction can always fetch up new family, like a wedding. It can establish a new set of relations – however distant – or a radically new way of experiencing old ones.

I hope you're finding all of this *relatable.*

Telepathy and Eros go together. Whether we are dealing with a nineteenth-century 'classic' such as George Eliot's *Daniel Deronda* or a 'modernist' novel such as Elizabeth Bowen's *The Hotel* or one of Blyton's *Famous Five* books, telepathic narration is the corporeal stirring and dissolving of distances and differences that enables a readerly immersion in others' perceptions, thoughts and feelings.

One of the reasons why novels just get better and better as you get older is that you come to appreciate more and more how much they function as time machines. A sun machine is always also a time machine. The preacher Ecclesiastes presumes a timelessness when he says that 'there is no new thing under the sun' (Ecclesiastes 1:9). He said this somewhere between the third and fifth century BCE. Then in the early sixteenth century, Copernicus came to the idea that the sun doesn't move. But the sun is not fixed and eternal. It's a hive of activity and it's not going to stick around forever. As an undergraduate in the late 1970s I got interested in photography of the sun, which had begun in 1845. I should have been reading Dickens, but I found solar photography, with all the associated talk of macula and facula, dreamier and more compelling.

The sun has a history. It began and it will end. In a few billion years it will become a *red giant*: we may note the mythopoetic, grandly anthropomorphic language. Even the scientists talk of giants. In any case, you can't think about the sun without thinking about time, and that is what novels also do – they mix the sun with the time.

Books of fiction are always written in a time that is distinct from the time that they are written *about*. Some works, such as Alain Robbe-Grillet's *Jealousy* (1957) or J. M. Coetzee's *Waiting for the Barbarians* (1980) or Jenny Offill's *Weather* (2020), may seem to reside in the present tense. They may lull us into supposing that the time of writing coincides with the time of the events and experiences recounted. But there is always temporal discrepancy. There is always two-timing. Immediacy is a fiction.

It is a *construct*, as some people like to say. I must admit I am not fond of that word. It suggests something easy but clunky, done and dusted, empty of life. Identity is a construct. Reality is a construct. A novel is a construct. Ugh!

But then I can readily imagine one of you saying:

– Hey but hang on a minute! What's your theory of the sun machine if it isn't a *construct*?

To which I would say:

– No, not exactly.

This sun machine I've been talking about doesn't exist. It's not an actual object, any more than its understanding can be confined to a song by Bowie, a story by Ray Bradbury, a book by Enid Blyton or a poem by Yeats. You know when people talk about a website as still 'under construction'? That's how I think of the sun machine. Like a time machine, in fact: it is in process. It's got future feel. It's less about the apparently fixed nature of a piece of writing or music and more about reading or listening as something underway. It's about the response – how you respond, what you can make of it, where it might take you.

Recall the marvellous opening sentence of Franz Kafka's 'The Burrow': 'I have completed the construction of my burrow and it seems to be successful.' The construct, the very construction of the sentence, comes apart at the – uncertainty of the – 'seems'. Just as love is in the present but also has a futural dimension – like a promise – a sun machine is coming. *The sun machine is coming down.* The sun machine might be invisible or it might be strangely luminous, like a silver vessel 'in the yellow haze of the sun' (to recall Neil Young's beautiful song from 1970, 'After the Goldrush'). But it's never just about one person, whether the writer or musician as sovereign constructor, or the reader or listener as sovereign constructor of the meaning of the work.

The sun machine is a work of alien engineering. People associate the word 'engineering' with science and objectivity. Engineering is a so-called STEM subject, right? But actually it has a spirit or genie inside it. To engineer is literally to spirit up. A sun machine is about forces of ingenuity that don't belong to anyone and aren't in anyone's control. It's about the undermind.

We are all familiar with the ideas of flashback and flashforward. That is to say, in classical rhetorical guise, *analepsis* and *prolepsis.* These occur in films and on TV *because* they occur in novels. Like Native Americans, novels got there first. And to pursue that analogy in more spirited fashion, I would note that their manner of being there first was not to stick a flag in the ground like some self-regarding empire landing on the moon, but to attune to the singularity of the environment, to its flora and fauna and weather, in ways that have nothing to do with land-rights or the blood and soil of nationalism.

I was just eleven at the time of the US Apollo 11 landing, on 20 July 1969. Although it was the middle of the night, I was allowed to watch it on TV with my father. I had never stayed up so late in my life. This vigilance produced a kind of groggy, quasi-hallucinatory state marvellously suited to the unearthliness of what my father and I were watching. But I still vividly recall my astonishment at seeing these people arriving on the surface of another world and sticking a Stars 'n' Stripes flag in the ground. It struck me as ludicrous and obscene.

The only nationality that interests me is the literary kind. *Literary nationality*: I borrow this phrase from one of my favourite writers, Hélène Cixous. Literary nationality makes a mockery of patriotism and undoes all blood-and-soil nationalistic ties. It is a coming together in a spirit of music and poetic thinking. It finds only comedy in the designations of 'English' or 'American' or 'Russian' or any other presumed nationality.

A book might drift, limp, glide or hurtle about from one time to another. As I hope you might agree, if you cast your mind back over a novel you've read, supposing you will have done so, the temporal perspective veers about, not just from one paragraph or chapter to another, but within a single sentence. As in the one I just enunciated. Writing is an unpatented box of tricks and disguises of different times and tenses.

Enid Blyton is especially fond of 'in the meanwhile'. She regularly turns attention to something that someone was doing, or something that was happening, *in the meanwhile*. 'And what was so and so doing all this time?' She loves that kind of formula. It allows her to tilt and go back in time and then catch up again. Analepsis, prolepsis. Time-shunts. Fictions of simultaneity. It's an aspect of her fascination with the power of the unknown, the effects of things happening at the same time without characters being aware of them. Like her father conducting an extra-marital affair with Florence Agnes Delattre and finally walking out of the family home, shortly before her thirteenth birthday, never to return.

A novel, then, is a time machine, but *so is the reader*. I am sorry to announce that there is essential engineering work taking place here. This is due to a collision, two kinds of time machine coming together. To operate as a time machine, a book needs the time machine more familiarly known as *a reader*. How you read a work of fiction when you're twenty is not how you read it when you're forty or seventy. Every book contains other forms and possibilities of yourself in the meanwhile.

Yourself in the meanwhile is, I submit, a peculiar phrase. A time oddity, perhaps, as much as a space oddity. Later on in these lectures I'll try to talk more about certain late Bowie songs, such as 'Where Are We Now?' and 'Love is Lost', as examples of time oddity.

Yourself in the meanwhile gestures towards strange happenings, peculiar goings-on within you, of which you are not aware. It's akin to what Wordsworth, in his Intimations 'Ode', called 'moving about in worlds not realised'. It's not about the mentality of the *could have, should have, would have.* It's about how the books we love can also be uncanny archives, so that when we return to them, they tell us things about ourselves that we had quite forgotten or had never apprehended.

The phrase 'time machine' is indelibly associated with H. G. Wells. His novel of that name was published in 1895. If I tell you that Wells was born in Bromley (at 162 High Street, to be precise), you might suppose that I am going to make something of this – the peculiarity whereby all things seem to point to Bromley, the fact that these figures I'm talking about – David Bowie, Enid Blyton and now H. G. Wells – all emerge from the same location.

One or two of you, for all I know, may be privately dreading that I am going to launch into some mystical exposition of what the Romans called *genius loci* or 'spirit of place'. Others possibly, of a more hermeneutics-of-suspicion bent, may be puzzling over the fact that my name is anagrammatically contained in 'Bromley', as if this entire elaboration of sun and time machines originated in that wordplay, and they may even suspect (should they not be particularly familiar with the boroughs of South London) that I've made 'Bromley' up.

I have no such extravagant schemes in mind. I am simply remarking the coincidence. What I really want to do is talk about my Dad.

When he was a young man, my father read the novels of H. G. Wells with great enthusiasm. This enthusiasm he sought to replicate, or lovingly transfer to me, and I therefore – like any other rebellious, contrary son – declined to oblige. But things are not so simple, as has by now become clear to me. A son's opposition to his father's desire is also a form of fidelity. Sigmund Freud, who thought quite a lot about such things, came up with the term 'deferred obedience'. It's a matter of delayed compliance – a lurking submission, to be made real in the future.

Deferred obedience is a phrase you might like to note down on a post-it or other slip of paper and stick on the fridge or the table beside your head as you sleep, and think about for the rest of your life. It's the idea that when you are young, you behave in a way that is quite distinct from how your father or mother behaves, but then years later, when you get to your thirties or forties, you clock that you now feel or think or do exactly the same as your mother or your father. It can be disconcerting, dispossessing, uncanny. That's deferred obedience.

The Time Machine just bubbled up for me here. I hadn't planned to talk about it at all. It reminds me of a funny image evoked by Hanif Kureishi, another Bromley boy: it's the idea of people such as himself (but perhaps me too now) as a bunch of 'H. G. Wells clerks'.

I thought I could use the phrase 'time machine' and just leave it there, without getting drawn into a whole H. G. Wells, My Father and the Workings of Deferred Obedience shenanigans. It landed without my noticing. If you want to check out one of the places where Freud talks about deferred obedience, have a look at his book *Totem and Taboo*. It's full of fascinating things, especially regarding the magic of art and the omnipotence of thoughts. It is perhaps his most sustained meditation on the *undermindful* idea that everyday language – every verb, every noun, every proper name – is 'nothing other than watered-down magic'.

In *The Importance of Being Earnest*, Oscar Wilde has Algernon say: 'All women become like their mothers. That is their tragedy. No man does. That's his.' Jack, in response, wonders if this is simply 'clever'. It's not just clever but funny. Algernon's is a beautifully turned aphorism but, if I'm being earnest about it, I'm not sure whether the tragedy of being a man isn't in fact comic and the cleverness lies in supposing that, if he is able to dispense with at least some of the completely unnecessary coercions and artificial constraints which bind and blind him, a man can come to see more and more, as time passes, how much he is also his mother. Or indeed his grandmother.

What if we loosen up the parameters of deferred obedience and suppose that it doesn't stop at one's relation to a parent but extends backwards, in a mode of transgenerational haunting, into preceding generations? What if deferred obedience, for example, were not from the father, so much as from the father's mother?

What is going on here? I suspect I am trying to tell you about something strange and painful that probably doesn't belong in a public lecture. Then again, it is not clear to me where it should belong. *It's confusing these days*. But I remain committed to the form of the lecture, and to the lecture theatre as a space that facilitates imaginative and intellectual explosions – however private.

Elizabeth Bowen recounts that when she read Rider Haggard's novel *She* for the first time, at the age of 12, she realised that a book could be like a bomb that goes off in your hands. Elsewhere, in her short story 'Mysterious Kôr', a character talks about the idea that, if you can blow places out of existence, you can also blow them into existence. Thoughts light as moondust. That is how I fantasise these lectures might work.

But it's hopeless. Time and tide stayeth for no proverb. I'm going to have to conclude today's lecture, but I feel I've hardly begun telling you what I most wanted to say – about how listening to certain David Bowie songs, in conjunction with returning to Enid Blyton's *Famous Five* books after a gap of fifty years and more, transported me, as if in a TARDIS, into a world of unexpected revelations. It's all to do with what Elizabeth Bowen calls the 'echo-track[s] of sensation' – from being read to and reading as a child, to reading again many years later. It corresponds with something that H. G. Wells talks about in *The Time Machine*, namely 'recalling an incident very vividly' and journeying, as a kind of extraterrestrial, into other 'mental existences'. It has to do with my father and mourning, with untapped and unfinished memories.

When Blyton goes down into the undermind, the children are there. The children have to go under as well. Under the swell, under a spell, as well. But the darkness needs to be visible. Battery-operated torches are tremendously important. So are the moon and stars. Time is arrested. As Freud said of the unconscious, timelessness reigns. The children never age. Every *Famous Five* book is a perennial annual. Every new volume it's the holidays again and the exhilaration and thrills of another adventure.

As a child, Blyton loved *Peter Pan*. She was aware of J. M. Barrie's words: *To die will be an awfully big adventure.* There are plenty of orphans in Blyton's books, although details about the nature of deaths, parental or otherwise, are kept minimal. She isn't interested in dying. In fact, I would say she avoids it like the plague. Death is always on the cards and the children have a variety of ways of talking about this – as they clamber up or down a steep cliff-face or set out in a little boat at sea in the dark; as they find themselves incarcerated by villains in the cellar of an isolated old house; or as they are forced to make their way along a seemingly unending subterranean passage. But 'death' scarcely features. In this respect Enid Blyton is close to that otherwise quite different writer of the undermind, Franz Kafka.

I want to finish here today with 'Golden Years', from the album *Station to Station* in 1976 – a song about sunny golden times that keeps taking me back, running for the shadows. Bowie apparently wrote it with Elvis Presley in mind. He identified with Presley not just because he loved his voice and music, but also because they had the same birthday. There is a kind of fantasy of shared musical birth. To be born in music, *born once again*, is of course also the subject of 'Word on a Wing', the track that follows 'Golden Years' on *Station to Station.*

'Golden Years' is another of those songs I always hear with my brother. We listened to it together numberless times, yet he died scarcely a decade after its release. Like other Bowie songs, the music and lyrics race away in so many directions, opening strange doors and pulling double strings. Whop whop whop! It is funky and bizarre, soulful and unreal, retro and futuristic, like nothing else on *Station to Station* or indeed any other album. The phrase 'golden years' appears to echo H. G. Wells's short story 'The Chronic Argonauts' (1888), a sort of proto-text for *The Time Machine.* Wells evokes a shadowy voyage in time, veering between being 'in the very jaws of death' and experiencing 'undreamt-of joys'. Wells's protagonist asks: 'Will you come? Will you walk among the people of the Golden Years? …' Bowie's song is likewise suggestive of surreal time travel. Its golden years stretch out across the centuries, in the unspoken name of a loved one. Its running shadows embrace the thought and desire of sticking with this person 'for a thousand years'. That image comes back in the magnificently over-the-top, seven-minute version of 'Cat People (Putting Out Fire)' – someone staring at you *for a thousand years.*

[Play David Bowie, 'Golden Years']

The Croydon Bookshop (fifth lecture)

Hello, this is your ghost speaker, your teacher *condamné*, once again. Welcome back. I begin today with a dream. I did, literally, begin today with a dream. Perhaps you did too, even if you don't remember. Not the same dream, obviously. But then, when is a dream ever the same? Dreams shift every time you think about them. I would like to imagine that you are able to listen to my dream in silence, though I appreciate that that is a contradiction in terms.

I wanted to talk about the idea of silence at the end of the last lecture, especially what I think of as the sort of 'golden' silence at the end of the title track of 'Station to Station', before 'Golden Years' begins. As I remember it now, listening with my young brother (who was then just 16), the silence wasn't total of course – you could perhaps hear the very faint sound of the needle as the record was going round on the turntable … But I'd like to suggest that *that* silence, the silence at the end of 'Station to Station', is completely different from the silence after 'TVC15', before 'Stay'. In fact I'd like to imagine – however bizarre it might seem – a theory of 'Silent Bowie'. I'm not going to elaborate on that at any length – at least not, er, vocally. But I am thinking of the silences between certain tracks, the silences Bowie leaves *in* his songs, the sounds of a silent age and the invitations to silence (*Don't let me hear you say …*), the workings of mime and meditation, the silence in the effects of the fragmentary, paused or unfinished. Bruce Robb, the owner of Cherokee Studios where the album *Station to Station* was recorded, makes a suggestive observation in this context. He says that Bowie 'could hear what wasn't there'. This relates to a sense of silence not as privation but rather as a state in which, as Jean-Luc Nancy describes it, 'you hear your own body resonate, your own breath, your heart and all its surrounding cave'.

In his marvellous poem 'Frost at Midnight', Samuel Taylor Coleridge evokes the night with the words: 'Sea, and hill, and wood, / With all the numberless goings on of life, / Inaudible as dreams!' Today's lecture comes to you out of the silence of this dream. I appreciate that recounting a dream can be self-indulgent and ridiculous. It can be as boring as listening to someone regaling you with their thoughts when they're really drunk or stoned. I hope you'll forgive me – and see its curious relevance and interest here.

I woke up in my bed at home in Sussex by the sea in the middle of having dinner with Gerald Doherty and Randall Stevenson in Helsinki. The fact that one can be asleep in Seaford (where I live) but then, in the sloppy mess of waking up, be in the capital city of Finland is a readily recognisable idea. It's about the liminal or transitional space of the hypnagogic, where you are neither properly asleep nor properly awake. This out-of-place feeling relates to a phenomenon that I propose to call the Croydon Effect. This lecture itself, for reasons that will I hope become clear, is called 'The Croydon Bookshop'.

My friend Gerald Doherty has been dead for several years, so it makes no sense that I'd be having dinner with him – but that's dreams for you. Randall Stevenson, on the other hand, I met only once, about twenty-five years ago, in Edinburgh. Recently, however, I acquired his book *Reading the Times* – that's not a book about reading the newspaper, it's about *Temporality and History in Twentieth Century Fiction* (as the subtitle runs) – and I had been dipping into it. *Reading the Times* is (to borrow a phrase from Enid Blyton) a very 'dippable-into book'.

Dipping is of course a form of swimming (children in Blyton's books are forever doing it), but also flying (as a bird might dip into a bush). And of course it's about chance – as in a lucky dip. I don't know about you, but I like to take several dips every day. Sometimes I can't stop. A five-minute dip in *Reading the Times* will turn up something intriguing, I promise you. Yesterday evening for me it was Stevenson's discussion of Henri Bergson. In an essay called 'Dreams' (1901), Bergson describes how memories experienced in the present carry underneath them 'thousands on thousands' of others. 'Our past life is there,' writes Bergson, 'preserved even to the minutest details; nothing is forgotten; all we have perceived, thought, willed, from the first awakening of consciousness, persists indefinitely.'

Gerald Doherty was deeply interested in meditation and Eastern philosophy. He wrote a lot about D. H. Lawrence and James Joyce, especially in relation to desire. There's *Oriental Lawrence: The Quest for the Secrets of Sex*, for example, and a book about Joyce's *Dubliners* called *The Games Narrators Play*. I recommend dipping into all and any of his books. I would not have thought of Gerald as a time machine thinker: it took a dream to make me realise. Desire is always time-sensitive. All games are games with time.

Gerald and I never met in Helsinki. He lived in the Finnish countryside somewhere in the region of Turku. I used to go and stay with him and his stardust-spangled larger-than-life wife Pam and their imperiously large cats, in a marvellously peaceful house in what felt like the middle of a bucolic nowhere. It was in fact on an island, surrounded by forest and sea, with the more or less unpronounceable name Rymättylä.

Why dine together in Helsinki? 'Dine', as I've already noted, is an anagram of 'Enid'. The dream work is always doing overtime. As Lewis Carroll's Humpty Dumpty might say, these dream workers should be paid extra. 'Together' also requires clarification. Initially I was at a different table, with another friend, Liz Walker, a colleague at the university, a member of what is nowadays called Professional Services (implying that there might also be a distinct group of employees who provide Unprofessional Services, but let's leave that aside for now). Liz took voluntary severance last year. Like many other colleagues, I miss her. Anyway, Liz and I were having a very enjoyable chat, while eating some exquisite cake that she had insisted we have, and then I saw Gerald, a few tables away. I caught his eye, or he caught mine, and I knew we had to speak. I had to say goodbye.

Dreams in which dead loved ones come back to life have something of the beauty of the songs one loves. In the love of music, memory is shared. Love is preserved and ready at any second to return.

It's there in the word 'record'. Songs are forms of resurrection. David Bowie understood this, perhaps better than anyone.

Where are we now?

How does one say goodbye to someone who is already dead? In the dream I was vaguely aware of that aporia. I loved Gerald Doherty and never wanted to say goodbye to him. I suppose that is the simplicity of Catullus when he ends his elegy to his dead brother: *atque in perpetuum, frater, ave atque vale.* How should we translate this line? *And forever, brother, hail and farewell. And so for always … in perpetuity, brother … hail and farewell.*

You can never stop wanting to greet once more the one to whom you are saying goodbye.

That is the subject of the catchy but rather banal 1967 Beatles song, 'Hello, Goodbye': the hello as goodbye. More poignant and anguished, Bowie's music seems haunted by the *hail and farewell*: 'This is Major Tom to Ground Control …' The 'hallo' comes with a 'bye bye love'. 'Everyone says hi' means everyone says 'bye'. 'Say goodbye' is 'say hallo'. Bowie seems deeply interested in the power of music as greeting or valediction and especially both at the same time. It's not just the explicit instances of 'Hallo Spaceboy', 'Everyone Says Hi' or 'Love is Lost': there's a sort of persistent, loving, dissolving hail and farewell that recurs throughout his catalogue.

But back to the dream … Draped over the shoulders and tables of other diners – strung out between the table where I was sitting with Liz and the table where Gerald was sitting with Randall – was an inordinately long measuring tape. You know the metal sort that, if you retract it too quickly, can cut like a whip? It belonged, I realised, to Randall, and because I was aware of the inconvenience and annoyance it was causing to other diners, while he himself was apparently oblivious, I made it my priority, on parting from Liz and making my way across to their table, to tell him about the awkwardness of his tape measure.

It was a beautiful summer evening – that sort of ethereal white night one gets in Finnish summer – and the tables were all outside. My most urgent wish, however, was to talk to my dead friend Gerald.

'Sometimes a cigar is just a cigar.' So Freud supposedly once said, apropos the sexual symbolism of objects in dreams. This way he got to mark a limit and suggest that people shouldn't get so het up, looking for hidden or deeper meanings all the time. And also he could carry on smoking cigars and getting throat cancer without guilt or symbolic overkill.

Sometimes a measuring tape is just a measuring tape.

Seriously? That seems about as convincing as saying that sometimes a snake is just a snake.

But I'd prefer not to pin down any dream-object. Dreams resemble fairy tales in having no end. Like the grandmother's cat asleep by the fireside, truth purrs, curled up in the endless possibilities of relating. The undermind isn't where you get to stop the show and cry *Eureka!* as if to general applause and back-slapping. On the contrary, the undermind is about carrying on, alive or dead. It's like Blyton's only novel not written for children, *The Caravan Goes On.* Like a dream, it is no longer, the manuscript was not preserved, it has vanished, but in a caravanish way it goes on and on.

Freud suggests, in one of his many improvised lectures, that a snake is always uncanny. The way I understand this is that a snake never comes to rest. You can never get the final measure of a dream. The measuring tape was about the size of the cake – the impossibility of having and eating it. The retraction of the measuring tape was 'retirement'; the cutting edge of 'voluntary severance'. The measuring tape figuratively and literally 'came out' of *Reading the Times*, a book that is richly informative about measuring and calibrating time and times. The measuring tape was a snake. It was castration. It was homosexual longing. It was having a baby. It was reaching out. And so on and so on.

Last night, at bedtime, I was reading *The River*, the last of Enid Blyton's *Adventure* series, to my youngest son. You may know this book, characteristically strong on story, but deeply objectionable in terms of its colonialist representations of race and ethnicity, above all in its implicit assumption of some kind of 'white supremacy'. This is one of the more bizarre demands that reading Enid Blyton aloud makes on the contemporary reader: it's excellent practice, I suppose, if you have any desire to become a professional censor. I found I was having to pause and explain certain details, or simply cut and skip various sentences and phrases, as I was going along.

All of that aside, however, there is a boy called Philip, who has an implausibly strong and consistent special relationship with virtually all non-human animals. In particular, he has a highly poisonous bargua snake which – I kid you not – he keeps down his front. There are various references to taking it out and stroking it. There is a hilarious passage somewhere around the middle of the book where Philip is playing with the snake inside his shirt and putting 'gentle pressure' on the snake, which consequently wriggles with delight, and Blyton seems not to have any awkwardness about this – she might be playing with a less childlike reader's sense of humour, but just as plausibly, I suspect, she is merely down in the undermind, not giving a toss about whether it's innuendo or in your end don't. It's just an especially dramatic instance of that queer slippery-slidy space in which her writing takes shape.

I should add that the bargua, by the way, does not exist. I believe that it is the only animal in all of Enid Blyton's books that is merely fabulous.

OK. End of dream talk. It's time to play some music.

[Play David Bowie, 'Station to Station']

I hope that you enjoyed the silence at the end.

Perhaps you weren't listening? Let me play it again. (Joking.)

That was the title-track from David Bowie's *Station to Station* (1976), regarded by many people as his finest album. Famously not so much by Bowie himself who – due to his cocaine, amphetamine and baby elephant tranquilliser habits at the time – claimed to remember virtually nothing whatsoever about making it. This gives a new inflection to the phrase *avant-garde-a-clue.*

Just because people aren't present doesn't mean they're not doing stuff. That's one of the ideas I'm exploring here. Think of it as a trip into the golden years of the undermind.

When I was a teenager I developed a love of second-hand and antiquarian books. Not out of a love of reading – no, obviously not, as I've said I was too young for that – but rather out of sheer naked bibliophilia, a beautiful illness that my father transmitted to me and that afflicts me to this day. He had many an old tome at home. No doubt my love of books was originally nurtured there. But it was massively enhanced by the discovery of other buildings also containing old books. Look! Other people have shelves and shelves of old books too, and what's even better, these books are for sale!

Once upon a time there was a place called the Croydon Bookshop. It was on the A232, not long after you'd left Sutton, heading towards Carshalton. My father and I would visit regularly, of a Saturday morning. If you arrived promptly, just as it was sorting out its awning in the fresh bright sunshine of 10 o'clock, you could get one of the two designated car-parking spaces on the pavement directly outside. The Croydon Bookshop was a kind of heaven.

In those days every town in England had one or more second-hand bookshops. My father and I would go somewhere different every weekend. Occasionally, we'd drive as far afield as Chichester or Salisbury, but usually we stayed much closer to home. The Croydon Bookshop was our favourite. Its only real competitor was the ancient and labyrinthine Thomas Thorp's, at the top of Guildford High Street, a shop that is also long since departed.

The Croydon Bookshop was not cavernous like Thorp's, but it stretched away and back and had plentiful aisles, with books from floor to ceiling, in which to disappear. A small step-ladder, if desired, was never far away. I bought many books, down the years, at the Croydon Bookshop, especially nineteenth- and early twentieth-century poetry. Also, seventeenth- and eighteenth-century odd volumes, in original calf or vellum bindings. These were usually in Latin or works of English theology, but sometimes natural history or topography. I also developed a special interest in collecting copies of *The Rubáiyát of Omar Khayyám*, a poem first published by Edward Fitzgerald in 1859, said to be verses or *rubáiyát* translated from (or at any rate inspired by) Omar Khayyám, the twelfth-century Persian poet and astronomer.

As I recall this fact, I realise that it might have been this poem that really first set me thinking about books as sun machines. That would take my interest in this idea back to a time even earlier than Bowie's 'Memory of a Free Festival'. The idea of a sun machine is, after all, perhaps most easily thought about in the condensed form of a poem. As in those golden apples of the sun in Yeats that I talked about in an earlier lecture. The opening verses of *The Rubáiyát of Omar Khayyám* are all about the violent coming up or down of the sun ('Awake! for Morning in the Bowl of Night / Has flung the Stone that puts the Stars to Flight …'). And the quatrain I loved best was all about human phantasmagoria and an artificial sun:

For in and out, above, about, below,
'Tis nothing but a magic Shadow-show,
Play'd in a Box whose Candle is the Sun,
Round which we Phantom Figures come and go.

But the draw of the *Rubáiyát* was as much as anything else the illustrations, and the sheer variety of illustrated editions one could track down.

Books in the Croydon Bookshop were not necessarily in very good condition (or VGC, as lightly scribbled in pencil on the flyleaf). The worst – and I was not averse to this species – was WAF (with all faults). But whatever state the books were in, they were – for an enthusiastic teenager whose sole income derived from a bit of weekly pocket-money and doing a Sunday paper round – deliciously within price-range. I purchased, for example, a copy of Gilbert Abbott A'Beckett's *Comic History of England* for just a pound. A very tatty copy, to be sure, but with the hand-coloured John Leech plates all in VGC.

It is lying on my desk in front of me as I speak, in all its faded beauty of green cloth and gilt embossment. I remember the man in the shop's rather chilling term for it. A *breaker.* I became enamoured of the desire to *write* a breaker. A comic history of my own. Is that what is finally happening? Is that a possible variant title for these ghost lectures? *An Alternative Comic History of England.* Or perhaps better: *Reflections on How It Might Still Be Possible to Happily Describe Oneself as English, at Least at Moments, Without Immediately Wanting to Top Oneself in Embarrassment, Shame and Disgust.*

Listening to these words – as, in my mind's ear, I know he is – my father would be gladdened by the tacit correlation here, in accord with a classic conception, of comedy and happiness, but he would undoubtedly query the split infinitive, especially in a title. He would produce a very mild, scarcely audible sigh, signifying the gentlest *tsk.* But he would love me no less for the transgression, happily.

My father and I were never on first-name terms with the man who ran the Croydon Bookshop. He was rather gruff and distant but not unbenign, a lanky, bespectacled fellow who had a position in the shop behind a glass partition, so that he resembled a clerk at the post office or a pilot in the cockpit of an aeroplane. The glass encasement in which he sat makes him seem now merely protecting himself against a pandemic, fifty years ahead of his time.

One could attempt to chivvy him into conversation, but he was not a man of many words – at least not that he would expend in our hearing. He was manifestly serious about books, however, and about reading. When he wasn't, for his sins, attending as briskly as possible to some purchase or request from a customer, he was invariably reading a book. That's how I most clearly remember him: calmly setting aside the indubitable challenges of flying the world's first prototype bookshop-aeroplane, in order to settle back down at his table behind the glass partition and get on with what really mattered.

But what I loved most of all about the Croydon Bookshop was that it wasn't in Croydon. It wasn't even close. It might quite unassumingly have called itself the Sutton Bookshop or the Carshalton Bookshop, but 'Croydon Bookshop' just made no sense. My father and I more than once raised an eyebrow in unison on this topic, but we would never have countenanced pursuing an investigation. It might have been a simple matter, I suppose: *Good morning, how are you? We've been wondering, can you tell us, why is your bookshop called the Croydon Bookshop when it's not in Croydon?*

No, Alan, if that was his name – for in this abrupt fast-fading memory lane that has opened up, I vaguely hear someone one sunny Saturday morning addressing him as 'Alan' (in the same way that the woman at the bank in Frank O'Hara's poem about Billie Holiday, 'The Day Lady Died', was thought to be called Linda), unless it was 'Anyone', for in a sense *Anyone* is as beautiful as a name, I don't mean that Alan isn't a nice name, on the contrary I've always had a particular fondness for people called

Alan, and its orthographic variants (Allan, Alun, Allen), but there is something enchanting about the idea of a person called Anyone (that, after all, is surely Emily Dickinson's point in her poem about frogs and public advertising, when she speaks of a 'Nobody' that could just as well be an 'Anyone': 'I'm Nobody! Who are you? / Are you – Nobody – Too?') – no, Alan, if that was his name, if confronted with the question 'Why is your bookshop called the Croydon Bookshop?' (and one would have to put it in that slimmed-down form because one wouldn't, in the event, actually dare to add the killer clause 'when it's not in Croydon', one could only enquire, as courteously as possible, as if to say, 'Please, Alan, I'm sorry, I believe that's your name, I hope you don't consider it unduly forward to address you as such but why, if I may ask, are these premises – I mean, this location in which we are currently situated – called the Croydon Bookshop?'), if so confronted, well, there's no knowing how he might have responded.

Responded or reacted. In certain contemporary forms of psychotherapeutic practice there is a clear distinction: your *response* to something is not the same as your *reaction*. And some of you may be thinking that if Alan, or at any rate the man, the owner of the establishment in question, had *responded*, it would have been with some gruff but nonetheless helpful, simple, enigma-destroying clarification such as 'It *used* to be in Croydon' or, a shade more poignantly, 'I used to be in Croydon', or, relieved to be able to come out with it, 'It's hard to say really, but I always wanted to have a bookshop called the Croydon and this, geographically speaking, is as near as I've managed to get' or, with disarming alacrity, 'What's in a name, sonny-boy?' or, unable to take any more, 'That's it! How many times do I have to field this idiotic question? Enough of your soulless prying! Clear out of my aircraft this minute, pedantic fool!' And others may suppose that if Alan, or the nameless person to whom by this point I am feeling closer than at any point in my life, had *reacted*, he would – out of his tall, vaguely Venusian being (for I now realise he was just like one of those tall Venusian beings passing through, in Bowie's 'Memory of a Free Festival') – have mustered up a calmly measured fist and landed me a sanguinary punch on the nose, or drawn up, alternatively, the locomotive energy for a forceful knee in the groin.

Thankfully, however, the distinction between response and reaction is not so hard and fast, and indeed to acknowledge this is itself, I think, not only to start to see how humans are no more or less special in this regard than many non-human animals, and thus to nurture a more humble and enlightened, less anthropocentric conception of the world, but also to start to appreciate how a *Famous Five* book might have as much to tell us about the meaning of life as a novel by, say, Ian McEwan or Ali Smith. As with the necessarily disorienting question of what Timmy the dog would make of *you*, if you were to show up unexpectedly in his domain, whether he would take a favourable or a hostile attitude, and whether his behaviour towards you would constitute a response or a reaction or undecidably both, for instance in the form of a blithe and loving nip on hand or leg, no conundrum need detain us, since neither my father nor I ever had the gumption to ask the proprietor why his bookshop was 'the Croydon'.

So much pivots around Croydon. It's the point of connection and separation between Cheam and Beckenham. It's midway between the two. Cheam melds into the London borough of Sutton which slopes into Carshalton and Croydon. Beckenham morphs by South Norwood Country Park into Addiscombe which slides into Croydon and Carshalton. Cheam to Beckenham, Beckenham to Cheam: the A232 becomes the A222, or vice versa, and you're there. Bob's your uncle. Or Bobs your dog – but I'll come to that.

It was scarcely ten miles away, and yet I never went to Beckenham. Why would I have gone there, any more than Bowie would have come to Cheam? I know he came close, when he performed at the Toby Jug in Tolworth, before *Ziggy Stardust* came out. I was too young to go, but I vividly remember the older brother of a friend at school talking about having seen him the previous night. I recall not long after that, too, my first sight of the *Ziggy Stardust* album, just outside the toilets in the school playground. A boy called Michael Mariscotti had brought it in to show off. Not in a brash or loudmouthed way. I remember he was holding it lovingly, protective and a bit bashful, tucked under his right arm. It was the newest thing I knew to be the newest to be known and everyone else knew too. The sheen and glow of that album cover said so.

The closest I came to Beckenham was on my eleventh birthday (4 October 1968), when my parents took me and my brother to visit the caves at Chislehurst. It's the only childhood birthday of which I have any sharp recollection. I remember waiting in the queue, the air of anticipation, the strange actuality of the caves themselves, tunnels stretching in labyrinthine fashion, some open, others sealed off, for 23 miles underground. I remember the guide's warning not to walk off alone – and the darkness and fear at the thought of becoming utterly lost. Chislehurst is just a few miles east of Beckenham.

The caves must have been important for Enid Blyton: they make suddenly plausible the implausibly long and multiplicitous hidden tunnels and secret passageways in her books. They had a place too in David Bowie's life: he performed down there on at least four occasions. It was also where, in 1967, Bowie's half-brother Terry indeed wandered and got lost. According to Dylan Jones, he was down in the caves for 'eight days straight'. The guide's voice as he gave his warning to us now bears a ghostly inflection of what had happened to Terry Burns the previous year.

Until the autumn of 1976, when I left home to go to university, I was a long-term victim of what I called suburban abjection. Cheam was bad enough, but Croydon was beyond the pale. I remember visiting the Whitgift Shopping Centre when it was new. That must have been in or shortly before 1970. Croydon was the capital of suburban horror and despair.

It was the same for Bowie. As he recalled in 1999: Croydon 'represented everything I didn't want in my life, everything I wanted to get away from.' For him it was a powerful adjective: 'I think it's the most derogatory thing I can say about somebody or something: "God, it's so fucking Croydon!"'

As some of you may know, I wrote a book called *An English Guide to Birdwatching*. It's a book at least in part about the music of David Bowie, especially in what might be called the main death scene. But principally it's a story about a couple of undertakers called Silas and Ethel from Croydon. Where else would the undertakers of my undermind come from?

There once was a man from Croydon
Of whose gifts I could say 'I destroyed 'em!'
Without any need of a pardon
He had a perpetual hard-on,
Bringing 'Woodlock' to bear on each stiff
Till he drove us both off a cliff

The town for Bowie was closely connected to the tragic life of Terry Burns, who spent years in a mental hospital a few miles south at Coulsdon and died in the Mayday Hospital in Croydon in 1985. What I referred to earlier as Bowie's education system escape artistry was in part based on his inability or refusal to complete his studies at the Croydon School of Art.

More than fifty years earlier, D. H. Lawrence was likewise empowered by education in Croydon cut short. Around the time he officially ended his life as a teacher in Croydon, Lawrence wrote in a letter to his friend Arthur McLeod (23 February 1912): 'I loathe the idea of school more and more.' He was enraged by what he called 'the amount of blood and spirit I sold the Croydon Education Committee'. Croydon was a pivotal phase in losing himself as a young man and letting his 'demon' emerge, as he describes it in the Preface to his *Collected Poems*.

Soon after leaving Croydon, Lawrence left England altogether, to become a traveller, a terrestrial extra, a veerer, writing books that were and remain amazing works of resistance, escape and disguise. As he put it on another occasion: 'I can't bear art that you can walk around and admire. A book should either be a bandit or a rebel or a man in the crowd.' Through Terry, ten years his senior, Bowie as a teenager was particularly inspired by the writings of Jack Kerouac; but D. H. Lawrence was *on the road* long before that. Croydon is where it starts from. That's what Lawrence and Bowie teach: get away from the Croydon of your life, fly over mountains, escape, be a bandit, be a rebel, mix in with the crowd, keep moving, keep changing.

I will always be grateful to Alan, if that is his name. Thanks to him, Croydon has always had an additional, otherworldly meaning, associated with the love of books. This Croydon is imaginary. It is a literary flying bookshop post-office.

England's first international airport was Croydon. London Heathrow and London Gatwick are mere Johnny-come-latelies. Neither of these latter airports is, of course, in London. I like to think that they only bear the name 'London' due to the Croydon Effect, after a bookshop that was not in Croydon. 'Croydon Effect' would thus constitute what linguists might term an *anachronistic back-formation*, except that linguists, in my experience, are invariably precise, methodical, clear-thinking people who are perfectly familiar with the concept of back-formation and suitably knowledgeable and disdainful regarding anachronism, so wouldn't be caught dead bundling them up together, not even if you paid them (to coin another absurd phrase) a barrowful of cryptocurrency.

The double sense of 'Croydon' – Bowie's derogatory adjective and then the soaring irenic bookshop post-office in flight – come together in 'Memory of a Free Festival'. It's like you just can't get away from it – that's what's so fucking Croydon. You can go to LA or Switzerland or Berlin or live in New York for years and years, or you can live in Finland or Scotland or Sussex by the sea, for years and years, but you still have Croydon following you around.

The location of Bowie's coming into his own, the concert in August 1969, was a McCallum and Hope cast-iron bandstand, put up in 1905 and now a Grade 2 listed building. It is now called, in memory of that day, the Bowie Bandstand. It is in a park in Beckenham. The name of this park is the Croydon Road Recreation Ground. It's not in Croydon but named after it. It was here too, by the way, that 'Life on Mars?' emerged. Bowie recalls how the song came to him on 'a really beautiful day in the park, sitting on the steps of the bandstand'.

A few years prior to the construction of the bandstand, in 1902, the UK's first manned airmail flight – delivering post to three locations in Kent, before going on to Calais – departed from Croydon Road Rec in a hot-air balloon. The first post-office flying machine. Enid would have been just five, watching it float up over the trees.

It's the white balloon in 'Memory of a Free Festival', it's what children of summer send, at the end of summer, it's Bowie's song, his letter – to Hermione, to Peter, to his father, to his mother, to Terry, to Alan, to all, a sun machine in memory of place.

I draw today's lecture to a close not with a reprise, however, but with a song from *Hunky Dory* called 'Quicksand', recorded in 1971. Here, just a couple of years after 'Memory of a Free Festival', is a song by someone who has come into his own. *Coming into one's own* means: to be able to sing in a beautifully assured way about being nobody or anyone, about giving up all the 'bullshit faith' of belief in self or any organised religion.

Evoking Aleister Crowley's 'Golden Dawn', Heinrich Himmler's 'sacred realm' and Winston Churchill's 'lies', 'Quicksand' is a song about occultism and fascism. As with the Thin White Duke in 'Station to Station' (whose 'white stains', for example, alludes to Crowley's cranky writings), occultist and fascist elements are part of the performance. Like so many other great Bowie numbers, 'Quicksand' is a meta-song, a song about thinking about music. About its power of captivation and subjugation, its seductive and dangerous magic. As Jean-Luc Nancy suggests (I am referring again here to his remarkable little book called *Listening*), music is haunted by the possibilities of fascism and other religious or quasi-religious phantasms: music's 'capacities of harnessing, mobilization and exaltation were not invented by the Nazis'. 'Quicksand' is not advocating that anyone should submit to some murderous leader. It's about a 'dream reality' and its dark but also quirky, surrealistically glittery 'imagery' – from the contemplation of 'kiss[ing] a viper's fang' to the strangeness of thinking itself as quicksand.

'Quicksand' is wonderfully layered. It's sung in the first person 'I', but it's all about losing oneself – disappearing, going under, into other spaces and other people. The interplay of 'I' and 'you' ('Don't believe in yourself') makes 'Quicksand' a double song, a submerging duet, a form of 'Shadow Man' dialogue in which one 'I' claims, fantastically, to have knowledge of death, singing from beyond the grave, to a 'you' still living on.

The sinking feelings of 'Quicksand' are not without buoyancy and uplift. Everything spreads out and proliferates. As Chris O'Leary has noted, the producer Ken Scott, inspired by recently working with Phil Spector on George Harrison's *All Things Must Pass*, uses overlaying techniques to create the impression of at least half a dozen acoustic guitars at work, not just one. Enjoy too the lovely disappearing tinkle of Rick Wakeman's piano …

[Play David Bowie, 'Quicksand']

Picture break

Hello again. This session is less a lecture than a sort of picture break. Let's call it that. I want to talk briefly about some images: I promised earlier that I would do this, but the pictures I am going to show you at this point are not the pictures I said I would get on to later. They are a surprise – to me, I mean, in the first instance. They've just turned up.

Dum scribo. I don't know if any of you are familiar with that Latin phrase. It means 'While I write' or 'While I am writing'. It's a quotation from René Descartes, who is a lot better known for saying *Cogito ergo sum*. There was always something a bit quick-sandy, to my mind, about that claim.

Enid Blyton and David Bowie both work with a *dum* aesthetic, if you'll forgive my homophone – *dum* as in 'while' is mostly what I mean, but also 'dumb' as in silent, and even 'dumb' as in acting stupid, corny and goonish. But mostly I am interested in this Cartesian or post-Cartesian 'while I write' – in how writing involves chance, the unforeseeable. It's about how strange things crop up while you are writing and these things need not be obstacles or hindrances but can be moments of illumination, discovery, even transformation.

These interferences or interruptions might seem to come from inside you. In which case it's about being open – whether we call it immersion in the undermind, or having the sort of 'grasshopper mind' Bowie had, apparently not knowing where it's going to land next. Or these disturbances might seem to come from the external world, like when you're under the bedcovers at night – this was how it was for me and David Bowie, not in the same bed obviously, I mean when you're a boy and you should be asleep, but you're under the covers listening to Radio Luxembourg or some other pirate radio station, and there's interference and you lose it and have to go from station to station, trying to tune in again.

Interference from inside or from outside. Either way, the *dum* is not within your control. Either way, in fact, it's to do with what is not yourself, it's some kind of outside. It's foreign – that's the meaning of the word 'foreign': outside. *It's happening outside.*

So *while I am writing*, having just gone down in the quicksand of music and thought, at the end of the previous lecture, I receive an email from a complete stranger …

Here I need to backtrack a bit and say that, as I started working on this lecture series, I talked about it with a few friends, and one of them told one of *his* friends and this friend of a friend, someone I don't know, totally out of the blue, sent me an email, and this person is a man called Stephen Finer. We fell into correspondence, this stranger and I, at first over email and then over the phone.

It is all quite cryptic and bemusing. He comes across as reserved, protective of his privacy and inclined to keep his distance. We've talked on the phone a few times now, but he's always called me, because he doesn't wish me to know his telephone number. It's charming. There's a nice suggestion of the clandestine and hugger-mugger. But the conversation itself is very easy and pleasant. I don't know what he thinks about me, but I often find myself laughing while we are talking.

In any case, Stephen Finer is a painter and his portrait of David Bowie is in the National Portrait Gallery in London. If you type 'Stephen Finer' and 'Bowie' into your search engine, you'll get the picture. It's an oil on canvas, painted in 1994. It was acquired by the gallery in 1995.

In his initial email Stephen expresses his enthusiasm for my project, saying it has special resonance for him because he himself grew up in Beckenham. He was born a couple of years after Bowie, in 1949. He also tells me that he has some unpublished photographs of Bowie, which I'd be welcome to use if I'm interested. I am, of course, interested, and I am happy to be able to share my screen with you and let you have a look at them here.

But first of all I'd like to say something about Stephen Finer's painting of Bowie, because I think it's rather remarkable. I suppose I must have seen it before, but to be very honest (as a football pundit might say) I'd never really given it much thought. I'm actually just being honest, but there's a football pundit (whose name I shan't announce because it might seem unkind to single him out in this way) who regularly says *If I'm very honest* or *To be very honest* and it always makes me want to laugh because, I mean, either you're being honest or you're not, right? There aren't calibrations here, like 'somewhat honest', 'honest', 'very honest', 'apocalyptically honest'.

In any case what I'm saying is: at first sight you may regard this picture as a huge, silvery, oil-encrusted mess; but let it sink in, or let yourself sink in a bit, and all kinds of things start occurring. The National Portrait Gallery website has the following brief but suggestive description of his portrait-painting:

> Stephen Finer's working practice involves long hours in the studio […] in which paint slowly accumulates on the canvas and is worked and re-worked to create an image which finally corresponds to the artist's experience of the other person.

There is no painting equivalent of *dum scribo* in Latin, though I do like the sound of *dum pingo*. As a painter, in any case, Finer is clearly interested in what 'slowly accumulates', in what emerges, impinges, coalesces *in the meanwhile*, in the process of working on the canvas.

Finer's Bowie is not exactly an anamorphosis in the manner of Holbein's *The Ambassadors*, but its forms of 'likeness' may emerge more clearly as you look at the painting from a distance or a different angle. There are the musician's small narrow shoulders and the bronze blond mop of streaked hair and a mouth here and an eye there. It's not the Elephant Man, a skull, a spaceman or an extraterrestrial, but all of these are in play.

There's a sense of madness and the demonic. It makes me think of Bowie's stunning vocals on 'I'm Deranged', a song dating from this period. There's bloodiness daubed and a devilish red eye, as well as suggestions of the gentler pinks and oranges of Aladdin Sane. It's a painting of controlled chaos, a superimposing of poetically slapped faceplants, driplines placed with loving care and attention to symmetry.

Above all, 'the artist's experience of the other person' seems to be richly, formidably layered.

Layered: that's how Bowie talks in 1995 about his new, 'scary, most experimental' album, *1. Outside*: 'I am definitely not a minimalist,' he says. 'Layer it on! The thicker the better!' As he observed of a characteristically thickly painted work by Stephen Finer's friend, Frank Auerbach: 'I want to sound like that looks.' The artist Tony Oursler remembers looking at a Jacqueline Humphries painting one day with Bowie, and Bowie remarking of her work: 'It's very similar to the way I think about constructing music. Overlapping patterns and layers scraped away to reveal other patterns.'

Photographs aren't layered like paintings. And the photos I am going to share with you here are in a sense the least layered kind of pictures imaginable: they are Polaroids, images that appear within a few moments of being snapped, the pictorial equivalent of service, if you're lucky and if you like that sort of thing, at McDonald's. And yet, down the decades, the Polaroid has continued to appeal.

Doubtless it's the sense of the single, immediately identifiable, square 'artefact', the physical photograph, grainy, manifestly amateur and of the moment. And Polaroids can become paintings. This was true for Bowie himself. Gail Ann Dorsey recalls that he took Polaroid pictures of each member of the band, on the final day of the *Outside* tour, then painted portraits of them all and gave them out as Christmas presents.

There are eight photos here in all. In a moment I will share my screen and let you see them. But first I would like to offer a few quick observations and reflections ...

The longest, funniest, least straightforward conversation I've had with Stephen was yesterday.

He calls me up at the agreed time: he knows that I am keen to ask him a few questions about the photos.

But I begin by wondering if he can say how he went about the 1994 portrait. There is a longish pause on the other end of the line before he replies: 'I'm not superstitious or anything, but no, sorry, I can't talk about that.'

Fair enough, I say. I feel that way when someone asks me about how I write.

So then I ask about the photographs. I know Stephen took them, but where? What was the location? 'I'm sorry,' he says, 'no, I'm afraid I can't tell you that.' I laugh. How could one not laugh? But he explains that he is concerned it might be considered indiscreet. I tell Stephen I respect this and then, for a moment, I feel rather baffled. In the absence of, er, finer details, what am I ever going to be able to say about the pictures?

So, moving on, I ask *when* the photos were taken. Stephen confirms that they were all on the same occasion, but he can't tell me the exact date. As we talk, however, certain details come back to him, and he also goes off on some intriguing 'sidetracks', as he calls them. In due course it becomes clear that the pictures date from 6 March 1995.

Stephen first met David Bowie in a small gallery in Cork Street in London, one day in 1994. Finer was there and Bowie happened to walk in. It transpired that Bowie already knew his work, having seen his picture of Marlene Dietrich at 'The Portrait Now' exhibition that ran at the National Portrait Gallery from 19 November 1993 to 6 February 1994. Stephen recalls precisely what David said to him: 'I like your paintings very much, Stephen. I'll certainly be in touch. Shall we go somewhere and have coffee?'

Finer painted Bowie in late 1994. Bowie thought the picture was 'wonderful' and said he would like to have bought it himself. But the National Portrait Gallery had beaten him to it.

You can see the portrait resting on the ground in five of the photos here. The photos belong to the period shortly before Bowie's own first art exhibition, 'Afro-Pagan and Work: 1975–95', at the Gallery, 28 Cork Street, London in April 1995.

I ask Stephen if he can recall what they talked about that day, whether Bowie had said anything specific about the recently completed portrait, why he was laughing in at least one of the pictures. Fittingly, perhaps, Stephen cannot recall what generated the laughter: the meeting took place so long ago. One touching stray detail emerges: although Stephen grew up in Beckenham, where his father was a GP, he never disclosed this to David.

A sidetrack shunts us away to Lawrence Ferlinghetti and *A Coney Island of the Mind.* I recall that I met Ferlinghetti once at the City Lights bookstore in San Francisco, more than thirty years ago. I think of Bowie's line on the song 'Slip Away' about 'sailing over Coney Island'. I recall – but I don't mention – Bowie referring somewhere to Ferlinghetti as the sort of 'stream of consciousness' literature he enjoys. 'Stream of consciousness' always makes me see birds – that was the context in which William James first used the phrase – but I'm not saying any of this to Stephen.

Everything seems to be moving steadily more off-topic. In the silence I feel my brain leaking away … I fear I have nothing to say, nothing to ask, nothing to write.

But then there is *Hamlet.*

Stephen suddenly remembers that there were two productions of *Hamlet* on in London at that time. There was Stephen Dillane at the Gielgud Theatre on Shaftesbury Avenue, directed by Peter Hall, and Ralph Fiennes at the Hackney Empire, directed by Jonathan Kent. Finer had been to both. Bowie was going to get along to the Ralph Fiennes.

There is something strangely provoking about this abrupt remembering of *Hamlet.* It's so much a play about remembering and forgetting, grief and melancholy, isolation and time out of joint. Mentally speaking, at the time of these photos David Bowie couldn't have been further away from me. I wasn't living in England then. I was in Dunblane, in Scotland. I had drifted away from Bowie. I suppose I'd kind of dropped him, in the same way he seemed to drop people.

It's only been in the past few years, following his death, that I've gone back and really listened to the music he was producing in this period. *1. Outside* (1994) contains some beautiful songs. So when I look at these photos they give me great pleasure, but also sadness. No doubt it's to do with 'that rather terrible thing' that Roland Barthes talks about in *Camera Lucida*, the way photography is doomed to figure 'the return of the dead', but also how a picture, especially a Polaroid, frames a person in their isolation.

In their grainy, of-the-moment ordinariness, these images highlight my sense of Bowie as the great singer of isolation. More than Elvis Presley, John Lennon, Bob Dylan, Scott Walker or even Leonard Cohen, there is in Bowie a 'vulnerable sensuality'. That phrase appears in the sleeve notes to *The Man Who Sold the World.* There's a vulnerable sensuality or (perhaps better) a sensual vulnerability in all his work, and it's in these photographs too.

The three unsmiling head-and-shoulders pictures here seem especially striking in this respect. In a sense they could be anyone. There's a definite air of the mugshot in a couple of them. There's a criminal in David Bowie: that's a strong feature of the *Outside* album, but it's there in so many songs, right up to *The Next Day* and *Blackstar*. An innocent criminal: the man guilty of sensual vulnerability. In these three photos especially, I think, one sees the Bowie who found it easy to disappear. The Bowie who could don a hat and sunglasses and read a Greek newspaper while riding the New York subway and never be noticed. The singularity of the face is a reservoir of resemblances. There are, perhaps, layers after all.

Especially in the photo where Stephen's painting is just visible in the right-hand corner, he reminds me of a schoolfriend with whom I sadly lost touch, a fellow admirer of Bowie's music who, as Andrew Eldritch, became lead singer of The Sisters of Mercy. Weirdly, Bowie in this picture looks a little reminiscent of Andrew in the 1970s.

Time's script is you and me, but so are his pictures.

These Polaroids could be anyone but they're also not. It's David Bowie. His manner of looking at the camera has something of the intensity of focus described by Dylan Jones: 'It was all about focus. He could look at a situation and gauge its importance and its repercussions like a man watching sand run out of an hourglass.'

I love the fact that Bowie's smile and laughter also appear in these photographs. His humour is integral to what I love about his music. But while there is pleasure and even hilarity in the playfulness of the subject in the presence of the photographer's own recent painting of him, in the characteristic posing of hand on hip, in the leaning forward rather earnestly, his left arm extended and his right hand resting on his left knee, his elf-like right ear forming a funny, slightly uncanny rhyme with the handle of the coffee cup on the table, there is also something poignant.

The word 'poignant' comes from the Latin verb *pungere*, to prick. 'We prick you', to echo a phrase from *1. Outside*. That's what's going on in Barthes's concept of the *punctum*, the capacity that photographs have for making a wound, leaving a mark on the viewer. There is something painful, a haunting sadness in these pictures. That is what I am going to try to talk about next time.

OK, that's the end of my spiel. Here are the pictures.

What a big memory you have, Grandmother! (sixth lecture)

Hi and welcome once again from the virtual interlocutory device aka your phantom lecturer. This session is called 'What a big memory you have, Grandmother!' I'll explain in a bit. But first, a track from *Ziggy Stardust* (1972).

[Play David Bowie, 'Five Years']

You all know this song. It's been talked about quite a bit recently: David Bowie singing about the end times. It's all about chords and melodies. About where his voice takes you. He said he always found it difficult to articulate anything, except in chords and melodies: 'There, in the chords and melodies, is everything I want to say.'

When Bowie died, in January 2016, I felt bereft. It was ridiculous. I never knew the man. I saw him perform on a couple of occasions in the 1970s. Later, from the mid-1980s onward, I more or less lost track of him. But his death took me by surprise. It was a jolt into lost time. I was airdropped back into the late 1960s and early 1970s. And with that came a horrible feeling of injustice. The way we don't do justice to strangeness and beauty.

No one would ever hear the living Bowie sing or speak again. The raw enormity of a voice vanished. Its longing, its fluting desire, its drummed delirious, endlessly modulating richness and charm. Its guitared and feathered mimic octopus strangeness and grace. Its quicksand slides and saxophonic highs and lows.

Its changes, exchanges and pregnant stops. Its cocktail vapour trails of pathos and surrealism, candour and cosmic isolation, irony and laughter. All crystalline clarity, moan and exhalation, lift and sigh. Words sung, cried, whispered, screeched, squealed, crooned, burst.

I don't know if we have five years. The world feels deeply precarious. Perhaps we have fifty – or even, in some unimaginable shape and form, a hundred or more. But thanks to the current pandemic, we have it confirmed to us, more than ever, a sense of the ending, an apprehension of where it's heading. Long before *Young Americans*, Bowie's 'Five Years' is asking: *Can you hear me?* Alongside its plangent imaging of our world's ending, 'Five Years' encourages transformative thinking about the short-term.

In five years I will be David Bowie's age when he died. That's by the by. In what remains of these lectures I simply want to reflect a little on my life in teaching, and then try to say something about my grandmother. If that sounds random, I'm sorry. These things cohere, at least for me, and I want to share them with you.

I'd like to express my gratitude to you for listening and being here with me in the admittedly weird space of these asynchronous online audio presentations. There's no convention of a valedictory lecture. The Voluntary Severance Lecture is not a recognised genre. There's no institutional interest in hearing, let alone sanctioning any final words. On the contrary, to go quietly, with minimum disturbance, is what's expected of a scholar at the end of the day.

I don't wish to be noisy, any more than I want to be 'disruptive by design'. A line from 'Up the Hill Backwards' comes to mind: *It's got nothing to do with you, if one can grasp it.*

Still, I've always hoped good things might happen. In W. H. Auden's phrase, *all I have is a voice.* That's the meaning of *vocation.* All I have is a voice in which to disappear, like a creature going down into its burrow.

What is the point of studying English Literature at university? Whatever is the point?

Plenty of people today consider these very words, 'English' and 'literature', no longer fit for purpose. This seems to me a terrible blindness, a misguided idea that is – deliberately or not – in league with the work of those committed to ideological daylight Blobbery, in other words with all those child-despising, vicious and deeply stupid politicians (the true 'Blobs') who have connived to weaken and destroy one of the most imaginatively rich and intellectually valuable dimensions of national and transnational culture.

Absolutely at odds with the idiocies, sadism and vandalism of a variety of 'education system' politicians too contemptible to name stands the reality of studying literature – of actually reading books and feeling and thinking about them. IMHO, 'English' and 'literature', separately and together, are the names of mysterious things still to be dreamed. Still to be thought, still to be invented.

I'd like to try to illustrate this with some words by Walter Pater, pivoting on a phrase that I've used a couple of times already in these lectures without actually pointing out that it's a quotation. I'm referring to 'art and song', a phrase that occurs in the little text he wrote at the conclusion to his book *The Renaissance*. The Conclusion is only a few pages long, but at the conclusion to the Conclusion to *The Renaissance*, in the very last paragraph, Pater writes:

> we have an interval, and then our place knows us no more. Some spend this interval in listlessness, some in high passions, the wisest, at least among 'the children of this world', in art and song.

It seems to me that, in these thirty-six words (not even two full sentences), Pater says a lot.

Life is an interval – it's worse than *Waiting for Godot* in that sense. We don't even get to be in the play. But it's an interval we have. Time is *waiting in the wings*, as Bowie sings. We'd like to suppose that we're in the play, rather than just watching. *We should be on by now.*

The play started before us, and it may go on after us, assuredly without our knowing, but for now, there's this interval. *We should be on by now.* This theatrical 'interval' is not Pater's primary sense, but it whispers of life spent putting off, holding back, waiting for the right moment, not living the now. It prompts thoughts of Padgett Powell's dark but hilarious book *The Interrogative Mood*:

> Are you still living in such a way that suggests you are waiting for the real living to start at some later and unspecified date? Do you think this sense of delay or stalling would be wiped away were you told you had, say, twenty-two months to live, rock-solid certain you'll be gone in twenty-two months from, say, esophageal cancer – would you set about the *actual living* you have in theory been not yet doing?

But of course 'interval' is a rich word that leads off in other directions as well. Etymologically it has to do with what is between ramparts. I like the suggestion in that of something vulnerable, something in-between and even (if you will) erotic. 'Interval' is gentle and delicate.

We are born (but we know nothing about that) and then we die (but we know nothing about that), and what happens in between is the interval. There's a responsibility intimated in the having. If 'we have an interval', we have a responsibility for thinking critically about how we spend it. We have five years, that's all. Or, possibly, longer. Or less. Far less. Elsewhere in the Conclusion, Pater has a lovely image about how 'what is real in our lives fines itself down'. We might think of this distinguished Victorian gentleman as Walter *Not Later* Pater. There is a calm in his words, even if it has a sort of vertiginous quality as well, spinning into oblivion.

'And then …', he says: *we have an interval, and then* … He puts a comma after 'interval'. It's important. The comma is a mark of love and respect for the reality and preciousness of the interval.

'We have an interval, and then our place knows us no more.' The comma is like a forgotten tadpole wiggling away, but in its wake time becomes space, 'interval' becomes 'place' and by the same turn becomes something akin to what psychoanalysis calls 'the subject who is supposed to know', in other words the analyst. It's an anthropomorphism, of course, this suggestion that a place can know you.

I guess you might all have had some experience of returning to a town or street or house which was once important to you and now no longer recognises you. Beckenham and Berlin no longer know David Bowie, any more than Beckenham and Beaconsfield know Enid Blyton. It's a projection, a poetic fiction that a place no longer knows us. It is also euphemistic, literally a speaking well, a speaking gently of death. It's like my father saying to me, with what transpired to be uncanny prescience, on the eve of his death: 'These things happen from time to time.' That was my father's way of evoking the interval, and the phantasmagoric bell at the end.

Still, Pater's phrase 'and then our place knows us no more' carries the intimation of a kind of magical remainder: as if to say, it's the end, we are the dead, walking the dead, but our place, during that interval, did know us.

And then comes Pater's second sentence: 'Some spend this interval in listlessness, some in high passions, the wisest, at least among "the children of this world", in art and song.' How are you going to spend your interval? It is an enigmatic series of options. It looks like there are three: listlessness, high passions, and then art and song. Pater lets us hear the drag and dullness in that 'listlessness'. To be listless is to be without relish or inclination to move, like a boat that won't go anywhere. Listlessness is languid indifference and apathy. Like a sauteed couch potato that doesn't realise it's in the frying pan. It seems that 'high passions' would be good – it's offered as something of an opposition to the listlessness – but this is tempered by the third offering in the series, 'the wisest'.

It's not certain that wisdom is simply separate from passions. Pater implies an accretive or upward movement in which, once we let go of the folly of the couch potato, high passions can give way to the greatest thing, which is the wisdom of art and song.

You may remember my quoting, in the first lecture, Pater's famous remark (also in *The Renaissance*) that *All art constantly aspires towards the condition of music*. It's not by chance that the sentence we're talking about here ends with 'song'. You can see, I hope, or perhaps hear, the rightness (taking it all the right way, making it right), the sentence doing it right by ending in 'song'. It just wouldn't be the same if it ended 'song and art'. For Pater, it's all about voice and music. The wisdom is not ours, it's in the aspiration to what art and song can give.

And it's a wisdom curiously bound up with the child. We are, in Pater's phrase, 'the children of this world'. This idea puts him in the same zone as Enid Blyton and David Bowie. Of course, it's not Pater's own phrase. He pins it to the golden wall of his writing with silver quotation marks. He nicks the phrase from the Bible (Luke 16:8) and repurposes it, turning the sacred into the pleasure of art and song in itself, art and song for their own sake. That was perhaps the most quietly shocking thing about the Conclusion to *The Renaissance* when it was first published. Pater says nothing about an afterlife, Christian or otherwise. We have an interval, and then our place knows us no more. There's no pudding, no afters. Life is just, as he puts it, 'this short day of frost and sun'.

Some of you may be wondering why I have been going on so much about some old codger, Walter 'Not Later' Pater, who was writing a bunch of art history essays in the nineteenth century. But the point is that his radical conception of life is as urgent and pressing as it's ever been. I don't know if David Bowie ever read the Conclusion to *The Renaissance* (I imagine he did, because he read a lot), but we wouldn't have Jack Kerouac's *On the Road* without Pater. Bowie's emphasis on the *now* may have come through Kerouac but it's Not Later Pater who's behind all that, just as he's behind the so-called 'stream of consciousness' writing of Virginia Woolf.

Take, for example, this celebrated brief extract from Kerouac's novel:

> the only people for me are the mad ones, the ones who are mad to live, mad to talk, mad to be saved, desirous of everything at the same time, the ones who never yawn or say a commonplace thing, but burn, burn, burn like fabulous yellow roman candles exploding like spiders across the stars …

If Kerouac's 'spiders across the stars' foreshadow Bowie's from Mars, the burning candles are pure Pater. As Pater writes in the final paragraphs of *The Renaissance*: 'To burn always with this hard, gemlike flame, to maintain this ecstasy, is success in life.' But Pater's vision, his affirmation of the present moment is more radical. It's Kerouac without the Catholicism, without the candles having to be roman and without the talk of being saved.

'Art and song' is about sun machines. On 'this short day', *aka* life, a sun machine may be coming down thanks to some book or song or picture. A book or song or picture that aspires to the dissolution of all these categories. A sort of UMO perhaps: an unidentifiable musical object.

It will be evident to you by now, I hope, that my conception of a novel doesn't really sit comfortably with that of the publishing industry or academic canon-keeping. A book must seek to *do something*, besides give pleasure or tell stories. It has to make trouble with language or let language make trouble. It has to affirm chaos and the fact that language messes with identity. Language likes to go off by itself, it likes to dream. It won't rest, it can't be owned or controlled. In the realm of music, this is the David Bowie of the cut-up, the demonic, multiple and proliferating voices, prosopopoeia, the ghostly, the fragmentary and, perhaps most of all, aposiopesis …

The moment I say this, I realise I haven't until now actually mentioned 'aposiopesis' by name in these lectures. Aposiopesis is key. It's the rhetorical figure for … You must have heard me do this in a lecture before. I don't know how many times … It's my favourite joke, I'm sorry.

Aposiopesis is the name for the rhetorical figure in which …

Hold on, bear with me, I'm going to put on a straight face now: aposiopesis is an unfinished or incomplete …

I can practically hear you groaning. It's not fair or reasonable of me. But I'm talking about the interval and the strangeness of the now. I'm talking about suggestion and danger, love and dream. And permit me to take up this ellipsis, this little pause in the proceedings, to make what I hope is a pretty obvious point, namely that the love of 'art and song' is not something that happens *on the side*, it's not something that takes the place of revolutionary politics, the fight for justice, the work of NGOs and underground movements, resistance to the fascist manipulation of populations, waging war on the oligarchic obscenities of misinformation and fake news, but it's the pulse, the force that makes such passions possible.

Aposiopesis – I'm not going to keep this joke going any longer, it's really had its day, there's a limit, I know …

Aposiopesis is a trope or figure in rhetoric that refers to a sentence or statement that is interrupted, cut-off, incomplete, unfinished. OK: so now are you happy? Did you really need to know how it ended?

Aposiopesis doesn't end where it ends, that's the point, that's the point of the mischievous, multivalent, wavering 'I'm better' in Bowie's 'New Killer Star' ('I never said I'm better, I'm better, I'm better, I'm better than you') or, very differently, breath drawing out in a final embodiment, 'I can't', 'I can't give', 'I can't give everything', 'I can't give everything away …'

The title of the touring exhibition that began at the Victoria and Albert Museum in London in 2013 and ended at the Brooklyn Museum in New York City in 2018 would be another obvious example: *David Bowie Is*. David Bowie is what?

Aposiopesis is crucial to an understanding of his music. Much has been made of the cut-up (Bowie's indebtedness to Brion Gysin and William Burroughs), but I would argue that aposiopesis is more fundamental, more suggestive and illuminating of what

Nicholas Pegg calls the 'tantalising chinks' in Bowie's songs, more capable of opening the …

Do I need to explain what and where, and how it doesn't, how it never …?

Anyhow, I was trying to do one of those nicely arching 'On the one hand … On the other' things where 'art and song' is about making trouble – no beauty without danger, no life without veering – and at the same time it's also about *making the truth.* St Augustine wonders in his *Confessions* why it is necessary to confess to God when God already knows everything. We confess as a way of making the truth, Augustine suggests.

Let me be clear here. I'm not talking about authenticity. I don't think David Bowie, any more than Jacques Derrida, was interested in 'authenticating' anything. 'Authentic' is hardly an adjective that springs to mind in the context of Enid Blyton either. I'm talking more, I suppose, about candour and vulnerability. In the case of Bowie it's something you can hear perhaps most intimately in his early song 'Letter to Hermione', but it's still there in 'Five Years', for example, and it's there too in the final track on *Blackstar*, 'I Can't Give Everything Away'.

Something happens in the voice, in the saying, in the words as they tumble or stumble from our mouths or on to paper to make truth. There's a music of making truth.

We need sun machines that fly clear of all the lies and distortions around us. It might be a *Famous Five* by Enid Blyton or a memory-work by W. G. Sebald or a heliotropic fiction by Kazuo Ishiguro. Whatever we might choose to call them, they throw new light on the nature of the undermind, writing and memory, the gift of having an interval, and the mysteries and responsibilities of being a human. This is why, in an era of 'alternative facts', 'post-truth', fake news, misinformation, deep fakes and synthetic media, sun machines matter.

Up to this point, I haven't really talked about 'the life' of Enid Blyton. If you read, for example, the account given by her daughter

Imogen Smallwood in *A Childhood at Green Hedges* (1989) or Nadia Cohen's biography *The Real Enid Blyton* (2018) you encounter disturbing polarities. You find a woman who was intensely committed, who had a firm moral vision and who worked enormously hard for various charitable causes, but who also neglected and inflicted pain and suffering on those close to her, including her mother, her brothers, her daughters and her first husband.

So far, I've focused on 'the work' of Enid Blyton – especially on her *Famous Five* books, but also on what I see as the art and song of her 'writing for children'. I now want to shift focus a bit, however, and try to sound out a more biographical dimension.

I'm going under, I have to tell you. I'm letting in the dead.

Blyton is not immune to letting the dead speak. Her beloved black and white fox terrier Bobs does it. His letters in *Teachers' World* magazine continued to appear for years after his death.

One day my mother said to me: Your grandmother had an affair with Enid Blyton.

Those were her words. She might have put it differently. Your grandmother was of the other persuasion. Your grandmother and Enid Blyton were lesbian lovers. They were queer. They had a thing together. But it came in that rather formalised rendering: *Your grandmother had an affair with Enid Blyton.*

This is what came back to me in the pandemic, early on but late enough to be feeling already blitzed, bleary and blinded with the amount of Blyton I was reading to my young children every day. It was the oddest shadow running through those weeks turning into months. It was something I remembered but in remembering realised I'd never troubled to think about. It was like a foreign object in the garden that had always been there, but unconsidered. It was like a door in the house I'd forgotten was a door, or a dinosaur fossil suddenly flash-lit in the ceiling of a tunnel at the Chislehurst caves on my eleventh birthday.

It's a noteworthy revelation, I suppose, for the biographer who wonders, as Blyton biographers do seem to like to wonder: 'Did she lead a double life? Did she have a love affair with another woman?'

In what context did my mother make this announcement? It must be forty or more years since she said it. And it's almost half as long again since she died.

There are sunny spots of memory that come from no longer being a spring chicken. I appreciate, as I never did in my youth, how the recollection of this or that speech or event or experience doesn't exist in amber, like insects trapped in lovemaking fifty million years ago. The amber softens and sets anew every time you cast your mind back. Writing about my mother in recent years – and now preparing these lectures – has enabled me to appreciate as never before how the act of writing is a way of treating amber that is in certain respects more delving, and also therefore more capable of resurrecting, drawing up (like buckets from wells of the undermind), than any other mode of recall. Smells and sounds vividly return us to people and places, photographs restore a ghostly freshness, thinking with eyes closed and body at rest brings back remarkable silhouettes, but writing can lead us by the hand into passages and places previously unknown.

When Hamlet hears the ghost of his father, he rushes off to his tables to set down what he has heard. At first this may seem ridiculous. The Ghost has just said 'Remember me', and the son needs to *write that down*? But Hamlet's response is a dramatic statement of the vital connections between memory and writing. Indeed, in my lecturing career, I've sometimes evoked this moment in Shakespeare's play as a comical but also serious example of the need to take notes: if you don't jot it down, you won't remember it, even if you think you will. *Hamlet* is a masterpiece of bestial oblivion, but also of writing in memory.

As we may recognise from some of the most intense memory-writing of the twentieth century, such as Marcel Proust's *In Search of Lost Time* or Eileen Chang's *The Fall of the Pagoda*, remembering is bringing back, assembling, bit by bit. It's archaeology and modern design in one. But with writing – as distinct from merely sitting in an armchair or lying in bed, furrowing your brows, trying your damnedest, wracking your brains to reconstruct – there is always the chance of discovering another door, even a completely other building.

One day my mother told me that Enid Blyton and my grandmother were lovers. I hear her say it: *Your grandmother had an affair with Enid Blyton*. What kind of past tense was she using? What time frame was she conceiving?

My mother's tenses. They would merit a book in their own right. How to be doing it right to my mother's tenses? You had to 'listen in' to the grain of her speech. You had to enter her speech as a thought bubble.

She was not referring to her own but to my father's mother. She was not suggesting that my grandmother and Enid Blyton had been lovers over a period of many years. At least, at the time, I didn't think so. She wasn't suggesting that their affair had caused the breakup of the family. Depending on how one understands *breakup*. Or *affair*.

But why was she even talking about this topic? How did it ever come up in the first place? It couldn't have been apropos nothing. My mother was empress of rhetorical disjunction, but even *she* wouldn't just, out of the blue, as I'm making us our fourth cups of instant Nescafé Gold Blend of the day, declare: *Your grandmother had an affair with Enid Blyton.*

Of certain things I have no doubt. First, that my mother, for all her playfulness and capacity for mischief, wouldn't say something of this nature flippantly. Second, that she knew more than she was letting on. And third, that her interest in the love life of my grandmother and Enid Blyton was not in any way marked by disdain or disapproval.

Why is it that I don't recall anything else from the conversation that sunny morning – for, as I recollect, I find that sunlight has filled the kitchen, putting my mother with her cup of Nescafé and

Silk Cut cigarette in the shade, but shining more or less directly on me, in my eyes and face, as I stand beside the counter with my own coffee and cigarette? Motes of bright smoke hang in the air. We must have been speaking of my grandmother or else we must have been speaking of Enid Blyton. I'm inclined to suppose it was the former, but I draw a blank on what we might have been saying. I suppose it's neither here nor there. But what I find most bizarre is that, as far as I recall, my mother's remark was the last thing said on the subject.

What do you mean my grandmother had an affair with Enid Blyton? When did this happen? How do you know about this? Who else knew? What does my father think about it?

All of these questions now seem to me intensely interesting. Why on earth did I not put any of them to my mother at the time?

Your grandmother had an affair with Enid Blyton. You may reasonably wonder why it was my mother who was divulging this information about a skeleton in the family cupboard – for there was in her statement something of a grinning flash – and not my father whose mother she was talking about. But then you didn't know my father. There is no possible way that my father would ever have said such a thing to me. It is not remotely plausible to imagine my father saying any of the following phrases: *Enid Blyton and my mother were lovers, they had a lesbian affair, they had a romantic liaison, my mother and Enid went to bed together.* No words or phrases even faintly resembling these could ever have passed his lips. At least when speaking to me.

But my mother knew. I try to picture my father communicating this information. I have to suppose it possible: someone would have to have told her. It seems too weird to imagine that my father's *father* told my mother and that my father didn't know.

The mystery of one's parents!

Perhaps I should say something here about my mother's sexuality? How she would laugh at those words, *my mother's sexuality*! What bureaucratic psycho-drivel! Her satirical contempt for such pigeon-holing phrases was part of what made her alien to any education system, like others I've been discussing. My mother evidently had sex with my father on at least two occasions. Enough to bring two sons into the world. And she was in her own distinctive way – if I can say this with an inflection of her own high-pitched laugh of joy and derision – a highly sexualised being. She flirted with men of all types and backgrounds. I think of that as intimately bound up with her vocation as a nurse. Eros was everywhere. But I don't sense my mother much enjoyed sex with men. She had romantic affairs with other men before she met my father. But I never got the sense that the phallus much excited her.

Undoubtedly, she had sexual feelings for other women. On her hockey teacher at Putney High School for Girls, for example, she once told me she had a 'huge pash'. And her attractiveness to men seemed to be based in part on her very uninterestedness. Her tendency to flirt, to tease, to tickle with double entendre was the flipside of her lack of sexual interest in those with whom she got, with every further sally or riposte, ever more deceptively entangled. In her speech and in other ways, my mother was a force of liberation before anyone had invented 'women's lib'. So when she told me that my grandmother had a female lover, I knew she was not implying any negative judgement. On the contrary, she was affirming something about the truth and value of her own experiences. It is perfectly feasible that her observation about my grandmother was intended as a prelude to revealing something about her own past.

I'm sorry, I'm going to have to bring things to a pause for now. I'll have to come back to this next time. You sense perhaps what drove me to call this lecture 'What a big memory you have, Grandmother!' It feels huge. Literally colossal. And as yet, I sense, I'm only at the bright bubbled amber surface.

It's the world as memory of the grandmother. You'll hear in this, I hope, something of David Bowie's play on the phrase 'memory of', in 'Memory of a Free Festival'. 'Memory of' is always double. It's over but still happening, commemorated and commemorating.

It is what the memory is *of*, and it is 'in memory of' (now and into the future). That's what I hear in the line about the sun machine *coming down*. It's memory *in the present* and it's coming, so it's futural, it's not stopped happening, or not happened yet. There is the grandmother's memory and the memory of the grandmother.

For the moment I'm just going to suggest that the grandmother is the prettiest star, for a lad insane or a girl, and see you next time.

[Play David Bowie, 'The Prettiest Star']

But the clouds (seventh lecture)

[Play the first movement of Beethoven's 'Moonlight' sonata]

As you perhaps know, that was Beethoven's Piano Sonata No. 14 in C sharp minor, the 'Moonlight' sonata, in this case performed by Daniel Barenboim. I've played you just the first movement but, once again, I encourage you to listen to the whole thing. It's a sonata that Thomas Blyton liked to play to himself, and to his daughter upstairs in bed, or to anyone still awake, at night in Beckenham back in the days when he still lived there, before he walked off into another life.

What is a sonata? According to George MacDonald it is something shared, something that enables listeners to commune, to feel a 'consciousness of sympathy', but at the same time it 'seizes you and sweeps you away', into 'the region of the uncomprehended'. It is here that MacDonald sees a strong affinity between the sonata and the fairy tale.

It's that 'queer feeling' again, which I talked about earlier, of how music transports you back and away in time. The 'Moonlight' sonata is one of those pieces of music that my own father played, on a mono record player, on a Sunday evening when my brother and I were just boys, lying in bed. And I have to tell you I can't bear it. I played the first movement to you just now because I can't bear it. It's so packed to the rafters with loss. I cannot listen to it without feeling, like D. H. Lawrence in his poem 'Piano' (1913), 'cast / Down in the flood of remembrance'.

This is one of the flabbergasting things about being a time machine. In youth you scarcely notice it. As years go by, other perspectives and complexions slip in. It's necessary to go carefully. You might lose yourself in Regret. The land of Regret welcomes all. You can visit and even settle there without difficulty. Then, gradually, the borders harden. You discover it has changed its name. It is Anxiety, a messed-up principality under constant threat of Death's invasion.

On the matter of regret, as in so much else, I followed my mother. She loved to sing snatches of songs as she was sitting at the kitchen table, or as she moved around the house, or as we were out walking somewhere. Edith Piaf's 'Non, je ne regrette rien' and Frank Sinatra's 'My Way' (with its regrets 'too few to mention') were regular visitors to her lips. It is tempting to wonder how far such refrains were a testimony to the contrary – melodies haunted by regrets – but I accepted them as motherly reminders of the importance of not being earnest about their power to harm.

My father seemed likewise to have no inclination to regret. If challenged, he was fond of quoting the absurd words of *Candide*: 'All is for the best in this best of all possible worlds.' On other occasions he liked to say, 'All things are possible to him who believes', a remark attributable to St Mark in the New Testament, though I don't think my father was much concerned with its Christian provenance. Generally he lived in quiet accordance with his own idiosyncratic and inscrutable forms of eastern philosophy. He had no interest in the land of Regret, where longing is promoted as timeshare and people count their losses.

It's what you don't find in John Keats. It's what makes him such an affirmative, youthful poet. Keats is always looking ahead. He is what Paul de Man calls a *prospective*, not a retrospective thinker.

This is how I used to think of David Bowie as well. He's Keatsian. He's forward thinking, forward feeling, forward singing.

Bowie feels compelled to make every day 'as good as I can possibly make it'. He often speaks of not being interested in looking back, only in moving forward: 'I'm not hungry for the past,' he declares. Or as he sings in the finely saxophonised late piece, 'No Plan': 'All the things that are my life … Nothing to regret.'

But everyone has to spend time in the land of Regret, if only in transit or denial. And even if you're only planning a quick visit, you're in danger. This is where we can find Tennyson at his wildest and most deathly sweet. It's in the brief lyric I quoted in an earlier lecture, in the context of all the kissing in 'Memory of a Free Festival'. It's called 'Tears, Idle Tears':

Ah, sad and strange as in dark summer dawns
The earliest pipe of half-awaken'd birds
To dying ears, when unto dying eyes
The casement slowly grows a glimmering square;
So sad, so strange, the days that are no more.

Dear as remember'd kisses after death,
And sweet as those by hopeless fancy feign'd
On lips that are for others; deep as love,
Deep as first love, and wild with all regret;
O Death in Life, the days that are no more!

Regret has a way of suddenly becoming strange. What a simple but unfathomable word! Its first syllable suggests the clear but mistaken impression of something repeated. *Gret* again. As if James Joyce, in naming her Gretta in his story 'The Dead', wanted to imagine some original *gretter* before regretting.

I see the *egret* in the word. A figure in which, perhaps, regret meets grief. An egret is a small white heron but also the feathery pappus on certain plants, most notably the clock of a dandelion. Time blown away.

I recall the precious moments, travelling on the train to or from the university, passing through the port of Newhaven, when the tide was low in a small tributary close to where the Dieppe ferry comes in, and there, if I was lucky enough that day to see, was a solitary white egret, stood stock still in the shallow water, like something already from another time, a doomed planet, five years of mud and milkshake sucked up and gone.

By then East Sussex County Council had already given the go-ahead for 'developing', that is to say *destroying* the area, with the construction of a new road and bridge slicing a swathe out of the coastal nature reserve of Tide Mills, to enable the installation of a MediPower incinerator. It was a corner of the reserve that no one now would be able to visit or indeed come out of alive. Certainly not the egret. I am talking about a 'clinical waste plant', where up to 12 tonnes of medical waste, including human body parts, get burned every day.

Giving his unequivocal backing to the proposal, the Conservative Party councillor Bob Bowdler observed: 'I've read the report and I find it difficult to find anything not to like about it. I think it makes a good contribution environmentally …' You couldn't make this stuff up. Can you imagine a more bowdlerised account?

I find it difficult to find … I mean, I've had a good squint. I don't live in the area myself, but I've read the report and I can only conclude, if I may half-inch a locution better known to our environmentally unfriendly friends across the pond, *what's not to like?* I find it difficult to imagine [suppressed chortle] that anyone living nearby would have the slightest objection to a great bonfire of human body parts blazing away every day on their doorstep. I find it difficult to see why the great-crested newts and purple sandpipers and oyster-catchers and other superfluous creatures on the adjacent wetlands should be put out in the slightest. I admit I haven't looked into the question of the egret. Who knew there was an egret? In any case, as I was saying, what with not being familiar with the area but having read the report, I find it difficult to find … what was it? I find it difficult not to find, no! I find it difficult not to, I find, oh whatever, I tell you, I like it! Oh yes, liking it would be an understatement. Totally positive! Positive contribution to the environment. Bring it on, I say! Let's get those ancient wetlands drained, let's get those trucks rolling, looks like we got us a convoy, eh what! Let's raise a bridge and a glass or two – to gasification galore!

Please forgive that attempted impersonation of a Tory councillor I've never met. Really it was all about the egret, and about the sense that even in the few years since Bowie's death our world has changed in horrible ways. The egret is an eerie figure, for me, of the idea that climate emergency entails a new, necessarily deranged experience of regret.

I still think of David Bowie as the greatest singer of the present moment in modern times. The most haunting voice of the *now, not tomorrow*. But I've also come to appreciate how profoundly 'regret' features in later years – in songs such as 'Sunday', 'Slip Away' and 'Everyone Says Hi' (on *Heathen*), and 'Love is Lost' and 'Where Are We Now?' (on *The Next Day*). His engagement with regret in these late songs is rich and complex, magisterial and playful. It's distinctly *layered*, to recall the word I was talking about in our 'Picture Break'. Regret is staged, sung, performed.

Among other things – especially in the video of 'Where Are We Now?' – it's a matter of regret resonating out of a voice, music and images that are *in the present* but that 'fuck with the fabric of time', to borrow Tony Visconti's phrase. What is the 'now' – where we are now – of this song?

Correspondingly, 'Love is Lost' – particularly the ten-minute version on the EP of *The Next Day* (the 'Hello Steve Reich Mix by James Murphy for the DFA') – works on multiple levels in terms both of composition and production and of how it is to be heard or read. 'Love is Lost' is a brilliantly melodramatic lament for youth, yours or mine. It's an autobiographical lyric about being 22, having lost Hermione Farthingale. It's about the demonic – the 'lunatic men' who carry off everything. It's about the mortal vertigo of thinking like mad and knowing you know you know and still you must sing. Then in another sudden and surprising use of the second person ('you'), it's addressed to an enigmatic 'beautiful girl'. It's about the death of Bowie's friend John Lennon. It's about the chiasmatic purity, the no longer tenable innocence of 'love is real, real is love', in the song 'Love' on *John Lennon/Plastic Ono Band*, a song my mother and I used to listen to over and over when it came out, around Christmas 1970. It's about Bowie's own back-list, from 'Space Oddity' to the Berlin albums to 'Ashes to Ashes'. And so on …

But 'Love is Lost' is also, I just want to say, an uncanny cry across the years following Bowie's death, tapping into and out of the horror of Shakespeare's *Macbeth* – 'I am afraid to think what I have done', 'What's done cannot be undone' – to become a resounding and awful rhetorical question addressed to humanity in its current state: 'Oh, what have you done? What have you done?'

It's a question for each one of us: What have I done? And, equally, now what am I going to do about it?

The recondity of one's parents and the questions one didn't ask or didn't realise one might have asked …

What was my father doing in the Croydon Bookshop, apart from infecting me with bibliophilia?

What now seems odd – but didn't at the time – was the infrequency with which he himself purchased a book. My father's chief interests were in heraldry and genealogy. Such items were uncommon. On returning from one of our Saturday jaunts I would usually be proud possessor of at least a couple of new old books in a brown paper bag, but he would usually be empty-handed. It was the same with mail order. He subscribed to a weekly catalogue, listing second-hand and antiquarian books for sale. I can't recall the name of this publication, but I remember that the front cover featured the insignia of the Antiquarian Booksellers Association with its motto: AMOR LIBRORUM NOS UNIT. *The love of books unites us.* And I remember the excitement when, on a Wednesday or Thursday, the catalogue arrived in the post. My father read it first, before passing it on to me. In red ink he'd mark things up in the margins with a cross, a question mark or an exclamation mark, for himself but, more often, for me. In truth he rarely ordered anything himself.

Yet as I formulate these words, something comes back, overlooked and left behind. Something I hadn't allowed, hadn't seen I might have thought aloud. There was one other subject besides heraldry and genealogy in which my father took an interest, and now as never before I see how primary and profound this was. I see it suddenly thanks to Alan, if that was his name, and the time when …

The time when!

Like many other owners of second-hand and antiquarian bookshops in those days, the owner of the Croydon Bookshop had a couple of glass-fronted bookcases, close to the cockpit and indeed even inside it. Other antiquarian booksellers whose shops we visited likewise kept jealous guard of certain books. There were books that you could access if the owner didn't dislike the cut of your jib: he'd open up the relevant case with a key. But there were also books altogether more out of reach. In the case of the Croydon Bookshop, these were shelved in the cockpit or post-office interior. These books were in the shop but not for sale.

Extraordinary! Wonderful! Fascinating! Queer!

The time when: we were visiting the Croydon Bookshop one sunny Saturday bright and early, a warm but gusty day in spring, and Alan, if that was his name, after we'd entered the shop and he'd gruffly recognised my father, looked at him and said: *I've got something for you.* And this was all about the fact that my father had asked him at some point, possibly months or even years earlier, whether he had anything illustrated by an artist called Lola Onslow. And now I recall vividly, but for the first time in several decades, that this was a question he put to *every* bookdealer, when first visiting their shop. I even feel an empathic tremor of embarrassment in recollecting this, because my father was so averse to speaking to anyone unnecessarily, and this request was invariably the closest thing to a major social event in which he ever participated, involving a second-hand bookshop owner.

And whether what is happening in this act of remembering is a ravelling or an unravelling, an analysis or its collapse, I now see that *this* was the point of my most treasured times with my father, the joyous weekly trips to second-hand bookshops. This was the *raison d'être* of the lovely illness he bestowed upon me. My father was looking for his mother.

My passion for books, and above all for illustrated copies of *Omar Khayyám*, grew out of this unseen. It was really all about his mother, his longing, his grief. Over the years that we went to old bookshops I collected ninety-nine copies of the *Rubáiyát.* I don't know why I stopped one short of a hundred, but I did. They included early editions, limited editions on handmade paper, and a wide range of illustrated editions – picture-books with colour plates or other fine designs by René Bull, Willy Pogany, Annie Fish, Edmund Dulac, Edmund J. Sullivan, N. C. Wyeth and many others. I loved acquiring these books and my father loved to encourage me. But it is only now that I realise what, for him at least, it was all about, and why we went to any of these old bookshops in the first place.

Notionally we were always looking for the work of children's book illustrators, such as Dulac and Arthur Rackham. We knew about the desirability of Kay Nielsen's books as well, but we also knew that everyone else knew. Nielsen was out of our league. We weren't experts in this field in any sense, but my father had acquired and communicated to me an understanding that Kay Nielsen was special. We supposed that Kay Nielsen was a woman. We thought she was Swedish. In fact he was Danish. He commanded significantly higher prices than other illustrators. When we were in a shop that had a Nielsen book for sale, we were differently aware of its presence and location. We had a vaguely reverential way of approaching it – as if it were behind glass, which more often than not it literally was. There was something peculiar about this, as if consciously exaggerated or hyperbolic. After all, it wasn't a volume of Speed's maps or Ackermann's aquatints or Audubon's birds.

It was fairly easy to find other illustrated books at a modest price, especially if you were willing, as I was, to be flexible about their condition. It was on that basis, for example, that I acquired a first edition of *Peter Pan* with Rackham's colour plates for just £4. This was because it was WAF: many of the plates had been removed. It was another example of a breaker, a book singular and strange as much for what it was missing as for what remained. But I say *notionally* we were looking for books of this sort, because I've realised, as these memories come floating slowly or tumbling towards me, that actually what we were looking for, and what my father most of all was looking for, was his mother.

I've got something for you, said Alan, and entered the cockpit post-office and opened up one of the glass cases and extracted a slender volume and passed it to my father.

Extraordinary! Wonderful! Fascinating! Queer!

These were the words of Ronald Frankau, from a book called *'Oh, Dear, Dear!'*, sub-titled *Poems and Stories for Real Children*, published in 1929. That's the book Alan handed to my father that sunny breezy spring day, through the cockpit-window of the Croydon Air Balloon Recreational Post-Office Bookshop. He must have had some sense of what pleasure he was bringing to my father. If the transaction were happening today, I expect the vendor would bump the price up at least 400% to maximise profits. But for reasons no doubt clear to all, the Croydon Bookshop could never exist today. As it was, Alan (if that was his name) was the kind of fellow who charged £4.75. That was the very modest sum that my father was asked to pay for his *'Oh, Dear, Dear!'* It was a nice copy too – a bit of foxing, but still in its dustjacket – with a colour frontispiece and dozens of black and white line drawings by Lola Onslow. And I remember my father's face when he took possession of this book. It was radiant. It was beaming. His face shone like the sun.

I think of my father as a contented man, shy, reserved, stoical, meditative, a man of few words. But now as I recall his face at that moment with the Frankau book I realise anew how bereft and alone he was. And how much it meant to be able to go away, into the beyond, somewhere like an aeroplane-bookshop, with his son, for his son, but also, unspeakably, in search of his mother, in search of a place where he could be with her.

Extraordinary! Wonderful! Fascinating! Queer!

Marvellous! Incredible! Oh, dear, dear!

Unspeakably, because he never, or scarcely ever, spoke of her and even when he did he didn't, wouldn't, couldn't. There was no one to hear. Oh, dear, dear!

Back at home, in the solitude of his small, book-laden study upstairs, under the intense light of his angle-poise lamp, he would have opened Frankau's book and gazed at the line drawing of himself on the inside cover, aged three, marching in a little striped shirt and dark shorts with bare legs, wearing a paper hat and holding a toy sword upright in his right hand, dragging with his left a wooden cannon, along with marching toy soldiers.

My grandmother, Kathleen Viola Frances Onslow, was born in Victoria Road, Dublin, on 10 April 1898. Her parents, Frank Drew Onslow and Katherine May Blood, married in Dublin in July 1894. Kathleen (who came to be known as Lola) had an elder sister, Effie May Onslow, born in 1895. Frank Onslow was alcoholic and violent. (At least that's what my brother and I were led to believe.) Perhaps implausibly he was also Principal Tenor of the Dublin Opera Company. By the time of the Irish census of 1901 the two sisters were registered as 'stepdaughters', living in Atmospheric Road, Dalkey, with James Mahony and their mother, now Katherine Mahony. At some point in the following few years the mother developed the strategy of what James Joyce would later term 'silence, exile and cunning', escaping to England with her daughters and, in fear of the father coming after them, lodging the girls with two spinsters, Ella and Isabel Bazett. In the

1911 English census Effie and Lola (their ages given now as 15 and 13) are 'adopted', living with the Bazett sisters in Ealing. On 25 August 1923 Lola married my grandfather, George Anthony Royle ('Tony'), referring to her father on the marriage certificate as Frank Drew Onslow, 'actor'. She was 26, my grandfather 24. My father was born a couple of years later, in Avalon Road, West Ealing, on 15 October 1925. He would have been three when she was producing the illustrations for *'Oh, Dear, Dear!'* His brother Peter was born in February 1928 and another brother, Jeffrey, in September 1932. I'm sorry, that probably seems like too much information. At any rate it's more or less what's publicly known about my grandmother, and now it's out of the way.

In early paintings she signed herself 'K Royle', in capital letters. Later she became Lola Onslow. There is a beautiful watercolour study of a tree, undated, but signed 'K Royle', which was exhibited at the Chelsea Art Show. I think of this as the faraway tree. Even when she didn't put 'Lola Onslow' on a painting, literally, she signed all over with loving, gently sloping 'ell'- and 'o'-shapes, in languorously curling blades of grass or looping, rounding waves.

Her husband Tony was an artist too. He became successful and especially well-known for his cartoon strips: his 'Just Jake' and 'Belinda' appeared year after year in the *Daily Mirror*. At first Tony and Lola lived in Avalon Road – and indeed today there's a road just off it, wittily named after the family, called Royle Crescent. But later they moved a little to the west, to what was then the village of Perivale. They lived in an Elizabethan manor house called Perivale Grange. Of this house my father spoke always with deep love. There was an avenue of chestnut trees leading up to it. It stood on a large plot, with an expansive garden to the rear, including a pond and some woodland. Most of what I know of this house I know from a handful of old photographs and things my father told me.

Because it was an old house at the heart of Perivale there were rumours of an underground passageway running from the house to St Mary's Church, close to the banks of the River Brent, further along Perivale Lane. The house itself contained secret panelling. This is one of my earliest memories, visiting Perivale Grange in around 1960, shortly before my grandfather sold it. I was three years old. A few months later the whole place would go up in flames, enabling the new owner to build a lucrative block of flats. I remember the pond in the garden, and I remember the dark oak panelling of the interior of the house. Most of all I remember the secret panelling, the action of sliding it back to reveal a hidden room.

In his youth my father became obsessed with the idea of the underground tunnel to the church. A priest hole of some sort had to exist. Lola and Tony weren't happy with their eldest son, now in his early teens, digging in the house to find the entrance to an underground tunnel. But they gave him permission to dig in the garden. Over the course of a couple of years he toiled, especially around the periphery of the garden closest to St Mary's Church. He stuck at his task like Curdie, the little miner-boy in *The Princess and the Goblin*.

No secret tunnel transpired. He must have cut a sorrowful figure, for his parents then allowed him to pursue his dream and dig up the floor of the pantry. One summer in the late 1930s this was his principal occupation. In due course he found himself in a watery hole in a cloud of mosquitoes. No priest hole, no concealed passageway. But it did result, he claimed, in lifelong immunity to mosquito bites.

Where did this desire to dig come from? It stayed with him all his days. No doubt it was compounded by his wartime experience as a Bevan boy, working down the mines, near Worksop in Nottinghamshire. By his own account these were three very happy years. But in the last twenty-five years of his life, too, when our family moved to Devon, he loved to dig holes in the garden, especially in search of underground streams.

Lola Onslow died in a nursing home in West Ealing on 15 February 1952. My father and mother began courting a couple of years after that. Or at least my mother began courting my father. I don't believe my father could ever have courted anyone or anything. My mother always gave me to understand that when she met him, he was in mourning for his mother, and that that was the basis of their relationship. She saw herself, in part, as a substitute. My mother was another Kathleen. He always called her Kathleen, even when others called her Kate. In the intimacy of birthday and wedding anniversary cards he addressed her as 'Mlalao': knowingly or unconsciously, the suggestion of 'my Lola' in this hypocoristic seems to me unmistakable. He also, on occasion, called my mother 'K'. The 'K Royle' with which Lola signed some of her earlier paintings was perhaps a factor in my father's (and thus my own) mistaking Kay Nielsen as a woman.

My father was just 26 when Lola Onslow died. It must have totally blasted him. The family had all survived the Second World War, but his own private Hiroshima was still almost seven years away.

There's a pencil drawing by Lola of the village of Hartland in North Devon, where she and Tony used to go on holiday. It's a simple sketch, unsigned, but the name 'Hartland' is written, along with the date, '12. 8. 45'. The atom bombs had fallen in the preceding few days. The war was over. New disasters were underway. And Lola was sketching a Devon village on a hot summer's day – a street of thatched and tumbledown cottages, house windows variously reflecting the sun or indicating dark interiors, grass tufting up at the roadside, deep shadow cast over the street by the nearest building, the sense of the artist's place, also in the shade, observing. It's hot and there's no one about, except for a woman with her back to us, a rotund silhouette, apparently making her way up the road, wearing a hat and coat, with unnervingly thin legs, carrying a large bundle of what appear to be sticks. It's a starkly simple but haunting drawing that captures the hot stillness of Hartland on an August day. That day, that year.

I'm now going to share my screen with you again. I want you to have a look at this picture. It's gentle but sharp, tranquil yet provoking. Nothing about this sketch would seem to suggest magic or the supernatural, but if you look towards the upper right corner, you see that there is cloud. Despite the presence of the hot sun and the shadows cast, there are clouds, and this prompts me to think of nuances. Nuance is a slight difference or variation in meaning or feeling, a subtle difference of shade or tone, but also, in the context of music, a gentle gradation or alteration in musical expression. It's a French word that comes from the Latin *nūbēs*. In English there is an adjective which I suspect none of you have ever used or indeed ever will use. I confess I have never till now uttered the word either: *nubilous*. It means 'clouded in appearance; misty, foggy'.

Of course, the nuances of clouds or the clouds of nuance are one of the great topoi of literary thinking, going back at least to Aristophanes' comedy, *The Clouds*, written around 423 BCE and considered, when first staged in 419, a complete flop. When Hamlet and

Pencil sketch of Hartland, North Devon, by Lola Onslow

Polonius have that manifestly ridiculous exchange, around two thousand years later, about whether a certain cloud looks like a whale or a weasel, they are harking back to Socrates in the Aristophanes play who wonders: 'Have you not sometimes seen clouds in the sky like a centaur, a leopard, a wolf or a bull?'

The ancient echo is even clearer in Shakespeare's *Antony and Cleopatra* when Antony, in the presence of his loyal servant and friend Enobarbus, drifts into a reverie beginning 'Sometimes we see a cloud that's dragonish, / A vapour sometime like a bear or lion …' Everyone is a cloud, Antony suggests – a sort of 'freecloud' perhaps … We are all vapours. Everyone is in a state of falling to pieces. We are all dissolving – being dislimned.

Like clouds, we are never separable from the fantastical and fabulous. Clouds change, and how we see them changes. Socrates sees a centaur. Antony sees a dragon. We see a mushroom. Or, perhaps, some alien life.

Detail of pencil sketch of Hartland

If you look carefully at the left edge of the cloud here, in the upper right of the picture, just to the right of the solitary seagull in the sky, there is the profile of the face of a creature with a little snub nose and one shut eye. A child or a fairy or an alien.

The Lola Onslow pictures that hung on the wall at home when I was growing up were perhaps not especially representative of her work, at least in terms of its place in the public imagination. 'Public imagination' is a nubilous kind of phrase, but I don't know how else to say it. She was known, in so far as she was known at all, as a children's illustrator, and she was admired, in so far as she was admired, for her paintings of fairies and goblins and talking animals. The pictures we had up on the wall at home were largely in a naturalistic vein, such as the watercolour of the tree I mentioned.

I've been going on for a while, so I'm going to stop here for today, but, as I do so, it occurs to me that I haven't told you the title of this lecture. It's called 'But the clouds'. This phrase comes from 'The Tower', a poem by W. B. Yeats published in 1926. Samuel Beckett thought it one of Yeats's most beautiful lines and he wrote a play about it, also called '… but the clouds …' (1976). Beckett put three dots before and three dots after, suggesting the cloudlike nature of dots themselves, as well as the importance of ellipsis and aposio—

Yeats's 'The Tower' is about an imagined future of study – being a sun machine student, if I can say that. (Yeats, like Bowie and Blyton, had no university education.) It's a poem about a fear of *the time when* – not the time when you remember something, and the memory and the meaning of your past transmogrifies as you do so. Rather, in wistfully anticipatory mode, as if playing with the future of regret, Yeats evokes the time when the breathtaking beauty of someone's face, the look in a lover's eye, the preciousness of a lost loved one, has all gone cloudy and dark. It's the time when

> The death of friends, or death
> Of every brilliant eye
> That made a catch in the breath –

Seem but the clouds of the sky
When the horizon fades;
Or a bird's sleepy cry
Among the deepening shades.

'The Tower' is a formidably death-laden poem. When are the clouds *but* the clouds? What role does the sun play? How does the horizon fade? Who is to say that birdsong is sleepy? Who is awake or asleep, who is the wakeful and who is the sleepy one, when it comes to listening to birds?

I leave you with those questions – and with the song of a nightingale, recorded by Nick Penny in Northamptonshire in the spring of 2008.

[Play https://www.youtube.com/watch?v=BTkZRO-FYTM]

Fairy
(eighth lecture)

Hi, once again, everyone. Still only half-awake, I thought of beginning this final lecture with some reflections on How to Become an Irish Writer, or Why There is No Such Thing as English Literature and That is Good. This is the reason I am taking on here, if only for a few short moments, what I hope is recognisably an Irish accent. It comes very easily to me, especially in this somewhat hypnagogic state. Hi.

But then so does speaking English like a French person – or a German – or an American – or an Englishman. Everyone says Hi.

Hi. In beginning with that word, I think of Wallace Stevens's follow-up sentence: 'The creator too is blind.' Stevens would have delivered those words in an American accent. But given that we live in what he called 'an old chaos of the sun', he also knew that his stars came from Ireland and an Irish accent is just as possible: 'Hi. The creator too is blind.'

I can also just as comfortably be an English-speaking mole. I should explain that, as I say these words, I have on a hand-puppet called Mole who is invisibly addressing you even now. Think of him as *en route* to his burrow and remarking *sotto voce*:

– I wouldn't be speaking Irish, or even English in an Irish accent, would I?

Mole is referring to a phone conversation I had earlier today with my friend Matthew. Mole wasn't here at the time but down in his underworld he hears virtually everything. Can it really be true, I'd wondered, that there are no moles in Ireland? You'd imagine that they might have got across somehow, I'd said. Following a pause Matthew said: Although they can't swim. We'd laughed about this. Now briefly up and nosing about, Mole wishes to make two observations:

– First, this is typical small-minded anthropocentrism and a climate disaster no one thinks about: other mammals managed to make it, but the level of the Irish Sea or whatever you want to call it rose so quick at the end of the Ice Age we never had time. Let that be a lesson, my friend. And then, are you so certain we can't swim? How else conceive the primary activity of these fabulously feisty fossors? It's underground swimming – and on an Olympic scale!

So if I switched from Irish to English Mole, it wasn't to assault your ears. It's about dreaming and fantastical roots – as in the radicalism, say, of old trees. It has nothing to do with national identity. What matters in art and song has nothing to do with nation or nationhood. What matters sheers clear of all belonging.

Tune into the comic cosmic strangeness of your voice as a shadow-show of accents, tones and registers, a play of other voices.

This is what David Bowie sings.

I'm trying to get back to my grandmother, but first I wanted to play you a song. 'Absolute Beginners' is a love song about love songs. It's also an elegy to Bowie's half-brother Terry, who had died a year earlier. It's about the dangerous desires that I associate with studying 'English' at university. 'Absolute Beginners' also has that sensual vulnerability I was talking about earlier – a sensual vulnerability that is characteristic of Bowie's finest songs – along with irony. It's a kind of musical desiring machine. (Bowie would have come across 'desire machines', I imagine, in his reading of Angela Carter.) And then 'Absolute Beginners' is also a sort of canny stranger to itself.

The song conveys an erotic spontaneity, as if the words, even the refrain, have only just occurred to him. As if the voice, the lyrics themselves are absolute beginners. And then at the same time, the song is very aware of what it is doing. It knows that it is – to borrow a fine formulation from Paul Morley – 'the sort of melody that people will use to bring back the past they want to remember'. Or, we might add, to bring back the past people didn't realise they knew or didn't realise they had to remember. 'Absolute Beginners' was released in March 1986, the month my dying brother's only child, Sam, was born. I hear all of this in Don Weller's saxophony.

[Play David Bowie, 'Absolute Beginners']

Lola Onslow was Irish. And just now as we were listening to 'Absolute Beginners', I thought of a new word, a funny neologism that's at least double. I have more than once wondered, while assembling these lectures, what genre they might best be described as fitting into. I confess I don't know. I suppose this is connected to Angela Carter as well. A tale, she says, 'retains a singular moral function – that of provoking unease'. There's nothing wrong with a bit of unease in a lecture either. And unease is integral to Bowie's songs too. But the word that came to me has a soft, anodyne feel: *memoirish*. The oddity only hit me afterwards, when I saw the 'Irish' in it. Forget *life writing*. Forget *autobiography*. These lectures have been composed, without me realising, in Memoirish. To do with the grandmother.

'Irish grandmother' has, perhaps, a strangely familiar ring. For David Bowie, one has to go back a further generation, on his mother's side: his great-grandmother, Mary Eileen Heaton, was born in County Tipperary in 1852. But Enid Blyton readily recalls her own Irish grandmother: 'I sometimes find her long-ago voice whispering in my mind still, when I think of leprechauns and banshees!' It's a matter of the fairy or otherworldly, and of voice. It's about the lilt and quality of Irish rhythms, as much perhaps as the tales spun or spilled.

A provoking recent analogy here might be Claire-Louise Bennett's *Pond* (2015). Her book is neither novel nor autobiography.

It's more like a pooling of lyrical narrative reflections. Bennett is not Irish. She grew up in Wiltshire and studied literature and drama at Roehampton, in Surrey; but *Pond* is a book about living in the west of Ireland. Her writing seems, among other things, to be an immersion in Irish soundscapes, an Irish voice-pool or voice-spool. Or then again, in a quite different way, we may think of Samuel Beckett who, after the Second World War, sought his own silence, exile and cunning by writing in French, as if to get away from the smother of all mother tongues.

As I ponder (no pun intended, for to be sure there's little fun in a pun – or for that matter a punt – on a pond), I recall in turn that my father enjoyed mimicking accents other than his default altogether-rather-precise softly spoken Home Counties English. His favourite and best was his Irish. It was light and gentle, and all these years I never considered what is suddenly blindingly obvious – that it was his mother's voice he'd have been picking up, replaying, hearkening after.

A staggering moment in *King Lear* comes when the blinded Gloucester recognises the King: 'I know that voice'. Irony and pathos crawl over one another in the dark. The blind man remembers 'the trick of that voice', but the man whose voice it is is no longer himself, merely a 'ruined piece of nature'. And then the man who has led Gloucester to this scene of recognition, his son Edgar – disguised like a beggar who is in turn possessed by some fiend – has *not* been recognised by his voice. As they are talking, Gloucester notices that the beggar's voice is not consistent – 'Methinks thy voice is altered', he tells Edgar at one point – but he fails to recognise the voice of his son.

I've just failed to recognise the voice of my father, but it's not a matter of a moment, it's a failure that has lasted all my life till now. How we miss people in their voices. How much there is, clamouring to be heard, that we suppress or ignore. How strange this sudden recall, this posthumous scene of deferred recognition!

A coach and horses of loss, lolling and nodding with sable plumes, drives slowly, airily through a person's speech, invisible to every listener.

I never heard Lola Onslow's voice, other than by ghostly ventriloquy. Her own mother, Katherine ('Irma') Blood, used to sing on the stage in Dublin. This was presumably how she met Frank Drew Onslow. There was one song she sang to her daughter who sang it to my father who sang it to me and my brother. I remember only a few lines. It's about a young Japanese soldier called (at least in my memory) San Mori San. It's a song about the Russo-Japanese War (1904–05), so I suppose my father's grandmother was singing it around that time.

It's half a century since I was a choirboy at school, but I hope you will forgive me if I sing:

O my San Mori San,
Come back to me, do,
Don't fight that Russian man,
He's much bigger than you!

O my San Mori San,
Come back to me quick,
Come back, my happy, Jappy soldier boy!

I cannot say anything about this fragment. I can only – and then very poorly – sing it.

Even or especially when we are most alive, the voices of the dead live on in us.

I recently located the sheet music for a song called 'Happy Jappy Soldier Man', with words by Paul West and music by John W. Bratton. The correspondences with the song as I remember it are evident, but the printed version is also curiously different. Dated 1914, its chorus runs: 'Oh, my Satsuma San / Come back to me do / Don't fight that Russian man / He's a bigger than you / Your geisha's mighty sad / Here in old Japan, / Come back my happy, Jappy soldier man.'

I never imagined that my grandmother would come to be the focus of my 'academic research'. She died several years before I was born. She was not my grandmother, except posthumously. How does that work? She has about her, irrepressibly, something of a fairy grandmother, phantom granny, granphantasma.

Writing these lectures has enabled me to see how my love of art and song is bound up with this woman I never met. Freud had next to nothing to say about the importance or meaning of a grandmother. He was too busy thinking about father and son, and developing a theory of the son machine called the Oedipus Complex. The ancient Greek for 'grandmother' is τήθη – which may be transliterated as *tethe*, a word that would rhyme with the great river of forgetfulness, Lethe.

Keats says 'Lethe-wards', we say *tethe*-wards. If this word seems dismayingly liable to forgetfulness in turn, permit me to offer a little ditty to aid the memory:

It might look a little teethy,
But any nibble or nip
Is merely a love of lip.
'Tis well-aligned with the leafy
And slow flow of the Liffey,
But finally it's all wreathy,
In memory of loves unsigned
The future of the undermind,
Entwining sounds of Tethe.

If there is an Oedipus complex, there is also a Tethe. But it's not a complex: it's not something shameful, to be endured or solved or dissolved. I'd prefer to think of it as an implex. Let's note that, anagrammatically, this would be an implex with *teeth* in it. This is signalled in the lines I just quoted. You can't see it of course, and I'm not going to read it out again but, by chance, the ditty also contains an acrostic: *I BIT, A BITE.*

The *OED* classifies the word 'implex' as obsolete. I propose we resurrect it. Samuel Johnson defined the adjectival 'implex' as 'involved, having a complicated plot'. It's from the Latin *implectĕre*, to entwine: *plectĕre* means to twist or plait. Naturally my attraction to 'implex' includes the charm of the *imp* and all the playful effects of a *lex*, a lexical or lexicon artist. And while it is precisely not a *complex*, the tethe implex would certainly challenge the idea of the Oedipus complex, in various ways complicating, dislocating and undermining it.

I thus find myself, for the first time in these lectures, talking about undermining – a special resource of the undermind. The *tethe implex* is, I think, preferable without capital letters: it's all about questioning the proper and reconstruing the authority of the father. The tethe implex is not a matter of anguish and neurosis, regret or unhappiness. It's about the realisation and affirmation of a transgenerational force of the mother, a force of art and song, Gran Phantasma, sweeping away all fear and hatred, especially misogyny, and watching over with love and laughter.

Close to the end of his life, the psychiatrist Eric Berne wrote: 'No one who has ever known his grandmother is an atheist, even if she herself was one, for all grandmothers, good or evil, are watching somewhere out there.' I don't know about the theism or the atheism, perhaps in part because I never knew my grandmother (although I do know she was definitely *not* a practising Christian, at least in later life), but it seems to me that Berne is uncannily right in his supposition of the grandmother's watchfulness. The mother watches, but the grandmother's vigilance is less locatable, more like a ghostly Lady Grinning Soul.

I've noted previously that a crucial book for Enid Blyton was George MacDonald's *The Princess and the Goblin* (1872). When she was growing up, as she tells us in *The Story of My Life*, she read it 'at least twelve times'. It's a haunting sun machine of a book. It's about the workings of light and shadow, the 'sun people' as well as the goblins of a subterranean underworld. MacDonald's fairy stories are richly interesting photological experiments. If you want to read a shorter piece, try 'The Shadows' or 'The Golden Key'.

But something else that *The Princess and the Goblin* gives us is the world of the grandmother. This is integral, I think, to what Blyton refers to as the 'strange "feel"' of MacDonald's book. The grandmother is the presiding genius, the implex figure who appears to the Princess and later to Curdie the little miner boy. The grandmother is the mostly invisible heart and hinge of the story. She is upstairs, hidden away somewhere, obscure, cryptic, but loving, gentle, sapient, seemingly faraway and inaccessible – but just a matter of going upstairs, if you can find the door. She is a sort of nineteenth-century inversion of what Gilbert and Gubar famously called the 'madwoman in the attic'. The grandmother is upstairs in the undermind.

I referred to Lola Onslow a few moments ago as a ghost granny. Fairy grandmother, I said, and perhaps that sounded a bit silly. But I meant it in at once the most playful and the most serious and far-reaching sense. That's the title of this lecture: 'Fairy'.

Among the various Lola Onslow paintings on the walls at home as we were growing up, one was the apple of my father's eye. It's of a fairy child or – I don't know how to spell 'faery' and I'm in deep water already. It seems apt that you can't see how I'm spelling the word: I like to imagine it silently, invisibly wavering about between fairy, faerie and other forms, more or less fair, various fare, fayrie, feerie … I'm in deep water, I was saying, because I always feel in deep water the moment I start trying to talk about a picture – for how does one do it, really? It's like the Polaroids we encountered earlier.

Bowie talks about how you should 'Always go a little further into the water than you feel you're capable of being in. Go a little bit out of your depth.' But I'm talking about being completely adrift or already capsized. What incompetence has one already demonstrated in saying, as I did a moment ago, that the painting in question is 'of' a fairy child? What does 'of' mean?

In the previous lecture I said to you, Here is a sketch *of* Hartland village, and then today, in just a few moments, I'm proposing to show you a painting *of* a faerie child. The 'of' is where the strangeness of resemblance dissolves into the calm of substitution, or vice versa. It's a pointless attempt to fix what cannot be placed. But it's also where imagination takes off. From the off, *of* is a fairy word.

I hope you can still remember the exquisite song of the nightingale we listened to at the end of the previous lecture. I'll save you a full-length disquisition on birds and David Bowie, and instead simply suggest that the sun machine as I have been talking about it is inseparable from what I'd call bird-dreams, that is to say *dreams of flying and foreign song*. Bowie, let's remember, was never remotely interested in actually going into space. But he *was* passionately interested in taking flight, taking off, flying up and away. He was passionately interested, also, in the foreignness of song, in being possessed by song like an unidentifiable bird; and in the prayer-like possibilities of words on a wing.

'And haply the Queen-Moon is on her throne / Cluster'd around by all her starry Fays': that's how Keats describes the night sky in Hampstead, just over two hundred years ago, in his great 'Ode to a Nightingale'. Who in their right mind would describe the moon as a queen on her throne, or the stars as her fairies?

'Fairy' is a French word. In the twelfth century it meant 'witchcraft', 'enchantment'. By the thirteenth century it had come to designate a realm of fairies. From the late fourteenth century onwards we find 'fay' as a synonym for 'fairy', especially in the sense of a supernatural being with magical powers who interferes in human affairs, whether for good or evil. 'Fay' goes back to the Latin for the Fates (*fāta*) and fate (*fātum*).

Literature is inseparable from fairy. Of course, fairies don't exist – so what? *Fairy* is a word that keeps veering. It can also mean beautiful, seductive, often used of a woman; or small, fine, delicate; or effeminate, a male homosexual. 'Fairy' goes to the heart of Englishness, in part because it seems to be indissociably bound up with embarrassment, the English capacity for embarrassment and the embarrassment of being English. 'Fairy' reaches down into the deepest strata of culture and society. It speaks of structural misogyny, homophobia, fear of the bisexual.

When I was nine years old – it would have been 1967, the year when, so late, so anachronistically, the Sexual Offences Act made homosexuality legal – I was taken by a family friend to watch Fulham play at Craven Cottage. The West London club had recently signed a striker called Allan Clarke from Walsall for a record sum. It was a trifling amount in comparison with today's bloated obscenities, but still enough to make Fulham fans expect or hope for something special. I remember standing (as one did then) on the crowded terrace at the Putney End and seeing Clarke loft the ball over the opponents' crossbar and send it close enough for me to reach out as it was passed back down, to get a touch of what James Joyce quaintly calls the 'leather orb', and someone a few yards behind us shouting furiously, 'You fucking fairy, Clarke!'

I remember the sense of shock, in the immediacy of the ball – the actual, unbelievably beautiful white leather ball that had broken through the fourth wall and was almost resting in my hands – and the venomous rage of the 'fairy' clearly audible to Clarke himself in the still air, in the split-second of that shot over the bar and the subsiding of the home supporters' groans of disappointment.

'Fairy' is the F-word that has stayed with me. What does it mean to call someone a fairy? What is the fairy realm?

Actually I should say that the alliterative 'fucking fairy' has stayed with me too. I still wonder at its possibilities: what are fucking fairies? What are they like fucking? How do they do this? Is there not perhaps a beautiful fucking fairy or many fucking fairies in each one of us?

I also like the fact that this footballer was called Allan. It's just chance, obviously. Clarke had a lovely touch. He went on to win nineteen caps for England. He had the nickname 'Sniffer', on account of his predatory instincts in front of goal. It reminds me of Walter Pater, once again, in his Conclusion to *The Renaissance*:

'Not to discriminate every moment some passionate attitude in those about us, and in the very brilliancy of their gifts some tragic dividing of forces on their ways, is, on this short day of frost and sun, to sleep before evening.' Don't lose the plot, Pater says, don't stop noticing and appreciating, till the last sunlit second.

Allan Clarke was dainty. He was a fairy, yes, I want to say that, but in doing so I want to blow off all the homophobic cobwebs, to brush away all the misogyny and wrongness attached to the word. I want to counter everything that fuelled the hatred of that angry fan more than fifty years ago, who sought to express his own problems by calling the footballer by that name. Every fan, male or female, has inner fairies. But as Marina Warner has observed, we don't talk much about maleness and masculinity in the context of fairies: society continues to be structured by 'a general retreat from even thinking about boys and fairy tales'.

David Bowie was a fairy. He was the greatest fairy of our time. He brought the comedy, strangeness and beauty of the fairy into the twenty-first century.

In the context of Enid Blyton, on the other hand, readers, critics, librarians and publishers alike categorically distinguish between fairy books and non-fairy books. She herself encourages us to think in such terms. Her own time-machine space-travel works, such as *The Faraway Tree* and *The Adventures of the Wishing Chair*, along with many other books, are, evidently, fairy stories. The *Famous Five* books, on the other hand, are full of 'strange happenings' resolutely kept in check. Anne, Dick, George and Julian never enter the faery realm. But this, as I've been trying to make clear, is misleading.

It is misleading, first, in terms of the idea of the undermind. The undermind is the force that drives the flower of a *Famous Five* book just as much as any of Blyton's so-called fairy stories. It's about absence of control, and an openness to chance and the unforeseeable. As Marina Warner notes: 'The impenetrability of destiny and the helplessness of humans in the grip of chance count among the sharpest messages of fairy tale.' And it is misleading also because the *Famous Five* books are structured, composed, made possible by magical thinking. Child and dog telepathy is the basis of their narration.

Blyton's writing emerges from the undermind, where all is mimicry and disguise, resemblance and composite figures, ventriloquy and subterfuge. It is not the author who presides in the undermind, but the three fairies, Flow, Follow and Interrupt. The true storyteller, as Walter Benjamin observed with a characteristic twinkle, is always 'the teller of fairy tales'.

Keats's 'Ode to a Nightingale' is a fairy poem. It's about the voice, the music, the telling – a faring, a fairying, through the undermind. It is a work of strange synaesthesia, mixing sound and vision, sound and scents. Despite its title, Keats's poem is an attempt not so much to address a bird, as to *become* birdsong, lost in the sound that 'oft-times hath / Charm'd magic casements, opening on the foam / Of perilous seas, in faery lands forlorn'. And then that single word, 'forlorn', is the clanger that closes everything off, tolls the poet out again.

> Forlorn! The very word is like a bell
>   To toll me back from thee to my sole self!
> Adieu! the fancy cannot cheat so well
>   As she is fam'd to do, deceiving elf.

We might hear in these lines Keats's altogether gentler version of Beckett's reference to God in *Endgame*: 'The bastard! He doesn't exist!' Even as the poet-listener is washed away from those 'faery lands' that have been charmed into being by birdsong, even as the limited powers of 'fancy' are acknowledged, the 'deceiving elf' remains.

For me, the faerie music of Keats's nightingale comes, as it has always come, through this painting by Lola Onslow that I'm going to show you (I promise!) in a moment. The painting is as round as a balloon or a bubble or the 'O' of her name. It is a tondo in a circular frame measuring just over thirteen inches across and, as an object on the wall, it rhymed, in our house as we were growing up, with one of those 1920s round mirrors, in a similarly ornate and knobbly stucco-style gilt frame, so that sometimes you could find yourself misplacing the painting and the mirror in your mind and take the painting to be where the mirror was or the mirror the painting.

It is a painting of ... It is a child, apparently an infant. The word 'infant', as you perhaps know, is from the Latin *infans*, meaning 'speechless', 'without speech'. All painting is speechless, I hear you say, but that is only the beginning of the story. Once again, it's about prosopopoeia, the rhetorical figure of voice-from-beyond-the-grave. What leads us to suppose that the child in this picture is an infant? And where does speech begin anyway? It's a cry, a sigh, an elemental 'O'. If literature is inseparable from prosopopoeia, it is also inseparable from a love of language that goes back to the mother, to a love of the mother lodged in the earliest coos and babbles. It's down there, in the most interior depths of poetic thinking.

The goodness of 'maternal sounds' is what Wallace Stevens calls it. 'The semiotic' is the phrase bestowed by Julia Kristeva. But I don't want to name-fix. I'm trying to think about the way a painting can sing or coo or gurgle or cry in the vicinity of what Pater is saying about all art aspiring to the condition of music. If you check out the context in which Pater makes his celebrated remark, by the way, you'll find that the example he gives is a landscape etching by Alphonse Legros.

The question of whether or how or what sounds a picture makes, takes us, like absolute beginners, into the realm of phantasmagoric synaesthesia. Phantasmagoric synaesthesia is a fairy space. That's where we have to go, to catch a sun machine. We say a picture is enchanting. It's about singing. Like the air of fascination, a demon that moves from station to station, or the telepathic isolation of a starman.

My father painted a little, mostly in oils, in his spare time. On my parents' marriage certificate, in 1956, he is described as a 'heraldic artist'. He worked for *Burke's Peerage*, painstakingly producing coats-of-arms with *fleur-de-lys* and lions rampant, bold blazons and fine hatching on a bend sinister et cetera, in a mode that already then seemed antiquarian. But then, as I hope these lectures have made clear, in everyday life, as in art and song, anachronism is the law. After *Burke's*, he got a job in a technical drawings company, working as what people would later term a graphic design artist. He was a competent painter but, he evidently felt, no more than that. It fell to his younger son Simon to become the painter my father wasn't. But my brother died before reaching even half the age of Lola Onslow.

Art is an unfinished business in our family. So much for 'spare time'. Did I really just use that phrase? Spare time, spare us the tears, driving us all spare.

My father always maintained that the fairy child was him, in the bath. I suppose it was painted in 1926 or 1927. So here is Lola's firstborn, Maxwell Anthony, aged one or thereabouts. He sits naked and snug, the tiny toes of his right foot as clear and careful as in a Leonardo cartoon, his small round knees up almost against his puppy-fat tummy, the fingers of the right hand fanned out in infant fascination, the left hand holding a clay pipe. He has a little snub nose and rosy cheeks and wisps of golden curly hair. He is tucked up in a coracle in the form of a seashell.

He is all at sea. The lower half of the painting is a great swirl of water, with tongues of waves jetting up behind him and descending over his head. It is a soft, tranquillised version of Hokusai's *Under the Wave off Kanagawa*, painted almost a hundred years earlier, with the wave coming from right to left rather than left to right. And instead of Mount Fuji, an infant beneath the wave.

Tondo of a fairy child by Lola Onslow

The child is not troubled by the cascading water, or by the large white seabirds in the air. With comically raised eyebrow and exquisitely long lashes, his big blue staring eye is focused on a bubble directly in front of him, almost the size of his own head. We infer that the child has blown this bubble from the pipe poised perfectly in his hand: the popular American song 'I'm Forever Blowing Bubbles' dates from a few years earlier, although the idea that a human is just a bubble (*Homo bulla est*) is familiar from earlier paintings, such as Salvator Rosa's dark masterpiece *Human Frailty* (1656).

But the provenance of the bubble seems beside the point. This bubble is a glistening event in suspense, watched by the child on one side and a seabird on the other. It is in mid-air, with dawn clouds piled on the horizon below and behind it, and a twilight blue above. The bubble captivates the gaze of the child as if it were a mirror, just as it attracts the seabirds. It is a bubble that sparkles and reflects. It gives off the blues of sea and sky and pale whites of the coming or going day and clouds and coracle and child and birds, but inside the bubble there is also green.

It is what in heraldry is called a *mise en abîme*: a bubble-image of the planet earth of which this scene is a part, the image of a mirror in which everything is seen or reflected, an image of the painting as a whole enclosed within the bubble.

Then you see more bubbles, in the air above and behind the child and in the foreground of the sea. The bubbles make a homophone of the see. A number of these bubbles, especially in front of the clouds, draw in the viewer's eye differently. Each has two symmetrically placed ruddy flecks in the upper left and upper right, a tiny spot of darkness in the centre, and a shadow-line where you might think to look for a mouth. These bubbles have faces, they are little clown ghosts or unborn cloud-creatures, almost imperceptible unearthlings looking at us.

Without wings this would be a painting of a human infant. But my father has wings. My extraordinary fairy father. They are small and very close to the waves that surge up behind him. *Opening on the foam of perilous seas.* They are golden like the creature's curly locks, with roseate ocellations.

Paintings wash over generations. This tondo is the Lola Onslow painting of my childhood, as well as my father's, and doubtless also of her own. It's a bubble, a microcosmic translucent balloon-mirror, like the sea-green ball of glass on the mantelpiece reflecting my study a few feet away from me as I write these words. My father had this old glass fishing float in his study when we were children. It was never described in that matter-of-fact fisherman way. When we were small, my brother and I firmly believed that it was ancient and magical.

This painting was the portal to Lola Onslow when we were children. 'Portal' now has computer connotations, but its links to the fantastic and eerie are, as always, open. You may recall the ghost that 'goes even now out at the portal' in *Hamlet*: ghosts and portals go together. It's about those dream doors I've been talking about at various moments in these lectures. Not that these are site-specific moments: the point, on the contrary, is that a ghost portal can open up anywhere at any moment, at the drop of a hat or swoop of a bird.

'Portal' is also Shakespeare's word, in his earlier play *Richard II*, for what I've been calling a sun machine. There he evokes the sun in 'the fiery portal of the east'. The sun rises, on this short fairy tale of life, in the east. It's a fiery fairy portal, the strange thing that is not a thing but a portal in the place of the east. The east wouldn't exist without it. Nothing would exist without the portal of the sun.

When I first heard someone say 'portal', I thought it was *porthole*. Because of this painting by Lola Onslow, they have always mingled in my mind. As if 'porthole' were like 'wassail' or 'victuals' or the Cornish seaside village Mousehole, pronounced 'muzzle'. Gazing at this painting in its rondel, in the round, is like looking through the magic casement of a porthole.

As I was growing up, I used to wonder at this infant, abandoned in the world of its painting, the original snow-globe of my memory. I used to wonder at the birds that seemed as audible as the sea and child. I hear them still in the gulls that haunt the seafront where I live and the kittiwakes in the cliff-face beside the ruins of Splash Point Hotel, at the end of Seaford esplanade.

Lola's birds are the original airborne creatures of my imaginary – precursors to the prehistoric fliers in the Zdenek Burian painting of an eerily desolate seascape, in the big dinosaur book that my father gave me on my eighth birthday. Lola Onslow's painting speaks of the Celtic Twilight, leaving the viewer uncertain whether day or night is to follow. She must have known Yeats's 'The Wanderings of Oisin' (1889), where 'clothed in a misty ray / I saw a foam-white seagull drift and float', and 'The White Birds' (1892), in which the poet writes: 'I would we were changed to white birds on the wandering foam: I and you!' But for me Yeats's birds come *after* her painting.

Towards the bottom left is her name, a signature in the sea, with the letters at once afloat and writ in water, the 'LO' and 'LA' of 'Lola' on top of one another, and the first letter of the forename ('L') and first letter of the surname ('O') bigger than the rest – a slow load of LO's.

Coda

I hope you will permit me the indulgence of a Coda. I have never written one before. The word is Italian, from the Latin *cauda*, meaning 'tail'. That seems apt.

Enid Blyton must have been half in love with my grandmother's name before they ever met. Here was someone with a low name of her own of a piece with the lull and slowness of childhood, like the soft notes of a song in flight, with just the same number of letters in her first and second names as herself. What a charming match, what simple symmetry, when Enid Blyton met Lola Onslow.

There is a recognised golden age of children's book illustration, running from the 1880s to the late 1920s. These were the golden years, full of fairies. Lola's shadow flits across this golden age. Her collaboration with Enid began with the *Enid Blyton Book of Fairies*, for which she did the beautiful cover image of fairyland, complete with seascape and magic mountain, published in 1924. They also worked together on the *Merry Moments Annual (Uncollected Stories from the 1920s, No. 1)*, published in the same year. Blyton wrote, and Onslow illustrated, three of the stories: 'Gamene at the Palace', 'The Fairy Castle' and 'The Land of P's and Q's'. In the same book Lola also provided the illustration for a poem called 'The Fairy Bird'. Later, in 1934, her exquisite colour illustration of an underground fairy lake was included in the *News Chronicle Boys' and Girls' Story Book No. 2*.

A year or so before the birth of my father appears to have been their heyday. Enid married her first husband, Hugh Pollock, at Bromley Register Office on 28 August 1924. Lola had tied the knot with Tony the previous August.

Enid was living as a nursery-governess in Surbiton, from 1920 till 1924. It's barely a twenty-minute journey from Surbiton to West Ealing, but they could also meet in town.

Hugh began as an editor at the publisher Newnes in 1923 and was first in touch with Enid in January 1924, looking to collaborate. He oversaw the commissioning of *The Zoo Book* that year. Enid's book with Lola, the *Book of Fairies*, also with Newnes, was accepted in early June and published in October.

For a good while Enid didn't want Newnes to know of her relationship with Hugh. But then, with her ferocity for compartmentalising, she never seemed to want anyone to know who she was or wasn't in a relationship with. Her diary tells us little. Things went fast in early 1924. She and Hugh got engaged in June. Sex must have reared its ugly head, as my mother would say, at Easter, around Saturday 19 April. Along with her old friend Mabel Attenborough, Enid had slipped off with Hugh to spend the weekend at Seaford. Enid's diary records simply that it was 'the loveliest Easter that ever was'. They presumably stayed at the Splash Point Hotel, overlooking Ethel's Wharf.

Was Lola a married woman when she became Enid's lover? Or did the relationship begin in the spring and early summer prior to her marriage to Tony? Already by 1924 Enid was doing very well: she earned £500 for her books that year and would make more than double that the year after. She was developing a fan-base, with a weekly cache of letters from admiring readers. Lola was conscious of Enid's rising fame, deceiving elf. Enid was bold like George, but rather awkward too. Not George as in my grandfather, George Edward Anthony, but as in Georgina, still a phantasmatic twinkle in Enid's eye, in a future faraway. Lola, sylph-like, a year younger, with her Irish lilt, showed Enid a few of her paintings and sketches and blew her away. There was no need to say *let's go to bed.* In the heat of the morning Enid and Lola began.

Well – that is all I can tell you for now. This is supposed to be a lecture series, not a sex novel. I am at the end of the road and the end (as Joseph Conrad might say) of my tether.

I hope that these talks about David Bowie and Enid Blyton have been of some interest, and that some of the things I've touched on – the sun machine, the undermind, telepathy and all its starry fays, the flying post-office bookshop, the Croydon Effect, the tethe implex, the fairy – might prove helpful and indeed pleasurable to think about and perhaps do something with. But I can't pretend that this is not a sombre moment. I mean, regarding the precarious and threatened state of the world around us, but additionally – if I may be allowed to say this – in a personal sense. It's the end of my career. These are my parting words as an academic. Voluntary severance is about to take place. As clear as *this* – which you can't see – but I'm making a slitting throat gesture.

Now, at the end, I feel a great influx of strangeness around the thought that, having delivered these lectures, all the time – in the meanwhile – no one has been here. It takes me back to the deserted theatre at Epidaurus in the Greek Peloponnese, when I was alone, gazing down at the expanse of empty stone seats and stage, one dazzlingly bright early morning, more than thirty years ago.

But still, it's love and laughter that I most wanted to evoke in these lectures. There is a comic history of England, and it comes to us, like a ghost, from the future. It is a comic history of irony and play, affirming the life-giving forces of art and song, breaking free of any idea of education as 'system'. These are some of the things that, in my view, most deeply entwine Enid Blyton and David Bowie.

And as I write this, I recall something else, one more thing I hadn't remembered in years but now see, like a sound faint in the distance, has always been here. It's my father's laugh, the one entirely expressive, joyous, tear-streaming, body-aching release my brother and I associated with him, and then in it, the laugh of his father, Gugga Royle as we called him, who died in February 1966. I don't remember anything Tony said, but I remember his laugh – superb, engulfing, withholding nothing. And in that memory I catch a trace of what I never thought to hear till now, Lola Onslow's laughing with him.

Of all the hundreds of songs and versions of songs by David Bowie, I would like to conclude with 'Drive-In Saturday' from the album *Aladdin Sane*. Bowie supposedly wrote this song on a train at night, travelling from Seattle to Phoenix, in November 1972, struck by the weirdness of a series of huge silver domes out of the window. The song is a surreal, anachronistic throwback and forwards: with elements of the 1950s and 1960s deranged as they're shunted into the 1970s and beyond (Bowie once called it a song from 2033). It's about a post-apocalyptic world in which people have forgotten how to have sex. In their attempts to rediscover it, they turn to watching old videos, featuring 1960s icons such as Mick Jagger and Twiggy, and also to reading (borrowing a book, not from the library but from 'the strange ones in the dome').

I haven't said this till now, but there's something about my relationship to Bowie's music that corresponds with what he says about Fats Domino. As a lad, Bowie loved Fats Domino's songs but, he says, 'I couldn't understand the lyrics and that really made an impression on me – there was some secret information that I didn't have.' It was like that for me when I first got to know Bowie's songs. I couldn't make out half of the words but that was fine. In the sixties and seventies you were lucky if there was a lyrics sheet, so most often you were just left guessing. I fell in love with the voice and melodies. The nitty-gritty of the words trailed some way behind.

So I still find it a bit funny when commentators feel compelled to speculate, for example, on the influence of the famous Swiss psychoanalyst as intimated in the line 'Jung the foreman prayed at work'. I'm not wishing to imply that Bowie's lyrics are not fascinating. Indeed, I take very seriously his suggestion that making music for him is a form of being in analysis. And what his songs give in turn, I think, is a space for analytic floating attention of a new kind.

But all the parody and allusion in 'Drive-In Saturday' are, to my ear, secondary to the main pull of the music. For me it's a sort of crash-course song about falling in love, about being absolute beginners, about being children of the summer's end. I connect 'Drive-In Saturday' with starting afresh. It might be a new relationship, or the magic of leaving home and going to university, and the early days of autumn – the release of the end of the week, the meaning of Saturday.

What a strange, deceptively simple title-phrase it is – about time (Saturday, the weekend) becoming space (a drive-in). It's a song *about* the time machine of music. It's about uncertainty, and then it's also very sexy.

I will always associate it with the engulfing experience of falling in love, really in love, and going to bed. 'Drive-In Saturday' is a love song about that stuttering, funny, uncertain thing called *aposiopesis*, you remember this, surely you can't have forgotten, it's the rhetorical figure for a … *It's a* … *It's a* … *It's a* … And it's a song about reading as a form of love-making. It's about the erotic, suggestively telepathic scene of *reading alone together*, reading alone with the other.

[Play David Bowie, 'Drive-In Saturday']

Part III

Typewriter

Mummy and Daddy were in the same goldfish bowl going round and round and round. The relentless sun of the early months had dissipated. The nightmare of 'home schooling' subsided into a few weeks of pseudo-normal 'back at school'. Then it was the summer holidays. But because home schooling had never happened, Mummy and Daddy wondered if now wasn't the time for it to do so. Like a ghost, the irreality of home schooling returned. It didn't really seem like summer, and there was no holiday to go on anyway.

Mummy and Daddy still used the names of seasons and months and days of the week, but time was estranged. One afternoon at the kitchen counter Daddy wrote out the four letters of this word on a piece of paper, cut it up and moved the letters around: EMIT, ME IT, MITE. Then he wrote out the letters of ESTRANGED and cut out and added those: EDGES RANT, GREAT DENS, DANGEREST. Then he mixed them up to make DEEM IT STRANGE, RIG MEANS TESTED, SET DREAM TINGE.

Daddy showed his workings to Monty and Mole. Mole was attracted to these pale slivers of paper but disappointed to discover they were not earthworms. He wanted to eat them or at least bite off their heads to immobilise them and bear them away to his burrow. Monty offered to get Mole some worms from elsewhere. They were invisible but very tasty.

Some things were clear. Lots of people were being hospitalised and dying; but there was some progress towards finding a vaccine. Daddy's remark about timeframes of work and expectations of remuneration altering for good seemed to Mummy just as utopian and stupid as when first aired; but demonstrations and support across the world for the murdered Black man, George Floyd, and against structural and everyday racism everywhere generated a feeling of hope.

Zeph tired of the audiobooks of Jan Francis and the reruns of MotoGP. When he wasn't playing Dragon City on his iPad, he was reading one of Michelle Paver's *Chronicles of Ancient Darkness*. He had moved on from the *Famous Five*. But Monty's passion persisted. Mummy had stopped reading Blyton aloud. Daddy became the sole supply line. He read all the *Secret Seven* books and all the *Adventure* series to Monty, as well as the *Secret* series, the *Find-Outers* and *Malory Towers*. Monty liked them all, but he kept coming back to the *Famous Five*.

No matter how mixed up time seemed, it was also still passing. Or people were. Monty turned six, Zeph nine. Mummy and Daddy got older too. It was difficult to calibrate. You could see it best when people were asleep. The children were growing up, but this seemed more disturbing than relieving. All sorts of things missed, stunted, suspended. Mummy and Daddy were at a loss. And then too it seemed, in some eerie way, as if older people were going back in time. Daddy could see it behind the masks of faces as he walked about their hometown. They were living a sense of the ending and the principal location for their thinking and feeling was the past.

When Daddy went for a walk, he now tended to avoid the seafront. The esplanade was busier than it had ever been. People came by car from towns and villages inland, even from as far as London. They were thirsty for space, for open air. They came for the seaside summer that was not there.

Instead, he headed into the downs. On a handful of occasions Zeph or Monty joined him, but most often he went alone.

Daddy tried to explain to Mummy his appreciation of being in the downs by recalling the word that Elizabeth Bowen used in one of her stories from the 1940s: *immune.* The immune downs. It was strangely reassuring to walk alone in high green hills long unpopulated, but scattered with earthworks and burial mounds, enfolding signs of vital, bustling ancientness. Right down to the prehistoric creatures that composed the chalk beneath his feet.

Mummy and Daddy were constantly amazed by Monty's acuity and innocence. He was their dark sweet goblin, unawares. One morning Mummy came into the kitchen. Daddy was sitting quietly with his first cup of coffee of the day. Big brother Zeph was still asleep upstairs, but the naked Monty, the full Monty, the beatific creature was hanging on her back like a gibbon. Mummy deposited him in Daddy's lap and sat down next to them.

Then Mummy and Daddy talked about how he was six now, but still just the same as when he was born. Daddy said: 'You were wearing your birthday suit then.' Monty replied: 'What does that mean?' Daddy explained: 'You came into the world not wearing any clothes.' Straightaway Monty asked, full of curiosity: 'Did Zeph?'

When Daddy read to him, Monty showed an almost alarming attentiveness. He was all ears and all eyes, saying not a word. But then he might come out with some curiously resonant observation: 'That's the good thing about stories. You can suddenly make them *go home.*'

Mummy was becoming increasingly beautiful. Mummy said this was Daddy's Glenkinchie goggles. But Daddy said it was a fact. It was partly because Mummy was working out in the studio every day and her body was becoming so sharp and supple and defined. And it was partly because Mummy and Daddy were so shattered with everyminute allthetimeness that, day after day after day, they kept losing sight of the oasis of being alone together, in the same bed at the same time, for instance, and conscious.

Daddy was rejuvenated by giving what Mummy called his Imaginary Lectures. Daddy wondered if she meant revitalised, but she said rejuvenated. Because she didn't listen to any of them, and she and the children were out of the house each time that he was recording one, it was easy to think that they were imaginary. Daddy said that made them sound like Walter Pater's *Imaginary Portraits*. He said that was quite misleading because the lectures were a lot more real than when one of Mummy's friends sent her a text of her dachshund Jarvis mouthing *I love you* and calling Mummy by her first name.

– So, Mummy inquired, do the lectures use synthetic media?

Daddy thought of explaining in loving detail how David Bowie comes on stage at a click of one's finger and smiles and laughs and jokes, singing as never before in the room with you, a fairy in the palm of your hand, and then, with another click, the Famous Five in all their smelly sentient substantiality are joshing and picnicking and spilling ginger beer right on your lap, with Timmy's tail swishing your face, but actually he only said that the talks were inspired by Mummy even if she never listened to them.

Mummy and Daddy kept up the routines as best they could. They tried at least twice a day to play together as a family – simple card games such as Go Fish, and computer games such as Among Us.

They also tried to share an interest in what the children were watching on TV. One afternoon Daddy sat with Zeph viewing old MotoGP races. Zeph talked all the time, so that Daddy couldn't hear anything the commentators were saying. Zeph's brain must be going so much faster than those bikes, Daddy thought. Daddy couldn't talk as fast as that to save his life. Mummy and Daddy worried about Zeph.

In the commercial break there was an advert about erectile dysfunction. Zeph asked: *Daddy, what's erectile dysfunction?* Daddy replied: *Something that some adults suffer from.* They watched images of the explosive benefits of the pharmaceutical product being advertised. Then Zeph asked: *What do rocket launchers have to do with erectile dysfunction?*

Daddy had always loved the way David Bowie sang the word 'crazy'. But like crazy paving, it couldn't be everywhere. As Bowie understood, you have to resist, displace, outplay the craziness of the world. All the lunatic men and 'madness in the family': Bowie retained, after all, his own singular, crazy sanity till the end.

Since signing up for 'early retirement', Daddy felt crazier than he had in a long time. Mummy also seemed rather crazy. Zeph and even Monty too. Mummy and Daddy thought a lot about the emerging global mental health crisis, and the local one in their house. But they could hardly speak about it, in those brief patches when they were alone together.

Mummy went back on to antidepressants. It felt like the opposite of voluntary severance, but she didn't make that joke with Daddy. She was very disappointed because she had managed to stay off them for so long. She thought she had moved on to a place where they were no longer necessary. Her defeated feelings were about herself but, just as much, if not more, about the children.

Monty was too young to be diagnosed with anything, but Zeph was old enough to see a child psychologist and Mummy and Daddy booked him in with a play therapist who lived locally.

Once a week Daddy drove with Zeph to the lady's house and the lady came to the garden gate in her mask to welcome his son and Daddy walked back to wait in the car. Sometimes he read a book. Sometimes he simply sat listening to a single David Bowie track, such as 'Stay'. It was as much as he could take. He'd play the song once, sometimes twice, and then just think about it. He sat still, gazing dimly out through the windscreen, watching leaves fall from the trees as the dusk descended, for it was becoming autumn.

Daddy thought about *the light of the world*. There was a painting of that name by William Holman Hunt. He remembered seeing it when he was a teenager, in an Oxford college, and being affected by it in ways that the painter probably didn't intend. How can one know what a painter intends? 'The Light of the World' is a work of Christian allegory. Or, as Daddy thought at the time, Christian propaganda.

When he was younger, Daddy used to be angry about the very existence of Christianity. He felt contempt for religion of all kinds. Daddy no longer felt that way. He felt sad that so many forms of thinking and belief guided by principles of love and gentleness seemed condemned to perpetuate violence and suffering. But he still believed in a world of the now without religion.

Jesus is standing at a door, with his right arm raised in the act of knocking, and his left arm lowered holding a lantern. He is in the classic garb of a Semite. He could be Jewish or he could be Palestinian. The painting is based on a verse in the Book of Revelation, at the end of the Bible: 'Behold, I stand at the door, and knock: if any man hear my voice, and open the door, I will come in to him, and will sup with him, and he with me.'

It has to be 'any *man*'. It wouldn't work if it were a woman behind the door. Why should a woman open it up to some strange bloke? The invite to *sup* sounds odd too: it calls to mind 'supping with the devil'. There's a closed feeling to the picture, despite all the lighting. The door has no handle. It only opens from the inside.

The Book of Revelation doesn't say anything about Jesus as *the light of the world.* This phrase only occurs in the Gospels – once when Jesus is describing himself, and then another time when he refers to his followers. It's a light that jumps from speaker to listener.

The lighting in the painting is as detailed as a colour photograph but completely unreal at the same time. There's a brilliant night sky of turquoise and a halo that looks like a huge moon behind the man's head and a lantern generating so much light it's like the start of a firework display, as if the door itself is going to burst into flames.

One day Daddy took a walk along the seafront. It was early in the morning. There weren't yet many people about. He couldn't help being curious about what they were saying to one another, as he passed. He overheard two conversations, one at either end of the esplanade, in which one person asked the other, in a gentle but earnest manner: 'Is it because …?'

Daddy was interested in how literature and music inspired other ways of thinking about the light of the world. When he read *The Princess and the Goblin* to Monty, he was struck by a peculiar passage in which the Princess avoids surveillance by a goblin (a 'watching creature') and manages to get back to her grandmother:

> Speedily, yet softly, she walked down the hill, hoping to pass the watching creature unseen. Dark as it was, there was little danger now of choosing the wrong road. And – which was most strange – the light that filled her eyes from the lamp, instead of blinding them for a moment to the object upon which they next fell, enabled her for a moment to see it, despite the darkness. By looking at the lamp and then dropping her eyes, she could see the road for a yard or two in front of her, and this saved her from several falls, for the road was very rough.

Daddy had never read a description of lighting like that anywhere before. It was uncanny. That's not how he would have put it if he'd been talking to Mummy, but he never mentioned it to Mummy. There was no time for such things.

It reminded Daddy of when he went mad. He had eaten some magic mushrooms and sat with friends in the dark and they listened to David Bowie's new album *Heroes*. It was amazing. But then one of his friends said she was bored of sitting in the dark. So they considered the matter at some length and finally agreed to turn on the light. But turning on the light was a blinding cataclysm. Quickly they resolved to go outside. It was night time. But the meadow and the deer and the great elm trees where they walked were as brilliant as in broad daylight.

His eyes had turned into sources of light that could be switched on in the dark.

Daddy was very fragile for weeks after that. He had to leave the university and go home for a while. That was when Daddy stopped using drugs.

And now Daddy had left the university again but this time he was never going back and he had this vision of new lights of the world when he thought of the planet suddenly not in terms of all the fossil fuels and forest fires burning but in terms of sun machines – all the millions of sites across the world where people day and night were listening and reading, in love, and putting out fire with gasoline.

To Mummy, Daddy said nothing. Mummy had enough on her plate without having to worry about how crazy Daddy was going. In any case, Daddy told himself, it wasn't crazy. It was OK. It was like Camel, settling down in the warm ribbed sand for a big sleep, or Badger after a night out returning to his woodland sett along the babbling stream lit by glow-worms, or the narrator of *The Princess and the Goblin*, whose tone and address seemed so irenic. Daddy tried to tell Mummy about the pleasures of reading George MacDonald. He read aloud a sentence from one of MacDonald's essays, 'The Fantastic Imagination': 'I do not write for children, but for the childlike, whether of five, or fifty, or seventy-five.'

Daddy wanted to tell Mummy how topical this felt. He wanted to say something about how a line from a David Bowie song or a passing phrase from one of the children could illuminate the whole world differently. But Monty walked in on this oasis at 'seventy-five', wondering if Daddy could *do some book* with him.

Do some book. Had anyone ever before generated such mystery and brilliance in these three words?

This was where Monty had got to, in his passion for the *Famous Five*. He didn't simply wish to hear Daddy or Mummy or Jan Francis reading. He wanted to write the books himself. Or at any event, to oversee the task. He launched a cottage industry. If the house remained (at least by day) under the reign of Blyton, Monty now seemed bent on inscrutable usurpation.

He did very little himself. He couldn't write. What letters he *could* make were charmingly dyslexic. All of his numerals were in mirror-writing. Monty made rudimentary line drawings of what were evidently very complex scenarios, but he refused to let Daddy or Mummy add a caption to explain what was happening. And his power of listening seemed extraordinary. Monty would raise one eyebrow or gaze upwards and a little sidewise in reverie. His listening was radiant, as he entered the force field of a *Famous Five*. Mummy and Daddy loved to watch him, thinking and feeling, dreaming and scheming – inside the book with Enid Blyton.

Monty sat up at the kitchen counter and directed operations. Daddy found a few sheets of A4 paper and a stapler and scissors and pens and coloured pencils. Monty watched while Daddy carefully cut and folded up pieces of paper until he had a blank 64-page book. Then Daddy had to staple them together and insert page numbers. Then he had to do the 'bubble' writing for the front cover. This always included the words 'FAMOUS FIVE'. And the back cover gave information about other books in the series.

Monty was the dictator, Daddy the amanuensis. Sometimes Monty dictated so quickly that Daddy couldn't keep up and then Monty became angry. Had Monty learned to be moody like this from George? The text was divided up into chapters of 4 or 5 pages and each chapter ended with one of Monty's arcane 'stick' drawings. For example, there was the volume called *A Thrilling Time* in which Julian and George went out for a walk in the forest, and when they came back Anne was in the kitchen:

> 'What have you been up to?' said Anne.
>
> 'Well, just finding stuff out,' said Julian. 'Nothing else but finding stuff out. I mean, who *wouldn't* find stuff out staying out so long? It's almost lunchtime.'
>
> 'Have you finished?' asked Anne. 'Or are you going to talk some more?'
>
> And just then, before Julian could reply, Aunt Fanny, their mother, came in. And Aunt Fanny made lunch.

> After lunch they went upstairs and into Dick's bedroom. They heard Dick snoring. Then Dick finally woke up.
>
> And Dick didn't say anything. He just rushed downstairs to get his lunch.

What Daddy took down was mostly dialogue. Julian says this. Anne says that. It tended to be an inordinately long time before an adventure got underway. But then came a frenzy of activity and everything was wrapped up in a single sentence.

As onlooker, Mummy wondered who was amanuensis for whom. Monty was channelling Blyton but also channelling Daddy. Mummy spoke of this channelling thing when they were alone in the kitchen one evening. It was rare for Mummy even to come back downstairs after the children were asleep, but on this occasion she reappeared. This always made Daddy's heart wake up, even if he was also looking forward to putting on a series of Bowie songs very loud and listening to them for the umpteenth time.

Despite their exhausted state Mummy and Daddy always found pleasure in sharing reflections, however fuzzy or fragmentary, on Zeph and Monty. Daddy was drinking a bottle of Fuller's ESB. Mummy was drinking water. They were sitting in two adjacent chairs looking across the kitchen as if they were on an aeroplane. Mummy was sitting back resting her head and had her eyes closed, as if they were midway between London and Tokyo, suspended over Siberia.

Daddy thought of talking about the fact that Enid Blyton herself was channelling. That was what the undermind was about. But then Daddy considered that he had never said anything to Mummy about the undermind and now probably wasn't the time to start. So, instead, he said that Monty seemed to be channelling something in Blyton like no one else.

Daddy wondered if Mummy was asleep. He stood up, leaned down and kissed her very gently on the mouth. She smiled, without opening her eyes.

Mummy loved it when Daddy put her to sleep by talking about books. But he knew she wouldn't want to go to sleep where she was sitting. Mummy liked to be quite horizontal when asleep. Uncertain how fully she was attending, Daddy brought the dictionary up on his phone and began to satisfy his curiosity. He said quietly, in case she had already dropped off:

– 'Channelling' in the sense of acting as a medium for some spirit or extraterrestrial being is anachronistic. At least according to the dictionary.

– Uh? said Mummy, but then she closed her lips again.

So Daddy went on:

– Since the nineties it's been more about emulating or imitating or appearing to be inspired by.

Daddy waited to hear if Mummy had anything on this. But as she said nothing, he set his phone down and sipped his beer. He said:

– There's something rather crass about that sense, don't you think? As if there is an easily identified one-way passage. The psychotherapist's *aha!*

Daddy rather hoped that this, especially the 'aha!' bit, would arouse Mummy's attention. But it didn't. He sat with his glass of beer, looking at Mummy in Siberia.

'Channel' was originally a water-word. It was about a stream or length of water. In its earliest recorded usages it was about the hollow course of a waterway, rather than the water itself. As if *channelling* was channelling itself.

People didn't start talking about channelling until the 1970s. Bowie had a role in all of that. But there was no channelling in Blyton. It was after Blyton's time. But that, thought Daddy, was the point. Now everyone was *here*: out of time.

*

Then came the typewriter.

That was one of the things Daddy had in the Sussex-after-the-Bomb more usually referred to as his study. It was an Imperial Signet typewriter, made in Japan. Daddy's Mummy and Daddy gave it to him as a birthday present. It must have been 1969 or 1970. It rested in peace inside its faded, grey, bakelite case. Or *lid* as Daddy used to call it. Like an old car bonnet. All these decades it had never been more than a few feet away from Daddy in his study. Stood in a corner. Underminding its own business.

And then one morning, in the midst of all those feverish seemingly interminable days of home never alone, Daddy's eyes paused for a moment on the corner in question and he elected to clamber over the assembled chaos of boxes and books and small tables piled high with papers and pick it up. He could hardly believe how heavy it was. It reminded Daddy of Monty who had the gorgeous little body of a six-year-old but for some reason, when Daddy or Mummy tried to pick him up, felt like antimatter.

Daddy lugged the typewriter downstairs to the kitchen. Mummy was tidying some things that the children had left on the floor. Zeph was on his iPad. Monty was watching Daddy and what Daddy was carrying. He was watching with the quiet but imposing concentration of a previously unrecorded animal. Daddy placed the typewriter on the countertop and removed the lid. Daddy saw it with his own eyes but also with Monty's.

Zeph remained wrapped up in his computer game. But Mummy came over to look. Mummy was too young ever to have had a typewriter. She made an admiring noise, like the hum of a llama, but said:

– It can't still work.

Then she left the room.

At first Daddy simply stared.

It had been too long. The thing was too strong. At once so familiar and so peculiar. It was too personal, private, secret. Like a postscript he'd never read. Dense with memory and love, imagination and loss. And it was just a heap of metal, antiquated, pointless. Like the brown rusty agricultural implements one could still see on occasion at the overgrown edges of old fields or farmyards.

Daddy was transfixed by the inky and metallic odours. The unexpected depths and gaps. The carriage and platen. The keytop letters. The space bar. Daddy was suddenly struck by that name – a space bar for space oddities! And then there was the ribbon, and the rather grand silver lever for the return of the carriage when starting a new line. The hillside of type-bars going down into the illiterate valley of the type basket.

Daddy looked at Monty. Monty was agog. He had never seen such a thing.

It didn't occur to Daddy that the ink might be fresh after all these years. As Mummy had said: it couldn't still work. But the glitter in Monty's eyes suggested otherwise. At that moment he looked just as Daddy imagined the young Curdie in *The Princess and the Goblin* – 'with eyes as dark as the mines in which he worked and as sparkling as the crystals in their rocks'.

Daddy experienced a queer deliquescence in his own body. He found a blank piece of paper and slid it down and around the platen. He lined it up to begin typing as if it was fifty years ago, as if he were returning to a pivotal moment in his own past, only now recognising it. Daddy's hands knew what to do without a split-second's reflection. The snail-silvery black ribbon was still serviceable. He started typing a few random letters: p p s. He laughed at the exertion and Monty laughed too. The sheer physical effort required to get the keys to rise up and smack down to leave a legible symbol on the paper! The laborious clatter of every letter and item of punctuation!

Monty was literally squirming in his seat. He wanted to try. Daddy scrolled down a few spaces and put the machine in front of him. But the keys were too stiff, the letters on the keyboard too heavy. Monty couldn't manipulate the return.

Daddy found it strangely painful, having to replace the old thing in its case and return it to the corner of his study. It was like rescuing a friend from a mental hospital, then seeing them escorted back before anyone had had a chance to speak. But next day after breakfast, Mummy took Zeph and Monty out for a bike ride, and Daddy cleared space on the desk in his study and took up the old machine once again. He unhooked the lid and slid in a sheet of paper. He started typing. Within five minutes he had a page. Then he had two pages. Like stars in a night sky rushing out.

Part IV

Strangers meet we when

Lola Onslow

There was the room where the painter slept and kept her things and on a gorgeous sunny spring day only just introduced themselves to one another when her big sister Effie called up needing help with something downstairs and it wasn't supposed to take five minutes the younger had said fearing it might be twenty and flustered but trusting she'd made her apologies and would be back.

It was the dog had something stuck in his paw or cut it poor thing but she didn't want to explain because this was not a vet's surgery nor a day for Effie to be part of but the hour for showing the picture and settling the commission and the tea would stay hot under the cosy and Miss Blyton had said right out she'd something to read and was happy with her nose in it for as long as the painter needed.

No one to know her undermind the author closed her eyes.

Such a glorious morning and that girl so funny and full of go with her Dublin accent disappearing into English reminded her of her grandmother and what a lovely room with the fresh flowers in jugs in practically every corner and the warm sun stirring the Queen of the Suburbs out of the windows distant sounds of omnibus and car and carriage away across the park with all the trees coming into blossom and the birds singing as if the world was on fire in the gathering heat of the morning.

Strangers meet we when

There was the painter's easel with her latest work taking form and the newcomer might feign not to have noticed the splendour of its quietness a watercolour of a great tree she hadn't yet decided still its beauty gave her a queer sense of having seen it before.

For equally she might in these minutes have brazenly fingered the portfolio by the little bed doubtless placed conveniently for its owner to unfasten the little black ribbons and display but this she saw was a feat too far for the exacting bows and retying without notice and anyway that might spoil a pleasure.

But a roving eye was hers and she was hardly going to nestle in these cushions beside the tea-tray and bowl of something freshly baked under a neat starched tea-towel reading as if under obligation the book she'd brought with her for why would you do that when you're suddenly alone in a lovely stranger's room without the stranger.

Unless it was a book belonging to the stranger was how she saw it and it fell out when treading softly alert as a thief to a creaking board she dipped her face towards the narcissi on the table keen for the fragrance of their stems as much as flowers and skirting the pretty spray of cherry blossom in the fireplace after checking herself in the mirror over the mantelpiece to see the new red dress just right with the pearls.

Miss Blyton scanned the shelf skipping novels by Scott and Dickens and Henty and Wells and the poems of Yeats and de la Mare and Brooke and Drinkwater her eyes alighting on a slender black spine of more anonymous and lowly origins and how pleased she felt with this speed and felicity a gift she possessed like her powers of memory only glance at a page and have it by heart.

And so she slid out and proceeded to read knowing she shouldn't the Paris and Swiss Journal of Lola Onslow dated May 26th 1911 occupying the first forty pages of an otherwise blank notebook.

> We started off on Monday April 24th 1911 by the 6.15 train from West Ealing station to Victoria. A friend of ours, Irene Harman & Nellie, our cook saw us off. We were very excited. When we

> arrived at Victoria we had nearly an hour to wait, so Effie & I amused ourselves by exploring the station. When the train came in we secured our seats, & settled down for the journey to Newhaven. The train started at 8.45. A young friend of Miss Bazett's, Winnie Binning, was coming with us as far as Lausanne, where she was going to teach at a school. Effie & Winnie did not sleep at all during the journey to Newhaven, but I slept a little. We arrived at Newhaven at about 10.30. Our luggage had been [put, she must have meant] through to Paris, & so we had nothing to do with it, until we reached Paris. We went on board the SS Brighton, & went down into our cabin, there were two rows of berths round it. So Effie & I each secured a top one. We were given rugs to cover us with, by the stewardess, who was very nice. When the boat started, she turned down the lights. Beside our berths there were portholes, & Effie & I spent most of our time, looking out through them, at the waves.

O how powerfully in waves it brought back the excitement of her own first journey abroad with her beloved Louise to Annecy just two years later never to be forgotten.

It was bad form but awfully pleasing to read someone else's journal and a good reason she herself kept no record of what most mattered never to reveal the intimacies and intricacies of her rages and longings concerning her father and mother and brothers not to mention heady ambitions for writing and desires for other girls.

It was childlikeness before any betrayal made her a good Froebel teacher and now governess and what always outstripped in gaiety and innocence any respect for the world of the grown up for wasn't being a grown up the biggest betrayal of all wasn't de la Mare right when he said what was it he said 'children are butterflies' who most of them 'by a curious inversion of the processes of nature become half-comatose and purblind chrysalides'.

O to be off on an adventure with a sister how she always longed for a sister all at sea with her gazing through portholes.

Conscience and anticipation tingling she turned the pages absorbing the pleasure of this girl's continentalising and while poised at a second's notice for the door was ajar and she must certainly catch Miss Onslow's steps coming back up the stair to shut and replace the journal and appear merely to be surveying the volumes on the shelf she was unable to stop.

The prudent thing it occurred to her was to have an alibi volume to hand not merely gormless at the shelf and so she picked out *The Wilde Swans at Coole* setting it open on the book tops and returned to what she shouldn't have been doing.

She revelled in the girl's hand with its looping elegance and charming Q's and V's and I's and B's and ampersands and all her precision with the times of trains departing and arriving and the trees on the way from Dieppe with *large quantities of mistletoe* and the rain *coming down in torrents* and then the sun and churches in Paris and breakfast and dinner and supper and the *rolls and chocolate* and *drink of milk* in a café and lemonade for refreshment and the little steamer down the Seine and the Flower Market at La Sainte Chapelle and the museum with the candid admiration surely an interesting sign of the paintings of Rosa Bonheur at the Palais de Luxembourg *once an old palace but now a picture gallery* with all the little trips around the city by carriage and then the girl's *first ever journey in a taxi* making for the Gare de Lyon they *went whizzing along so quickly* seeing Paris by night *all lit up* before the train out of France.

Miss Blyton's fingers took her eyes to Switzerland.

> Tuesday May 2nd. In the morning we walked up to the Signal, to see a lovely view of the lake & mountains. When we got to the top we sat down & Miss Isa read to us. Then we came home, on the way we picked, cowslips, anemones, violets, cuckoo pint, primroses, primulas, and ranunculus. In the afternoon we had two Finland ladies to tea, & afterwards we went for a walk with them. Miss Isa & they sat down on a little hill, & Miss Bazett, Effie & I did a little exploring. We went through a dear little wood, where we saw enormous snails, which, Miss Bazett says, are eaten for consumption. Beyond the wood was a field &, in it we found our first small blue gentians. Afterwards we went home to supper, & bed.

> Wednesday. In the morning we walked to the village & back: and in the afternoon, went for a walk through some fields to look for some more gentians. A lady had told us of a place where she had found some. When we had passed a wood we had to go through first, and come to the field beyond, great was our surprise to find that it was the same place we had gone to the day before.
>
> Thursday. After breakfast we walked to 'Lake Bret'. It was a very pretty walk. We came home in time for dinner. After dinner we made friends with a little French girl whose grandmother was stay [staying, of course] at our Pension. Her name is Jeanne, & she had come over with her mother, with the purpose of going to Vevey, but instead she came with us for a walk, while her mother & grandmother went to Vevey. So we took some oranges & things, & set off for Lake Bret. We took with us some mountain sticks we had just bought in the village before we came out. We played by the lake for some time, & then sat down & had some refreshments. Jeanne fed a big snail with orange & it eat [or ate: a mistake I make too!] a lot of it. After we had finished we went for a little walk by the side of the lake, & then came home. Before supper, we played hide & seek, & after supper, patiences. At about 8.30 Jeanne had to go home. When she had gone Effie & I went to bed.

The visitor was streaming through the final entries when the step of her subject now thirteen years older sounded on the stair and she scrambled to stow the journal and picked up the Yeats and in her reverie having practically forgotten what Lola looked like felt a fresh flush of pleasure at the pale linen simplicity of her dress and bare feet and glad grace the pretty face and winning smile mingled with the triumph of concealment accomplished.

Less to cap the profusion of apologies and confirmation that the dog was fine than to close the chapter of her clandestine activity she recited as if by heart the start of the poem on the page she had happened to leave open.

> May God be praised for woman
> That gives up all her mind,
> A man may find in no man
> A friendship of her kind

> That covers all he has brought
> As with her flesh and bone,
> Nor quarrels with a thought
> Because it is not her own.

Miss Blyton visibly coloured at the irony and smiled and gave the title 'On Woman' before asking would Lola if she didn't mind first names would Lola like to show the picture now or sit and have tea and the painter tickled to be addressed as Lola but unsure at this momentary reversal of roles said tea when in truth she would have preferred settling the picture.

So they sat on the floor and drank tea still hot and Lola sliced lemon cake still flustered to think Miss Blyton no Enid really was so much the author already found herself divulging as she otherwise very well might not have done that *her* mother was an author too.

Enid looked at Lola and thought of the tomb of Captain Arkwright *who was lost in an avalanche on Mont Blanc and his body was not found until 31 years afterwards when it was discovered in the stream that runs underneath the glacier.*

That passage had frozen in her mind and she saw it as clearly as she saw the girl.

Said Lola:

– My mother is an author and she's published a book you won't know I'm sure.

At which the painter rose almost spilling her tea veering across the room to gather from a small shelf by the bed her mother's *Faces and How to Read Them.*

– It was published just two or three years ago.

And passing the book to the visitor she rushed to fill the space saying

– She publishes as Irma Blood but her real name is Katherine and my sister Effie says sometimes she's away with the fairies.

Which made Enid laugh and also Lola but for a moment more awkwardly.

– Mother thinks you can judge someone's character by the shape and size of their mouth or nose or the distance between their eyes and Effie says Mother is entitled to her opinions but Mother says she received the gift.

Truly there was something about this painter's elfin looks and lilt of voice and half swallowing words with her shyness but the author remarked only

– Delicious cake!

which Lola ignored as she was trying to explain:

– Her father worked on the railways in India when Mother was a girl and she was an only child in a vast foreign place left during the day to wander by herself and one morning she heard strange noises on the other side of the compound wall down among the trees and peered over to see a very old man simply lying by the roadside and she must have communicated with him but it can't have been in English as he wouldn't have spoken that language but it was hot already and he was resting against the wall in the shade of the trees.

Then the Indian Irish English girl as Enid was now thinking paused as if to let her own words catch up with her before carrying on.

– Mother must have been only so high herself.

And Lola raised a slender lovely bare arm again almost but not spilling her tea in the process.

– But she felt such pity for this wizened little fellow by the road I suppose one didn't need to speak the same language to know a body was hungry and she came to learn he was there every day propped up by the roadside in the shade of the tamarind trees and she carried a bowl of gruel to him each morning for breakfast because he had no teeth he was so old Mother said his bones had turned to jelly and later in the day friends would come and bear him to the marketplace and tie him in knots and when Mother had to leave India and return to Ireland on the final morning she took him his gruel and the old man my Mother says passed on to her the gift.

– Of tying people's limbs in knots? interposed Enid laughing.

– No not that at all but Mother's gift as a witch.

Then the visitor opened the book and half-inclined to giggle but maintaining a serious expression read off from the inside board the advertisements for other *Useful Handbooks on Character Reading and Fortune Telling.*

– *Hands and How to Read Them … Heads and How to Read Them … After-Dinner Sleights and Pocket Tricks … Card Tricks Without Sleight of Hand or Apparatus … Simple Conjuring Tricks that Anybody can Perform … Hand Shadows: The Complete Art of Shadowgraphy ….*

– *Shadowgraphy* repeated the visitor at the end and they both laughed because Enid without meaning for a moment to do so had pronounced this word with an Irish accent as if she were Lola or her own grandmother Mary Ann Hanly now.

Then the visitor turned a couple of pages and delivered in a voice at once sympathetic and playful words Lola well recognised.

– *There is something very fascinating about the study of faces; we can learn so much from the observation of our fellow-creatures. It is a useful study, too; so useful that it would be a wise thing for everyone to gain a slight knowledge, if no more, as a guide to the placing of trustworthy persons, or the reverse, either in our affections or in our business concerns.*

The young women both orphans of a sort regarded one another with laughing eyes and Lola hardly knew but as Enid passed the book back their hands touched in a mild but thrilling instant and enquired as if no one had ever posed such a question before

– Shall you show me your picture?

Which gave rise to a quite other giddiness for the painting Lola showed struck Enid as vivid with a delicacy and intricacy akin to Brueghel's *Landscape with the Fall of Icarus* a heavily turreted sunlit fairy castle occupying an island all of its own in the manner of Mont St Michel but with a dreamy bridge to a nearby land and magically impossibly tall-looking trees at whose roots beautiful young fairy women gazed at the approach of goblins and a great old ship set sail for the deep blue horizon.

She was in love with it without a word.

– You've always painted?

This was all Enid could say even though she knew already because the girl writing in her 1911 journal kept referring to the fact that she was painting and drawing and other images now flashed through her mind of Lola's picking *periwinkles and narcissi* and going to the post office to send *boxes of flowers back to England* and the *spray of white lilac* in the Swiss hotel foyer *for the wedding* and then she asked to see other pictures but hardly had to glance at a couple of these marvels of the Little People to wonder would Lola consider also painting a frontispiece for her work was so lovely and the author's heart was pounding so funnily in her chest she promptly sat down again on the floor and Lola joined her.

And Lola laughing plucked up her mother's book once more and read out the very end of the volume which was most amusing and had perhaps Enid would agree nothing whatsoever to say about faces but was all about sitting on the floor.

> *Many people are possessed of a great fondness for sitting on the floor, and those who do so will generally give some clue to their character in the way in which they make themselves comfortable in this position.*
>
> *For instance, should the 'floor-sitter' hug her knees (for these people are generally of the feminine sex) and rock to and fro, she is inclined to be imaginative and given to indulge in flights of fancy. She will more often than not prefer her own society to that of others, and will never be at a loss for amusement when alone.*
>
> *Should she sit with her legs tucked away under her, she will be youthful and unspoiled in mind; and, indeed, will often prove to be one of those most delightful of people, a 'grown-up child'.*
>
> *The energetic, clever and impetuous individual will throw herself down on the floor in any attitude, and will fidget and wriggle all the time she is sitting. She is very keen, though apt to be something of a disturbing element at times, owing to her restless, untiring nature.*
>
> *And, now, if you will follow my rules and facts, you will never be far wrong in your estimation of your fellow-creatures; and it is indeed a comforting notion that we are able to judge others fairly and that we have a safe and reliable guide to the characters and attributes of the people we encounter in our every-day affairs.*

Strangers meet we when

It was so funny.

It was so extremely funny that the breath of these young floor-sitters almost sisters sifters cysted stopped as clouds curling floated away and this room in the Queen of the Suburbs filled with sun true to no form before witnessed in the miracle of the blossoms of the cherry and almond trees and the great oaks and horse-chestnuts beyond the windows and the sweet swart goblins and gossamer fairies of an undermind in the coronal songs of so many birds both laughing knowing what was about to happen and the sun itself as they sat in its jets and spicules in its surges and flares rim after rim and limb after limb was actually exploding.

What is a sun machine? Afterword by Peter Boxall

Nicholas Royle's *David Bowie, Enid Blyton and the sun machine* is a book unlike any other that I have read, one that does not sit comfortably in any existing genre or form. I suspect that Royle would gently discourage us from describing his book as 'creative non-fiction' ('Personally', he says, the phrase 'makes me sad'). It is not memoir, precisely. It is not a novel, according to most definitions we have to hand. It is not 'theory', or literary criticism.

We have only one term with which to define *The Sun Machine*. It is a sun machine.

The Sun Machine is not a book *about* sun machines – or not just a book about sun machines. It is also a sun machine in its own right. In this respect, it belongs to a small but noble family of works whose effects rest on the blurred distinction between what they are 'about', and what they 'are'.

We might think of Franz Kafka's *The Burrow*. 'I have completed the construction of my burrow', the narrator of Kafka's story declares in an opening sentence that worms its way into Royle's book, 'and it seems to be successful'. The burrow in question, that has so recently been completed (even though, confusingly, it has also just begun), is the beautifully designed subterranean warren that Kafka's narrator – a peculiar kind of speaking mole – digs for himself, in order that he might live in peace, defended from his enemies. It is also the story that the narrator writes for himself, in order that he might find sanctuary in the 'passages' of which it is composed, which 'enclose me more peacefully and warmly than a bird is enclosed in its nest'.

The Burrow of *The Burrow* is at once *a* burrow and *The Burrow*. Or we might think of Charlotte Perkins Gilman's *The Yellow Wallpaper*. The protagonist and narrator of Gilman's story spends the duration of the tale becoming ever more obsessed with the wallpaper that decorates an upstairs room in which she has been confined by her coercive husband, a physician named John. She is gripped by an increasingly urgent need to read the wallpaper, to find in it a message of some kind, even a way out of her captivity. 'John was asleep, and I hated to waken him, so I kept still and watched the moonlight on that undulating wallpaper until I felt creepy.' The narrator reads her wallpaper, as we, Gilman's readers, read ours, until both she and we start to feel distinctly creepy. And the title, *The Yellow Wallpaper*, refers to both texts, the text that Gilman's story is about, and the text that it is.

David Bowie, Enid Blyton and the sun machine is a sun machine, and this fact unsettles many of the conventions that allow us to orient ourselves in relation to it, to determine where it begins and where it ends, what it is and what it isn't. Not least it complicates the terms in which we might conceive of an 'afterword'. It is not just that this blurred distinction between 'is' and 'about' tends to weaken the boundaries of the work, so that the opposition between what is inside the sun machine and what is outside it becomes difficult to sustain (although I will come back to this tendency shortly). It is also because it is a defining feature of the sun machine that it disturbs the passage of time in such a way that we might no longer feel very sure about what comes after, what comes before, what happens during, or meanwhile.

This is what Royle – in his guise as the 'phantom lecturer', the 'teacher *condamné*' – means when he says that 'a sun machine is always also a time machine'. Sun machines contain the past within them, as they contain the future, and so they tend to reveal to us the fictional nature of after, of coming after. They are time machines, in the way that H. G. Wells's *The Time Machine* is a time machine. Wells's text is another distinguished member of the small family of texts that are 'about' what they 'are'. The passage of time recorded in this brief novel is only a week, a little week. It starts on a Thursday, when the narrator visits the time traveller before he sets off on his travels, and it ends the following Thursday, on the evening when the traveller returns. But it is the magic of prose fiction, of fiction as time machine, that in the passage of an imaginary week the time traveller journeys to the very edge of time, and to the end of planetary history presaged by the death of the sun. The machine that is Wells's story allows us, with remarkable ease, to conceive of such a feat. 'So I travelled', the traveller says, 'drawn on by the mystery of the earth's fate, watching with a strange fascination the sun grow larger and duller in the westward sky.'

Works that are sun machines are time machines – and it is perhaps a feature of the novel, as a form, that it can serve as both. A novel can be a compound of a sun machine and a time machine, which makes of time not something that passes, but something that remains, held within the webbing, the underground passages, of its own architecture. Every sun machine awaits the reading that is to come, tomorrow, and tomorrow, and tomorrow, to the last syllable of recorded time. This makes it difficult for us to conceive of coming 'after' a sun machine – and it touches too on another difficulty presented by the prospect of writing or reading an afterword to such a text. That is, the question of how the sun that shines inside a sun machine relates to the sun that shines outside it, beyond its borders, as I am writing, now, beyond its borders. 'The sun itself', Royle says, 'the sun as we think and talk about it in everyday language, is a fictional thing.'

The sun belongs inside a fiction, inside the fiction that is a sun machine. We can only conceive of it in fictional terms. We say, as Royle observes, that it rises and sets. We might feel inclined to worship it, or to bathe in it. We might want to imagine, if we are in a sunny or childish mood, that the sun has got his hat on and he's coming out to play. But the sun does not rise or set. It is not a he, or a she, or a they. We cannot bathe in it, and it does not wear a hat.

Our idea of the sun comes about through the fictions that we tell ourselves and each other about it. But, at the same time, and in a perplexing contradiction that is native to the sun machine, there can be no fiction without the sun. To bring an imagined world into being – to usher a reader into the space of a text, like the sunlit kitchen in which the Mummy and Daddy of *The Sun Machine* read to their children during the COVID-19 pandemic – one has to light it with its own sun. 'What in me is dark', says the nearly blind poet at the opening of *Paradise Lost*, 'illumine'. A poem – like a novel, or a painting, or a song – has a sun within it, and to read it is to be drawn into the orbit of this sun, to see by its light, and to be warmed by its rays.

To read *David Bowie, Enid Blyton and the sun machine* is to be gathered into the world that it imagines, so we no longer feel ourselves to be situated beyond its borders. We are addressed by the narrative, summoned by it into a certain kind of being. We sit, slumberous and dreamy, listening to the lecture series *A Sense of the Ending*, and we are transported into the virtual, asynchronous lecture theatre that the lectures themselves create. The text weaves an auditory space, lit by its own spoken sun, as the voice itself becomes a kind of light ('By the voice', Samuel Beckett's narrator says in his miraculous late work *Company*, 'a faint light is shed. Dark lightens while it sounds.')

This effect, this feeling that narrative voice reverberates beyond its own imagined field, that its light and warmth radiate beyond its own world and passes into ours, is perhaps common to all acts of the literary imagination. But it is given a particular expression in Royle's work, both in *The Sun Machine* and elsewhere, where it becomes a singular kind of mental transmission. How does a literary text speak to us, through what effect of telepathy? This is a question to which Royle has consistently returned, since his first book, *Telepathy and Literature*, published in 1991. How does voice persist? Through what forms of prosopopoeia do the dead speak to us?

Royle has turned this question over in his works of theory, from his book on telepathy, to his 2003 book *The Uncanny*, to his 2011 book *Veering*. And in his fictions and hybrid works – in *Quilt*, in *An English Guide to Birdwatching*, in *Mother: A Memoir*, in *The Sun Machine* – this question is bound up with a meditation on how we mourn those we have lost, how we draw the people from our past into the present, and the future. The question of how to imagine the sun, how to light our world with a fictional sun, is for this reason conjoined, in Royle's work, with the question of how to imagine the son, how to be a son, how to have a son (as it is entangled, too, with the question of being or having a daughter, or a mother, or a grandmother). The sun machine, Royle says, with, I suspect, a line from *Hamlet* in the back of his mind, is also a 'son machine' ('the homophone of "s-o-n" is there to be heard'). The homophone is there to be heard, too, in *Hamlet*. Gertrude pleads with her gloomy son to cheer up, to try to get over the death of his father. 'Good Hamlet', she says, 'cast thy nighted colour off.' 'Do not forever with thy vailèd lids / Seek for thy noble father in the dust.' Claudius, too, is impatient with Hamlet's exorbitant grief. 'How is it', he says to his nephew, 'that the clouds still hang on you?' 'Not so, my lord', Hamlet replies. 'I am too much i' the sun.'

Hamlet is a sun machine, in which the father can at once be dead and be living on, a spectre made visible by the light of the sun and of the son, a literary sun that 'usurp'st this time of night' so that we can see with veiled and clouded eyes. It is a machine that allows us to see the continuity between death and life, and to hear the voices of the dead, as the voice of old Hamlet resounds from somewhere under the stage ('Ah ha', Hamlet says, giddy with the excitement of hearing his father's voice once more, 'You hear this fellow in the cellarage'). Old Hamlet, his son says, is an 'old mole' who 'canst work i'th' earth so fast', a speaking mole who returns in Kafka's

Burrow, and who returns again, in Royle's *Sun Machine*, in the form of a hand-puppet called Mole, a wise counsellor who speaks in a voice which is at once high and deep, and through whom the 'Daddy' of *The Sun Machine* talks to his sons, talks to us, talks to himself as a son. The voice of Royle's text is a telepathic voice, one which opens on to the ground which joins absence with presence, parent with child, darkness with light. It crosses boundaries, forms, genres. It is made at once of colour, sound and thought, of music, painting and writing, all bound together. It is made, above all, of the shared ground that it finds between David Bowie and Enid Blyton, the ground that we see by the light of Bowie's sun machine, in which the memory of a free festival is enclosed.

'The sun machine is coming down, and we're gonna have a party.' If you know that song, 'Memory of a Free Festival' by David Bowie, then you will be able to hear this refrain, you will be unable *not* to hear it. Even now, as I invoke it again, this melody will be playing in your mind's ear (as, throughout Royle's book, snatches of melody will rise from the seabed of your mind – 'Ground Control to Major Tom', or 'a crack in the sky and a hand reaching down to me', or 'I'll stick with you, baby, for a thousand years'). That's the magic of the sun machine. It is not just about something, it is that thing. Bowie's voice, its particular pitch and clarity, is here again, sounding in your head. 'Memory of a Free Festival', Royle says, 'is *about* a sun machine, but it also aspires to *be* the sun machine that it is about.' We do not need the audio-visual equipment in the lecture theatre of the imagination to play the song, because it is already here, already in our mind, or in the undermind, where melody is stored not only as sound, but as light, as memory, as feeling, as voice.

Bowie's music is a medium of memory in *The Sun Machine*, a recovered space in which Royle is still listening with his brother to 'Golden Years' or 'Station to Station'. The voice glides, both high and deep, over distances, differences and years. It opens pools of shared being in which Bowie's voice mingles with the sound of our own lives – and mingles, in *The Sun Machine*, with the voice of Enid Blyton. In the sun-drenched kitchen, in the stilled time of the pandemic, it is this junction that Royle's book brings to light. The 'listening with' that is preserved in Bowie's voice is entangled, in the revelatory moment that lies at the heart of this book, with the 'listening with' that is conjured by the work of Enid Blyton. Listening to Bowie becomes entangled with listening to Blyton – 'Daddy' listening to the audiobooks read by Jan Francis, Zeph and Monty listening to their parents reading the same text, 'Daddy' half-remembering the same books from his own boyhood, where they lie secreted in some cellared fold of mind.

Royle asks us to imagine Blyton and Bowie nearly crossing paths in a Beckenham street, Blyton ensconced in her Rolls. But really he is attending to their shared place in a collective memory, a community of the mind where one voice bleeds into the other, as music bleeds into prose. Blyton's work comes from an undermind – her own word for the cellarage from which she draws her imagined worlds. But it also produces an undermind of its own, a space that lies hidden, half-forgotten, in so many of our minds, where it is entangled with the sound of the parent's voice, reading to us in the dark. Nobody, until now, has shown us how this Blytonic undermind inhabits us, how it opens channels, underground passages between parents and children, between the past and the future. *The Sun Machine* holds Blyton's sun machine within it, so we can see it again, as if for the first time. It was only on reading *The Sun Machine* that I discovered how intimately I know Blyton's work, how vividly I can picture its sunshine, its islands and waterfalls, and also its various undergrounds, its dungeons, cellars and passages. This is a world that I know in the marrow of my mind, that was given to me in my own childhood bedroom, and that I have given to my children in theirs, but that has remained, until now, sequestered in its own storied domain, in its own still pool of bedtime light.

In capturing Blyton's sunshine in this way, in mixing Blyton's light and warmth and vitality with Bowie's, *The Sun Machine* acts as its own environment, its own imagined community, which we as readers are invited to join. This is an environment, a community, which does not partake of what Royle calls 'a sense of the ending', and which does not belong to the time of 'after', the time of this afterword. This is not to say that Royle's book is not everywhere concerned with the perception that things are ending. 'It seems to me', Royle says, that 'we have a *sense of the ending* as never before.' The pandemic in which the book takes place is an engine of this sense of an ending, an accelerant of the 'profound and palpable precarity' of contemporary life. It was difficult to avoid the feeling, when we were living through it, that the pandemic was a symptom of the larger eco-crisis with which it is so deeply intertwined. Whether we subscribe to the 'lab-leak' theory, or to the theory that COVID emerged as a result of 'animal spillover' in a wet market in Wuhan, it is clear that the disease is bound up with the ongoing crisis in the relation between human and non-human, between human and environment – the crisis that has led to and resulted from climate change.

The pandemic is a temporally immediate manifestation of the slower violence of climate change; and it has shone a bright light too on the other failures that are associated with the climate emergency. As governments around the world locked down their populations, as restaurants, pubs, museums and schools were closed, we entered into some global ground zero, in which we were granted a frighteningly immediate access to the ways in which our cultural lives are attached to our naked being. How do democratic institutions gather that being into the shared commons of social life? How might such institutions offer some kind of ameliorative address to the climate emergency, to the ecological despoliation that delivered us to this stasis? How might our cultural institutions – schools, theatres, cinemas – sustain a vital connection between a shared past, and the future that lies before us now?

These are the questions that are in the air, as Royle delivers his valedictory address, and we might think that the response he offers to such questions gives us little cheer. One of the institutions that appears to be ending, in this larger climate of finitude, is the university. The prospect of the asynchronous lecture – and of the lecturer as a 'virtual interlocutory device' – felt eerily eloquent of the contemporary erosion of the university as the guardian of a critical public sphere. This is a dismantlement of the university that Don DeLillo imagined, with his own eerie eloquence, in his 1971 novel *Americana*. Eventually, DeLillo's narrator says, the university will be winnowed down to a single room in which two television sets face each other. Tuition would begin when 'the videotape of the students would watch the videotape of the instructors'. As Royle's 'ghost academic' speaks into the dark, through the cloudy portal of his computer screen, one feels a longing for the space of the lecture theatre, that space that makes a transformative kind of critical assembly possible, and that feels so deeply endangered today. But if the pandemic university presents to us a gloomy prospect, it is the case, nevertheless, that *The Sun Machine* harbours its own brightness, its own forms of continuation, its own contact with a past, and with a future. *The Sun Machine* is not just *about* the university. It projects an image of the university as it might be. It summons voices and images from the past – the Irish accent of Royle's grandmother, Lola, carried in the intonations of his father; the artwork that is a lasting remnant of Lola's love affair with Blyton projected on the screen of the mind. It opens its own channels between sound and vision, the under and the above, before and after, channels into which we, who come after, are drawn, and drawn again.

Like all those other members of the family to which it belongs – the works of art which are what they are about – Royle's book produces new relations between literature and philosophy, between thinking and imagining, between listening and seeing. It is a free festival that generates a new kind of imaginative possibility, even as that possibility appears to be foreclosed, everywhere we look. *The Sun Machine* projects a visionary university, in which literature, painting and music live on, sustained by nothing other than the light and warmth of the sun.

Notes

In general, I have not provided music and film details here: the reader, I am supposing, can track them down easily enough if wished. All quotations from Enid Blyton's *Famous Five* books are from *The Famous Five*, in 22 volumes (London: Hodder and Stoughton, 1997). All quotations from Shakespeare are from the *RSC Shakespeare: Complete Works*, ed. Jonathan Bate and Eric Rasmussen (London: Macmillan, 2007). References to the *Oxford English Dictionary* (*OED*) are to the online version at https://www.oed.com/

Epigraphs

x Will you come?: H. G. Wells, 'The Chronic Argonauts' (1888), in *The Time Machine and Other Works* (Ware, Hertfordshire: Wordsworth Editions, 2017), 334.

x For if the exaltation: Virginia Woolf, *Jacob's Room* (1922; New York: Harcourt, 1978), 120. From the same novel of 1922 I would also like to propose a cryptic supplementary epigraph, in the form of Betty Flanders's words to her young son Archer: 'Think of the fairies … Shut your eyes, and think of the fairies, fast asleep, under the flowers' (*Jacob's Room*, 12). The submerged environs of an endnote seem a fitting place to point out that one of the concerns of the present book is to suggest an elided history of 'modernism', pivoting on the 1920s, in which fairies take on new significance. This would differ from Nicola Bown's argument that, in the wake of the First World War, along with the publication of the notorious Cottingley photographs, interest in fairies was 'killed off'. See Bown's richly interesting study *Fairies in Nineteenth-Century Art and Literature* (Cambridge: Cambridge University Press, 2001), 196.

Preface

xi **what Mark Twain calls *mental telegraphy***: See 'Mental Telegraphy' and 'Mental Telegraphy Again', in *The Complete Essays of Mark Twain*, ed. Charles Neider (n.p.: De Capo Press, 1991), 71–87, 160–5.

xi **funny and spooky**: See Jeff Hilson, 'The God-Awful Small Affair of the Invisible Organist: David Bowie Translated', in *English: The Journal of the English Association*, 69.267 (2020): 346–62, and Leah Kardos, *Blackstar Theory: The Last Works of David Bowie* (London: Bloomsbury, 2022).

xii **Wembley Empire Pool in May 1976**: The playlist ran: 'Station to Station', 'Suffragette City', 'Fame', 'Word on a Wing', 'Stay', 'Waiting for the Man', 'Queen Bitch', 'Life on Mars?', 'Five Years', 'Panic in Detroit', 'Changes', 'TVC15', 'Diamond Dogs', 'Rebel Rebel' and 'The Jean Genie'.

xiii **as Shakespeare's Friar Laurence says**: William Shakespeare, *Romeo and Juliet*, Act 2, scene 6, lines 9–11.

xiii **reality literature**: See Nicholas Royle, 'Afterword: Reality Literature', in *Quilt* (Oxford: Myriad, 2010), 152–61.

Part II Memory of a free festival (first lecture)

28 **all about feel**: Bruce Robb, quoted in Dylan Jones, *David Bowie: A Life* (London: Windmill Books, 2018), 236.

28 **future feel**: See Timothy Morton and Nicholas Royle, *Even the Plague Journal: Everything Is Happening* (forthcoming).

29 **death art**: See, for example, Dr Mark Taubert, quoted in Jones, *David Bowie*, 499.

29 **it was really about *life art***: See Leah Kardos, *Blackstar Theory: The Last Works of David Bowie* (London: Bloomsbury, 2022), 204.

29 **always aware [of] death**: David Bowie, quoted in Jones, *David Bowie*, 417.

29 **I worship life**: David Bowie, interview with Russell Harty, 1973, accessed at https://www.youtube.com/watch?v=_ZtHxP4EMVo (accessed 2 May 2023).

30 **'Satori' […] is the Japanese word**: See Jack Kerouac, *Satori in Paris* (London: Quartet Books, 1973), 1.

30 **Dear as remember'd kisses**: Alfred Tennyson, 'Tears, Idle Tears', from *The Princess*, in *The Poems of Tennyson*, ed. Christopher Ricks (London: Longmans, 1969), 784.

31 ***All art constantly aspires***: Walter Pater, 'The School of Giorgione', in *The Renaissance* (New York: Modern Library, 1919), 111, Pater's emphasis.

31 **because even in heaven**: Lawrence Ferlinghetti, lines from *Pictures of a Gone World* (1955), in *A Coney Island of the Mind* (New York: New Directions, 1958), 88.

32 **a sponge for the zeitgeist**: Mikel Jollet, in 'Such a Perfect Day', in *Bowie on Bowie: Interviews and Encounters with David Bowie*, ed. Sean Egan (Chicago: Chicago Review Press, 2017), 393.

33 **Education, er, education, maybe, education, not**: Accessed at https://www.theguardian.com/education/2010/feb/10/unkindest-cuts-in-university-funding (accessed 2 May 2023).

36 **David Bowie was very into *reading***: See, for example, Jones, *David Bowie*, 400, 411, 443; *Bowie on Bowie*, 150, 153, 270, 281, 347; and John O'Connell's succinct and excellent volume, *Bowie's Books: The Hundred Literary Heroes Who Changed His Life* (London: Bloomsbury, 2019). The 'perfect happiness' quotation appears on the back cover of O'Connell's book.

38 **He found it strangely pleasant**: Natsume Sōseki, *Sanshirō*, trans. Jay Rubin (London: Penguin, 2009), 60.

39 **a book centred on the sun**: Kazuo Ishiguro, *Klara and the Sun* (London: Faber and Faber, 2021), 117 and passim.

39 **Bowie as cloudlike**: See Lindsay Kemp, quoted in Jones, *David Bowie*, 39; and cf. 289.

40 **The sun, for sorrow**: William Shakespeare, *Romeo and Juliet*, Act 5, scene 3, line 316.

40 **Personally it makes me sad**: For further reflections on 'creative non-fiction' and related terms, see Nicholas Royle, 'Creative Critical', *Minnesota Review*, 99 (2022): 80–93.

40 **The sun shone, having no alternative**: Samuel Beckett, *Murphy*, ed. J. C. C. Mays (1938; London: Faber and Faber, 2009), 3.

40 **landscape still pale**: Elizabeth Bowen, *A World of Love* (1955; London: Penguin, 1983), 9.

40 **The fat sun stalls**: Zadie Smith, *NW* (London: Penguin, 2013), 3.

41 **bright book of life**: D. H. Lawrence, 'Why the Novel Matters', in *Phoenix: The Posthumous Papers of D. H. Lawrence*, ed. Edward D. McDonald (New York: Viking, 1972), 535.

41 **inconceivable idea**: Wallace Stevens, *Notes Toward a Supreme Fiction*, in *Collected Poetry and Prose* (n.p.: Library of America, 1997), 329.

41 **a bit of the flesh of God**: Ray Bradbury, 'The Golden Apples of the Sun', in *The Golden Apples of the Sun* (London: Grafton, 1977), 220.

41 **having dinner together**: See https://www.rollingstone.com/music/music-features/alice-cooper-on-his-dinner-with-david-bowie-and-ray-bradbury-92703/ (accessed 2 May 2023).

42 **walk among long dappled grass**: 'The Song of Wandering Aengus', in *The Collected Poems of W. B. Yeats* (London: Macmillan, 1977), 67.

42 **Let go, or be dragged**: David Bowie, quoted in Jones, *David Bowie*, 281.

The undermind (second lecture)

45 **Reading a 'Five book'**: In her autobiography, *The Story of My Life* (London: Pitkins, 1952), Blyton imagines children hungry for more of her work, chanting 'Another Five book, another Five book, another Five book … Another Five book!' (98).

46 **the fire in me now**: Samuel Beckett, *Krapp's Last Tape*, in *The Complete Dramatic Works* (London: Faber and Faber, 1986), 223.

46 **as if I were a dead man**: *The Autobiography of Charles Darwin*, accessed at https://www.gutenberg.org/files/2010/2010-h/2010-h.htm (accessed 2 May 2023).

47 **iron horse**: See Chinua Achebe, *Things Fall Apart* (1958; Oxford: Heinemann, 1986), 97.

48 **sunny pleasure-dome**: Samuel Taylor Coleridge, 'Kubla Khan', in *The Complete Poems*, ed. William Keach (London: Penguin, 1997), 251.

49 **undermind**: I follow Barbara Stoney in preferring to leave this word unhyphenated: see Stoney's *Enid Blyton: The Biography* (Stroud: The History Press, 2008), 146. Stoney includes as an Appendix Blyton's correspondence with Professor Peter McKellar (see 196–205). Here Blyton writes of the 'under-mind', and also offers the 'super-mind' or 'other-mind'. 'One learns to recognise it in other writings,' she goes on to suggest: 'Shakespeare is full of it' (198).

50 **the under-mind works at top speed**: Virginia Woolf, 'The Leaning Tower' (1940), in *The Moment and Other Essays* (1947), accessed at http://www.gutenberg.net.au/ebooks15/1500221h.html#ch18 (accessed 2 May 2023).

53 **the 100 books**: See John O'Connell, *Bowie's Books: The Hundred Literary Heroes Who Changed His Life* (London: Bloomsbury, 2019). Bowie was not, of course, unaware of Enid Blyton's connections with Beckenham. See, for example, his comically incongruous juxtaposition of Blyton with the Velvet Underground, quoted in Dylan Jones, *David Bowie: A Life* (London: Windmill Books, 2018), 182.

53 **snobbery or jealousy**: See Andrew Maunder, *Enid Blyton: A Literary Life* (Cham, Switzerland: Palgrave, 2021), 261.

54 infantile paralysis 'at the time': Blyton, *The Story of My Life*, 122.

54 voracious readers: I reference Bowie's passion for reading in the first lecture, 'Memory of a Free Festival' (above); Blyton discusses her own passion in 'About My Childhood – The Books I Read', in *The Story of My Life*, 47–52.

Telepathy (third lecture)

59 ecstasy of action: Nicholas Tucker, *The Child and the Book: A Psychological and Literary Exploration* (Cambridge: Cambridge University Press, 1981), 113, accessed at https://archive.org/stream/THECHILDANDTHEBOOK/THE%20CHILD%20AND%20THE%20BOOK_djvu.txt (accessed 2 May 2023).

63 the *uncanny way*: *Five Have a Mystery to Solve* (Book 20), 58. A less awkward instance of 'uncanny' appears in *Malory Towers* when the fifth-former Sally remarks that Alicia, another fifth-former, has 'practised that demon-sounding voice till it really sounds quite uncanny'. See *In the Fifth at Malory Towers* (1950; London: Hodder and Stoughton, 2019), 150.

63 'The Man Who Loved Islands': This begins: 'There was a man who loved islands. He was born on one, but it didn't suit him, as there were too many other people on it, besides himself. He wanted an island all of his own: not necessarily to be alone on it, but to make it a world of his own.' 'The Man Who Loved Islands', in *The Collected Short Stories of D. H. Lawrence* (London: Heinemann, 1974), 671–93: here 671. This Lawrentian man sounds like George when she enthuses about her *very own* Kirrin Island, which, nevertheless, she's happy to share with Julian, Dick and Anne. See *Five on a Treasure Island* (Book 1), 18, 21 and passim.

63 the great Leonardo remained like a child: Sigmund Freud, 'Leonardo da Vinci and a Memory of His Childhood', in *The Standard Edition of the Complete Psychological Works of Sigmund Freud*, trans. under the general editorship of James Strachey, in collaboration with Anna Freud, assisted by Alix Strachey and Alan Tyson (London: Vintage, 2001), vol. 11, 127.

63 radically childminded: For this playful sense of 'childminded' I am grateful to John McLeod, who generously shared with me a draft copy of his brilliant essay on Bowie, 'Calamity's Child' (forthcoming in *The Cambridge Companion to David Bowie*, ed. Denis Flannery).

63 that way madness lies: William Shakespeare, *King Lear*, Act 3, scene 4, line 23.

64 the characters make their way forward: See Enid Blyton, *The Story of My Life* (London: Pitkins, 1952), 82–8.

64 And we will leave them there: See *Five Run Away Together* (Book 3), 202.

65 a particularly strong influence: See Blyton, *The Story of My Life*, 48, 52, 82.

66 the 'feel' and 'atmosphere': Blyton, *The Story of My Life*, 52.

66 the *Alice* books are major nineteenth-century telepathy texts: For more on *Alice* and telepathy, permit me to refer to my book *Hélène Cixous: Dreamer, Realist, Analyst, Writing* (Manchester: Manchester University Press, 2021), esp. 110ff. More generally on telepathy in narrative, point of view and so on, see 'The "telepathy effect": Notes toward a reconsideration of narrative fiction', in *The Uncanny* (Manchester: Manchester University Press, 2003), 256–76.

66 You children *feel* this [...] You *think* this too: See Blyton, *The Story of My Life*, 16, 38, 45, 58, 60, 80, 100, 114 and passim.

67 churchgoing: For an exception, see *Five Go Down to the Sea* (Book 12), 46–7.

68 a storyteller, not a preacher: Blyton, *The Story of My Life*, 106.

68 based on the author herself: See Blyton, *The Story of My Life*, 113–14.

69 structure of feeling: Raymond Williams first used this term in his *Preface to Film*, co-authored with Michael Orrom (London: Film Drama, 1954). For an excellent account of 'structures of feeling', see Ben Highmore, 'Formations of Feelings, Constellations of Things', accessed at http://sro.sussex.ac.uk/id/eprint/60215/1/Formations%20of%20Feelings,%20Constellations%20of%20Things.pdf (accessed 2 May 2023).

70 Author of all being [...] Author of this universe: John Milton, *Paradise Lost*, ed. Gordon Teskey (New York: Norton, 2005), Book 3, line 374; Book 8, line 360.

71 when language *goes on holiday*: Ludwig Wittgenstein, *Philosophische Untersuchungen / Philosophical Investigations*, trans. G. E. M. Anscombe, P. M. S. Hacker and Joachim Schulte, rev. 4th edn by Hacker and Schulte (Oxford: Wiley-Blackwell, 2009), section 38; 23/23e. In fact, Wittgenstein's remarks are more bound up with notions of magical thinking, telepathy and occultism than readers might assume. He focuses on 'the conception of naming as a process that is, so to speak, occult'. He reflects on how philosophers '[try] to fathom' the '*strange* connection of a word with an object' (Wittgenstein's emphasis) and then observes: 'philosophical problems arise when language *goes on holiday*' (his emphasis). The original German for 'language *goes on holiday*' is 'die Sprache *feiert*', literally when language celebrates, revels, parties. Is the translation itself not in some sense an example of 'language on holiday'? Wittgenstein's translators appear to share something of Dick's enthusiasm at the beginning of *Five Have a Mystery to Solve*: 'The nicest word in the English language is holidays!' (*Famous Five*, vol. 20: 1).

71 **like a very good dinner**: Blyton, *The Story of My Life*, 52.

72 **propelled into an expectation**: Jean-Luc Nancy, *Listening*, trans. Charlotte Mendell (New York: Fordham University Press, 2007), 66.

72 **fracture everything**: 'Confessions of an Elitist', in *Bowie on Bowie: Interviews and Encounters with David Bowie*, ed. Sean Egan (Chicago: Chicago Review Press, 2017), 89.

73 **a major veerer**: For more on the figure of the veerer, permit me to refer to my *Veering: A Theory of Literature* (Edinburgh: Edinburgh University Press, 2011).

73 **the chameleon poet**: In a letter to his friend Richard Woodhouse (27 October 1818), Keats writes: 'What shocks the virtuous philosop[h]er, delights the camelion Poet. It does no harm from its relish of the dark side of things any more than from its taste for the bright one; because they both end in speculation. A Poet is the most unpoetical of any thing in existence; because he has no Identity [...].' *Letters of John Keats*, ed. Robert Gittings (Oxford: Oxford University Press, 1970), 157.

74 **polyphonico-rhythmic otherness**: David Wills, 'The Solicitation of Deconstruction: If I never see the English ...', *Nanocrit* (June 2022), accessed at https://nanocrit.com/issues/issue16/The-Solicitation-of-Deconstruction-If-I-never-see-the-English (accessed 2 May 2023).

74 **the childhood dog in you**: Cf. Bowie's remark: 'dogs really help kids give something to focus with'. See Dylan Jones, *David Bowie: A Life* (London: Windmill Books, 2018), 442.

74 **ambient menace**: Nicholas Pegg, *The Complete David Bowie*, 7th edn (London: Titan Books, 2016), 108.

75 **I mourn therefore I am**: I borrow this formulation from Jacques Derrida: see '*Istrice 2: Ick bünn all hier*', trans. Peggy Kamuf, in Jacques Derrida, *Points ... Interviews, 1974–1994*, ed. Elisabeth Weber (London: Routledge, 1995), 321.

The time machine (fourth lecture)

76 **her love of annuals**: See Enid Blyton, *The Story of My Life* (London: Pitkins, 1952), 50.

76 **What is the use of a book**: Lewis Carroll, *Alice's Adventures in Wonderland*, in *Alice in Wonderland*, ed. Donald J. Gray, 2nd edn (New York: Norton, 1992), 7.

77 **Mr Forster has the art of saying things**: Virginia Woolf, 'The Art of Fiction' (1927), in *The Moment and Other Essays* (1947), accessed at www.gutenberg.net.au/ebooks15/1500221h.html (accessed 2 May 2023).

77 **a queer feeling**: Blyton, *The Story of My Life*, 69.

78 the Nabokovian sun: For an astute discussion of the presence of Nabokov's *The Gift* in Bowie's 'I'd Rather Be High', see Nicholas Pegg, *The Complete David Bowie*, 7th edn (London: Titan Books, 2016), 126.

79 a kind of *lingophilia*: For more on lingophilia and its discontents, permit me to refer to my essay 'Lingophobia', in *French Thought and Literary Theory in the UK*, ed. Irving Goh (London: Routledge, 2020), 32–45.

80 Novels run on sex: Maud Ellmann, *Elizabeth Bowen: The Shadow Across the Page* (Edinburgh: Edinburgh University Press, 2003), 191.

81 it will become a *red giant*: Leah Kardos proposes the red giant as a figure for talking about that singular star, David Bowie, and his last works: 'To a red giant star, normal rules of engagement no longer apply. The work becomes a cannibalisation, a language of its own in dialogue with itself. Everything that the star is and has been becomes fuel that can be used and burned.' See Kardos, *Blackstar Theory: The Last Works of David Bowie* (London: Bloomsbury, 2022), 63.

82 I have completed the construction: Franz Kafka, 'The Burrow', trans. Willa and Edwin Muir, in *The Collected Short Stories of Franz Kafka*, ed. Nahum N. Glatzer (London: Penguin, 1988), 325.

83 literary nationality: See Hélène Cixous and Mireille Calle-Gruber, *Rootprints: Memory and Life Writing*, trans. Eric Prenowitz (London: Routledge, 1997), 204.

84 moving about in worlds not realised: William Wordsworth, Intimations 'Ode', in *William Wordsworth*, ed. Stephen Gill (Oxford: Oxford University Press, 1984), 301.

85 deferred obedience: See *Totem and Taboo* (1913), in *The Standard Edition of the Complete Psychological Works of Sigmund Freud*, trans. under the general editorship of James Strachey, in collaboration with Anna Freud, assisted by Alix Strachey and Alan Tyson (London: Vintage, 2001), vol. 13, 143, 145.

85 H. G. Wells clerks: Hanif Kureishi, quoted in Dylan Jones, *David Bowie: A Life* (London: Windmill Books, 2018), 19. Some years younger than Bowie, Kureishi also went to Bromley Tech.

86 nothing other than watered-down magic: This is an important aspect of *Totem and Taboo* (in *The Standard Edition*, vol. 13, 1–162); but the quoted phrase is actually from an earlier essay, 'Psychical (or Mental) Treatment' (1905), in *The Standard Edition*, vol. 7, 283.

86 All women become like their mothers: Oscar Wilde, *The Importance of Being Earnest*, in *The Importance of Being Earnest and Related Writings*, ed. Joseph Bristow (London: Routledge, 1992), 44.

86 a book could be like a bomb: See Elizabeth Bowen, 'Rider Haggard: *She*', in *The Mulberry Tree: Writings of Elizabeth Bowen*, ed. Hermione Lee (London: Virago, 1986), 250.

86 **you can also blow them into existence**: See Elizabeth Bowen, 'Mysterious Kôr', in *Collected Stories* (New York: Everyman's Library, 2019), 800.

87 **echo-track[s] of sensation**: Bowen, 'Rider Haggard: *She*', in *The Mulberry Tree*, 250.

87 **recalling an incident very vividly**: H. G. Wells, *The Time Machine: An Invention* (1895; Ware, Hertfordshire: Wordsworth Classics, 2017), 33. *The Time Machine* is also, of course, a remarkable text on the topic of the sun, as well as the Underworld that is solely accessed by 'wells' (pun doubtless intended).

87 **To die will be an awfully big adventure**: J. M. Barrie, *Peter Pan* (1911), accessed at https://www.gutenberg.org/files/16/16-h/16-h.htm (accessed 2 May 2023).

88 **The phrase 'golden years' appears to echo**: See H. G. Wells, 'The Chronic Argonauts', in *The Time Machine and Other Works* (Ware, Hertfordshire: Wordsworth Editions, 2017), 334.

The Croydon Bookshop (fifth lecture)

90 **could hear what wasn't there**: Bruce Robb, quoted in Dylan Jones, *David Bowie: A Life* (London: Windmill Books, 2018), 236.

90 **you hear your own body resonate**: Jean-Luc Nancy, *Listening*, trans. Charlotte Mendell (New York: Fordham University Press, 2007), 21.

90 **Sea, and hill, and wood**: Samuel Taylor Coleridge, 'Frost at Midnight', in *The Complete Poems*, ed. William Keach (London: Penguin, 1997), 231.

90 **dippable-into book**: Enid Blyton, *The Story of My Life* (London: Pitkins, 1952), 50. In fact, as she points out, the phrase was originally her brother's.

91 **Our past life is there**: Henri Bergson, 'Dreams' (1901), in *Mind-Energy: Lectures and Essays*, trans. H. Wildon Carr (New York: Henry Holt, 1920), 116; quoted in Randall Stevenson, *Reading the Times: Temporality and History in Twentieth Century Fiction* (Edinburgh: Edinburgh University Press, 2017), 97. Bergson goes on: 'But the memories which are preserved in these obscure depths are for us in the state of invisible phantoms. They aspire, perhaps, to the light' (116).

91 **paid extra**: On the question of meaning and the proliferation of the meanings of words, Humpty Dumpty tells Alice: 'When I make a word do a lot of work like that, I always pay it extra.' See Lewis Carroll, *Through the Looking-Glass and What Alice Found There*, in *Alice in Wonderland*, ed. Donald J. Gray, 2nd edn (New York: Norton, 1992), 164.

92 **atque in perpetuum:** Poem 101, in Catullus, *The Complete Poems*, trans. Guy Lee (Oxford: Oxford World's Classics, 1990), 138–41. Lee translates the line 'And forever, brother, greetings and farewell' (141). For a remarkable extended meditation on translating Poem 101, see Anne Carson, *Nox* (New York: New Directions, 2010).

94 **a snake is always uncanny**: See Freud's introductory lecture on 'Anxiety', in *The Standard Edition of the Complete Psychological Works of Sigmund Freud*, trans. under the general editorship of James Strachey, in collaboration with Anna Freud, assisted by Alix Strachey and Alan Tyson (London: Vintage, 2001), vol. 16, 399.

94 **'white supremacy'**: This is not Blyton's term, of course, but the idea is implicit here and elsewhere in her writings, as a disturbing aspect of her enthusiasm for what Andrew Maunder circumspectly calls 'the glamour of the colonial project': see Maunder, *Enid Blyton: A Literary Life* (Cham, Switzerland: Palgrave Macmillan, 2021), 62.

94 **gentle pressure**: Enid Blyton, *The River of Adventure* (1955; London: Macmillan, 2007), 128.

95 **avant-garde-a-clue**: In a 1997 interview with Linda Laban, Bowie uses the phrase 'avant-garde-a-clue' as if interchangeably with 'esoteric' and 'arty': see 'Bowie Retrospective', in *Bowie on Bowie: Interviews and Encounters with David Bowie*, ed. Sean Egan (Chicago: Chicago Review Press, 2017), 337. But this playful portmanteau is also suggestive of the undermind, adventuring into the unknown and, of course, laughter.

96 ***The Rubáiyát of Omar Khayyám***: All quotations are from the first edition of 1859 – not that I possess a copy of that volume. Very few copies of the original print run of 250 have survived and when one of them goes up for auction it commands a huge sum. The 1859 text is, however, the usual go-to version online, for example at https://www.omarkhayyamrubaiyat.com/text.htm (accessed 2 May 2023).

98 **thought to be called Linda**: See Frank O'Hara, 'The Day Lady Died', in *The Collected Poems of Frank O'Hara*, ed. Donald Allen (New York: Alfred A. Knopf, 1971), 325.

99 **I'm Nobody!**: *The Complete Poems of Emily Dickinson*, ed. Thomas H. Johnson (London: Faber and Faber, 1970), 133.

101 **eight days straight**: Jones, *David Bowie*, 37.

102 **It was the same for Bowie**: See 'Now Where Did I Put Those Tunes?' in *Bowie on Bowie*, 342.

102 **I loathe the idea of school**: *The Letters of D. H. Lawrence*, vol. 1: *1901–13*, ed. James T. Boulton (Cambridge: Cambridge University Press, 1979), 367.

102 **losing himself as a young man**: See Foreword to *Collected Poems* (1928), in *The Complete Poems of D. H. Lawrence*, ed. Vivian de Sola Pinto and F. Warren Roberts (New York: Viking, 1971), 849–52.

103 **I can't bear art that you can walk around and admire**: Letter to Carlo Linati (22 January 1925), in *The Letters of D. H. Lawrence*, vol. 5: *March 1924–March 1927*, ed. James T. Boulton and Lyndeth Vasey (Cambridge: Cambridge University Press, 1989), 201.

104 **a really beautiful day in the park**: David Bowie, quoted in Nicholas Pegg, *The Complete David Bowie*, 7th edn (London: Titan Books, 2016), 162.

104 **to Hermione, to Peter**: The proliferation of names is supposed to suggest the openness of the party. 'Letter to Hermione' – also on the second *David Bowie* album – is perhaps Bowie's most crystalline love song. Peter is evoked in 'Memory of a Free Festival': 'Peter tried to climb aboard but the captain shook his head …' In a strange but characteristic detail, the narrative speaks of 'climb[ing] aboard' without ever specifying what it is that one might or might not climb. This way to the mysterious sun machine!

105 **capacities of harnessing, mobilization and exaltation**: Nancy, *Listening*, 54.

105 **As Chris O'Leary has noted**: See his excellent 'Pushing Ahead of the Dame', accessed at https://bowiesongs.wordpress.com/?s=quicksand (accessed 2 May 2023).

Picture break

106 ***dum scribo***: I first came across this phrase in the eponymous essay on Descartes by Jean-Luc Nancy, trans. Ian McLeod, *Oxford Literary Review*, 3.2 (1978): 6–21.

106 **corny and goonish**: These are David Bowie's terms, quoted in Dylan Jones, *David Bowie: A Life* (London: Windmill Books, 2018), 469, 343. Bowie's love of acting stupid and other daft stuff is evident in his affection for comics such as *The Beano* and *Viz*, and novels such as John Kennedy Toole's *A Confederacy of Dunces* and Spike Milligan's *Puckoon*. See John O'Connell. *Bowie's Books: The Hundred Literary Heroes Who Changed His Life* (London: Bloomsbury, 2019), 59, 135, 54–5 and 250–1 respectively. But it is also evident in his attachment to Oogie and Bones Boy – those 'ridiculous puppets made out of ping-pong balls or somesuch' from *The Uncle Floyd Show* which nonetheless become key characters in the zany but moving song 'Slip Away' (on *Heathen*). Watching these puppets, Bowie recalls, 'We would be on the floor it was so funny.' See 'Rock's Heathen Speaks: Interview with David Bowie', 16 June 2002, accessed at http://www.concertlivewire.com/interviews/bowie.htm (accessed 2 May 2023).

107 **under the covers listening to Radio Luxembourg**: See Jones, *David Bowie*, 14.

108 Stephen Finer's working practice involves long hours: The National Portrait Gallery wording at https://www.npg.org.uk/collections/search/portrait/mw09556/David-Bowie (accessed 2 May 2023) can also be found in Robin Gibson, *The Portrait Now* (London: National Portrait Gallery, 1993), 103.

109 scary, most experimental: David Bowie, quoted in Jones, *David Bowie*, 397.

109 I am definitely not a minimalist: David Bowie, in 'The Artful Codger', in *Bowie on Bowie: Interviews and Encounters with David Bowie*, ed. Sean Egan (Chicago: Chicago Review Press, 2017), 283.

109 I want to sound like that looks: David Bowie, quoted in Jones, *David Bowie*, xii. Bowie's personal art collection included Auerbach's 'Head of Gerda Boehm' (1967). Stephen told me that his own friendship with Auerbach goes back many years; Auerbach painted two portraits of Finer in 1973–74.

109 It's very similar to the way: David Bowie, quoted in Jones, *David Bowie*, 411.

110 the single, immediately identifiable, square 'artefact' [...] of the moment: For this phrasing, I am almost entirely indebted to my friend Matthew Frost.

110 he took Polaroid pictures of every member of the band: See Jones, *David Bowie*, 463.

111 stream of consciousness: See *Bowie on Bowie*, 269.

112 he seemed to drop people: See Jones, *David Bowie*, 380.

112 that rather terrible thing: Roland Barthes, *Camera Lucida: Reflections on Photography*, trans. Richard Howard (London: Flamingo, 1984), 9.

112 the great singer of isolation: This seems to have been well established in Bowie from early on. It's evident, I think, in the mixing of the 'aloft' and 'lonely' that he encountered in the music of Neil Young. When Bowie got the album *I've Been Waiting For You* in 1969, he recalls, 'I was dazzled by the overall complexity of sound. It was so majestic but aloft or lonely sounding at the same time.' See 'Rock's Heathen Speaks: Interview with David Bowie', 16 June 2002, accessed at http://www.concertlivewire.com/interviews/bowie.htm (accessed 2 May 2023).

112 the sleeve notes to *The Man Who Sold the World*: The phrase 'vulnerable sensuality' appears on the sleeve of the RCA 1972 reissue of the album.

113 It was all about focus: Jones, *David Bowie*, 423.

113 Bowie's smile and laughter: Bowie's humour and easy laughter consistently feature in Dylan Jones's biography; see, for example, 323, 337, 339, 387, 410.

113 hand on hip: Cf. Nick Kent's reminiscence about the Spiders from Mars concert in London in February 1972, when the sound system fails – a terrible silence – and Bowie has to do something with it: 'what he did was put his guitar down, put his hands on his hips in this really camp way, and proceeded to give us all a rundown of what he was wearing. OK, boots Anello and Davide, trousers Freddie Burretti … He just did this camp routine, and then after about a minute the sound came back on. In that minute, Ziggy Stardust's destiny was manifest.' See Jones, *David Bowie*, 111–12.

What a big memory you have, Grandmother! (sixth lecture)

115 There, in the chords and melodies: 'Rock's Heathen Speaks: Interview with David Bowie', 16 June 2002, accessed at http://www.concertlivewire.com/interviews/bowie.htm (accessed 2 May 2023).

116 all I have is a voice: W. H. Auden, 'September 1, 1939', in *Selected Poems*, ed. Edward Mendelson (London: Faber and Faber, 1979), 88 (emphasis added).

117 we have an interval: Walter Pater, 'Conclusion', in *The Renaissance* (New York: Modern Library, 1919), 198.

118 Are you still living in such a way: Padgett Powell, *The Interrogative Mood: A Novel?* (London: Serpent's Tail, 2009), 158. I discuss Powell's remarkable book ('a novel?') at greater length in 'Interrogating Twilight', in *Literary Theories of Uncertainty*, ed. Mette Leonard Høeg (London: Bloomsbury, 2021), 178–99.

118 what is real in our lives: Pater, 'Conclusion', 196.

120 this short day of frost and sun: Pater, 'Conclusion', 197.

121 the only people for me are the mad ones: Jack Kerouac, *On the Road* (1957; London: Penguin, 2011), 7.

121 To burn always with this hard, gemlike flame: Pater, 'Conclusion', 197.

123 tantalising chinks: Nicholas Pegg, *The Complete David Bowie*, 7th edn (London: Titan Books, 2016), 173.

123 St Augustine wonders: See Saint Augustine, *Confessions*, trans. Henry Chadwick (Oxford: Oxford University Press, 1991), 180–1ff.

123 authenticating: As Derrida says, 'I do not seek to establish any kind of authenticity': see 'Limited Inc a b c …', trans. Samuel Weber, in Jacques Derrida, *Limited Inc.* (Evanston, IL: Northwestern University Press, 1988), 55.

124–5 Did she have a love affair with another woman?: Andrew Maunder, *Enid Blyton: A Literary Life* (Cham, Switzerland: Palgrave Macmillan, 2021), 11.

125 Remember me: William Shakespeare, *Hamlet*, Act 1, scene 5, line 96.

But the clouds (seventh lecture)

130 **According to George MacDonald it is something shared**: MacDonald remarks: 'The true fairytale is, to my mind, very like the sonata.' See 'The Fantastic Imagination', in *The Complete Fairy Tales*, ed. U. C. Knoepflmacher (London: Penguin, 1999), 8–9.

131 **cast / Down in the flood of remembrance**: 'Piano' (1913), in *The Complete Poems of D. H. Lawrence*, ed. Vivian de Sola Pinto and F. Warren Roberts (New York: Viking, 1971), 148.

131 **All is for the best**: See Voltaire, *Candide, or Optimism*, trans. Theo Cuffe (London: Penguin, 2006). Voltaire's novel is, of course, a sustained satirical rejection of the idea (embodied by the Leibnizian Pangloss). Candide's own conclusive view, at once resigned and enigmatic, is that 'we must cultivate our garden' (94).

131 **All things are possible**: The King James Bible has: 'All things are possible to him that believeth' (Mark 9:23).

131 ***a prospective*, not a retrospective thinker**: See Paul de Man, 'Introduction to the Poetry of John Keats', in *Critical Writings 1953–1978*, ed. Lindsay Waters (Minneapolis: University of Minnesota Press, 1989), 192.

132 **as good as I can possibly make it**: David Bowie, quoted in Dylan Jones, *David Bowie: A Life* (London: Windmill Books, 2018), 461.

132 **I'm not hungry for the past**: David Bowie, quoted in Jones, *David Bowie*, 404.

132 **Tears, Idle Tears**: Alfred Tennyson, 'Tears, Idle Tears', from *The Princess*, in *The Poems of Tennyson*, ed. Christopher Ricks (London: Longmans, 1969), 784–6.

133 **I've read the report and I find it difficult to find anything not to like**: See 'Medical waste plant is given the go-ahead', *The Argus*, 16 January 2019, accessed at https://www.theargus.co.uk/news/17363223.medical-waste-plant-given-go-ahead/ (accessed 2 May 2023).

134 **how profoundly 'regret' features**: I set aside here consideration of *Hours …* (1999), an album that is doubtless concerned with the idea of regret but – with the exception of 'Thursday's Child' and 'Seven' – seems to me among Bowie's less notable and less affecting works.

134 **fuck with the fabric of time**: Tony Visconti was speaking specifically about the Eventide harmoniser used for the drum sound on *Low*, but it's a phrase that can be extended to cover all the other technological possibilities used in the studio recording of a David Bowie song. See 'Tony Visconti on Berlin', interview at http://www.bowiewonderworld.com/features/tvuncut.htm (accessed 2 May 2023).

135 **I am afraid to think what I have done**: William Shakespeare, *Macbeth*, Act 2, scene 2, line 60.

135 What's done cannot be undone: *Macbeth*, Act 5, scene 1, line 50.

138 Extraordinary! Wonderful! Fascinating! Queer!: This is the refrain of the title-poem 'Oh, Dear, Dear!', in Ronald Frankau, *'Oh, Dear, Dear!' Poems and Stories for Real Children* (London: Frederick Warne, 1929), 3–9.

144 Have you not sometimes seen clouds: Aristophanes, *The Clouds*, accessed at http://classics.mit.edu/Aristophanes/clouds.html (accessed 2 May 2023).

144 Sometimes we see a cloud that's dragonish: William Shakespeare, *Antony and Cleopatra*, Act 4, scene 14, lines 3–4.

145 '… but the clouds …': Samuel Beckett, *The Complete Dramatic Works* (London: Faber and Faber, 1986), 415–22.

145–6 The death of friends: W. B. Yeats, 'The Tower', in *The Collected Poems of W. B. Yeats* (London: Macmillan, 1977), 224–5.

Fairy (eighth lecture)

147 The creator too is blind: Wallace Stevens, 'Negation', in *Collected Poetry and Prose* (n.p.: Library of America, 1997), 82.

147 an old chaos of the sun: Wallace Stevens, 'Sunday Morning', in *Collected Poetry and Prose*, 56.

148 on an Olympic scale: Mole here appears to be conflating the Olympic games with a reference to the gigantic molehill of Mount Olympus evoked by Laertes, standing in his sister's grave, at the end of Shakespeare's *Hamlet*: 'Now pile your dust upon the quick and dead, / Till of this flat a mountain you have made / To o'ertop old Pelion or the skyish head / Of blue Olympus' (Act 5, scene 1, lines 203–6).

149 the sort of melody that people will use: Paul Morley, *The Age of Bowie: How David Bowie Made a World of Difference* (London: Simon and Schuster, 2016), 231.

149 a singular moral function – that of provoking unease: Angela Carter, Afterword to *Fireworks*, in *Burning Your Boats: Collected Short Stories* (London: Vintage, 1996), 459.

149 I sometimes find her long-ago voice: Enid Blyton, *The Story of My Life* (London: Pitkins, 1952), 106.

150 I know that voice: William Shakespeare, *King Lear*, Act 4, scene 5, line 105.

150 the trick of that voice: *King Lear*, Act 4, scene 5, line 113.

150 ruined piece of nature: *King Lear*, Act 4, scene 5, line 139.

150 Methinks thy voice is altered: *King Lear*, Act 4, scene 5, line 10.

151 Oh, my Satsuma San: 'Happy Jappy Soldier Man: Japanese War Song', words by Paul West, music by John W. Bratton (New York and

London: M. Witmark, 1914). The publisher tells us that this version of the song has been 'Sung with Great Success by Eleanor Falk'.

152 **Lethe-wards**: 'Ode to a Nightingale', in *The Poems of John Keats*, ed. John Stillinger (London: Heinemann, 1978), 369.

153 **No one who has ever known his grandmother**: Eric Berne, *What Do You Say After You Say Hello? The Psychology of Human Destiny* (London: Corgi, 1975), 378.

153 **at least twelve times**: Blyton, *The Story of My Life*, 52.

154 **the 'strange "feel"' of MacDonald's book**: Blyton, *The Story of My Life*, 52.

154 **Always go a little further into the water**: David Bowie, quoted by Rob Harvilla, https://www.theringer.com/music/2018/1/8/16861842/last-five-years-bowie-documentary (accessed 2 May 2023).

155 **never remotely interested in actually going into space**: As Bowie once observed: 'I wouldn't dream of getting on a spaceship. It would scare the shit out of me.' Quoted by Rob Harvilla, www.theringer.com/music/2018/1/8/16861842/last-five-years-bowie-documentary (accessed 2 May 2023). As is well known, Bowie also had for many years a fear of flying on aeroplanes; hence, for example, the long train journey from Seattle to Phoenix which I discuss later.

155 **And haply the Queen-Moon**: 'Ode to a Nightingale', in *The Poems of John Keats*, 370.

155 **the night sky in Hampstead**: In a sort of ghostly Keatsian fashion, in the late 1960s David Bowie liked to go UFO spotting on Hampstead Heath; John O'Connell notes a link here with the line about 'scan[ning] the skies with rainbow eyes' in 'Memory of a Free Festival'. See O'Connell, *Bowie's Books: The Hundred Literary Heroes Who Changed His Life* (London: Bloomsbury, 2019), 181.

157 **Not to discriminate every moment some passionate attitude**: Walter Pater, 'Conclusion', in *The Renaissance* (New York: Modern Library, 1919), 197.

157 **a general retreat from even thinking**: Marina Warner, *Fairy Tale: A Very Short Introduction* (Oxford: Oxford University Press, 2018), 97.

157–8 **The impenetrability of destiny and the helplessness of humans**: Warner, *Fairy Tale*, 98.

158 **the teller of fairy tales**: Walter Benjamin, 'The Storyteller', trans. Harry Zohn, in *Illuminations: Essays and Reflections*, ed. Hannah Arendt (New York: Schocken Books, 1969), 102.

158 **oft-times hath**: 'Ode to a Nightingale', in *The Poems of John Keats*, 371.

158 **Forlorn! [...] deceiving elf**: 'Ode to a Nightingale', in *The Poems of John Keats*, 371–2.

158 **The bastard! He doesn't exist!**: Samuel Beckett, *Endgame*, in *The Complete Dramatic Works* (London: Faber and Faber, 1986), 119.

159 maternal sounds: Wallace Stevens, *An Ordinary Evening in New Haven*, in *Collected Poetry and Prose*, 411.

159 The semiotic: The semiotic is about sounds, rhythm and tone and the maternal body, *before* the imposition of fixed sense and meaning. See Julia Kristeva, *Desire in Language: A Semiotic Approach to Literature and Art*, trans. Thomas Gora, Alice Jardine and Leon S. Roudiez (1969; New York: Columbia University Press, 1980), and *Revolution in Poetic Language*, trans. Margaret Waller (1974; New York: Columbia University Press, 1984).

159 a landscape etching by Alphonse Legros: see Pater, *The Renaissance*, 111. I discuss this example in 'The Literary Turn', in *Veering: A Theory of Literature* (Edinburgh: Edinburgh University Press, 2011), 103–4.

160 anachronism is the law: Playing with this law is at the heart of David Bowie's music. It seems indeed to have been an aspect of his experience as a child: 'even when I was a kid, I would write about "old and other times" as though I had a lot of years behind me'. 'Rock's Heathen Speaks: Interview with David Bowie', 16 June 2002, accessed at http://www.concertlivewire.com/interviews/bowie.htm (accessed 2 May 2023).

162 goes even now out at the portal: William Shakespeare, *Hamlet*, Act 3, scene 4, line141.

163 the fiery portal of the east: William Shakespeare, *Richard II*, Act 3, scene 3, line 65.

163 clothed in a misty ray: 'The Wanderings of Oisin', in *The Collected Poems of W. B. Yeats* (London: Macmillan, 1977), 426.

163 I would we were changed to white birds: 'The White Birds', in *The Collected Poems of W. B. Yeats*, 47.

Coda

166 at Bromley Register Office: This was also, of course, where David Bowie first got married (to Angie Barnett, in 1970).

166 the loveliest Easter that ever was: Enid Blyton, quoted in Barbara Stoney, *Enid Blyton: The Biography* (Stroud: The History Press, 2008), 53.

166 Ethel's Wharf: Technically speaking, this is Terminal Groyne TV 48800 98205. The alternative name (an anagram of Lethe's wharf) appears in *An English Guide to Birdwatching* (Brighton: Myriad, 2017), 211ff.

168 I couldn't understand the lyrics: David Bowie, quoted in Dylan Jones, *David Bowie: A Life* (London: Windmill Books, 2018), 10.

Notes

Part III Typewriter

175 **immune downs**: Elizabeth Bowen, 'When Ivy Gripped the Steps', in *Collected Stories* (New York: Everyman's Library, 2019), 775.

177 **madness in the family**: In his *David Bowie: A Life* (London: Windmill Books, 2018), and in the Afterword (511–16) especially, Dylan Jones gives quite a bit of attention to this topic. His 'Was there, wasn't there?' approach tends to elide something more fundamental: there is always 'madness in the family', *families are crazy*.

179 **Speedily, yet softly, she walked down the hill**: George MacDonald, *The Princess and the Goblin* (London: Puffin Classics, 2016), 105.

180 **I do not write for children**: George MacDonald, 'The Fantastic Imagination', in *The Complete Fairy Tales*, ed. U. C. Knoepflmacher (London: Penguin, 1999), 7.

185 **with eyes as dark as the mines**: MacDonald, *The Princess and the Goblin*, 36.

Part IV Strangers meet we when

191–2 **We started off on Monday April 24th 1911**: Lola Onslow, *May 6th 1911, Paris and Swiss Journal* (unpublished). Further quotations are from this ms.

194–5 **May God be praised for woman**: 'On Woman', in *The Collected Poems of W. B. Yeats* (London: Macmillan, 1977), 164–5.

197 **There is something very fascinating about the study of faces**: Irma Blood, *Faces and How to Read Them* (London: C. Arthur Pearson, 1920), 7.

198 **Many people are possessed of a great fondness**: Blood, *Faces and How to Read Them*, 70–1.

199 **cysted**: My publisher asked me to provide some explanation for this word. I don't think I can very well; but it might be helpful to note that I talk about 'a "me"-cyst, a secret cyst, a hollow or cistern or crypt of "me" in "me"' in 'Protective Mimicry: Reflections on the Novel Today', in *Secrecy and Community in 21st-Century Fiction*, ed. María J. López and Pilar Villar-Argáiz (London: Bloomsbury, 2021), 44. There are connections here too with Jean-Luc Nancy's evocations of the 'hollow' or 'resonance chamber' and the 'drum' that is 'the space of the listening body'; see Jean-Luc Nancy, *Listening*, trans. Charlotte Mendell (New York: Fordham University Press, 2007), 38, 42.

Discography
Songs and music in order of appearance in the lectures

David Bowie, 'Memory of a Free Festival' (1969), from *Space Oddity* (2019 mix).
David Bowie, 'Space Oddity' (1969), from *Space Oddity* (2019 mix).
Johann Sebastian Bach, Concerto for Two Violins in D minor, perf. Christian Ferras and Yehudi Menuhin (1960).
David Bowie, 'There is a Happy Land', from *David Bowie* (1967).
David Bowie, 'When I'm Five' (1968), from *The 'Mercury' Demos* (with John 'Hutch' Hutchinson) (2019).
David Bowie, 'All the Madmen' (1971), from *The Man Who Sold the World* (2015 remaster).
Charles Mingus, 'Goodbye Pork Pie Hat', from *Mingus Ah Um* (1959).
Frédéric Chopin, Nocturne in E flat, Op. 9, No. 2, from *Chopin Nocturnes*, perf. François Chaplin (2010).
David Bowie, 'Golden Years' (1976), from *Station to Station* (2016 remaster).
David Bowie, 'Station to Station' (1976), from *Station to Station* (2016 remaster).
David Bowie, 'Quicksand' (1971), from *Hunky Dory* (2015 remaster).
David Bowie, 'Five Years' (1972), from *The Rise and Fall of Ziggy Stardust and the Spiders from Mars* (2015 remaster).
David Bowie, 'The Prettiest Star' (1973), from *Aladdin Sane* (2013 remaster).
Ludwig van Beethoven, 'Moonlight' sonata, from *Beethoven: The Piano Sonatas*, perf. Daniel Barenboim (1999).
Nick Penny, recording of nightingale song (2008), accessed at https://www.youtube.com/watch?v=BTkZRO-FYTM (accessed 2 May 2023).
David Bowie, 'Absolute Beginners' (1986), from *Nothing Has Changed* (2014).
David Bowie, 'Drive-In Saturday' (1973), from *Aladdin Sane* (2013 remaster).

Acknowledgements

I have always found this peritextual genre – 'Acknowledgements' – the most difficult to write. Where to begin? Or end? There is an expectation of conventionality and politeness, but should the Acknowledgements not also attempt – perhaps in quite strange and unexpected ways – to respond to the singular character of what the book has, thanks to those acknowledged, sought to do?

Acknowledgements are quicksand. The book would like to disappear into them.

My deepest gratitude is to my wife Jinan, and to my children – Augustus, William, Elena, Alexi and Sebastian – for keeping me crazy. *The Sun Machine* could not have been written without them.

Huge thanks to Matthew Frost, my editor at Manchester. His enthusiasm and support, his thoughtfulness, knowledge and laughter have been integral to this project. The book is dedicated to him.

My heartfelt gratitude, also, to Peter Boxall – not only for providing the Afterword, but for the many conversations we have had about this book in the process of its assemblage. I am immensely grateful for his thoughts and comments on the manuscript – from the earliest to the final draft.

Other friends offered astute and helpful reflections on earlier drafts or specific aspects of the book: I warmly thank Andrew

Bennett, Naomi Booth, Abi Curtis, Tom Dutoit, Maud Ellmann, Jackie Hall, Ben Hilton, Gabriel Josipovici, Candida Lacey, Allan Marriott-Smith, Rob Penhallurick, Pam Thurschwell, Tamar Wang and Sarah Wood.

My memories of listening to Bowie in the mid-1970s are indissociably linked to my friend Colin Mackrell. He was there with me at my first Bowie concert in May 1976 and he was also able to confirm the second we went to, at Earl's Court Arena, in the summer of 1978. My love and lifelong thanks to him.

This book is also in loving memory of Vanessa Royle (1966–2018), who shared my love of Bowie's music and understood more than she could ever say.

I am grateful to many others who helped me think about what I was doing in the process of working on this project: Emily Baker, Rachel Bowlby, Hélène Cixous, Rowan Deer, Mat Dimmock, Stephen Finer, Denis Flannery, Duncan Fraser, Simon Glendinning, Jeff Hilson, Sarah Jonckheere, Leah Kardos, Richard Madden, Elissa Marder, Ulrika Maude, John McLeod, Michael Morgan, Timothy Morton, Steve Pearce, Eric Prenowitz, Minoli Salgado, Nick Smith, Bethan Stevens, Becky Thomas, Tom Tomaszewski, Rick Watson and Mariam Zia.

In addition, I would like to express my gratitude to the University of Sussex, where I had the honour and great pleasure of working for more than twenty years. Despite the institutional difficulties of recent times, the School of English (lately amalgamated into the School of Media, Arts and Humanities) was an amazing place to teach and pursue research. I feel enormously indebted to all my colleagues and to all the students who helped make it such a brilliant place to be.

Mention must also be made here of a key counter-institution in my life, the *Oxford Literary Review*. For their friendship, writing and collaboration, I am grateful, as ever, to my co-editors on the journal: Geoff Bennington, Tim Clark, Michael Naas and Peggy Kamuf.

Acknowledgements

One of the most remarkable spots in the town of Seaford where I live is the thirteenth-century undercroft called the Crypt, hidden in an otherwise nondescript building on Church Street. My special thanks to Chris Goode for inviting me to Seaford LitFest at the Crypt in October 2021 and giving me an opportunity to speak publicly about this book for the first time. Additional thanks to Peter Boxall (once again) for being my interlocutor on that occasion. It means a great deal to me that this book, like *Quilt* (in 2010), *An English Guide to Birdwatching* (in 2017) and *Mother* (in February 2020), had its initial airing in the underground intimacy and wonderful acoustics of the Crypt.

Finally, I would like to say a few words about Hilary Mantel, who died on 22 September 2022. We never met in person, but we had some email exchanges over the past few years. I will always feel warmly grateful for her generous support and appreciation of *Mother: A Memoir* (2020), and for her deepening my interest in the enigmatic world of memoir-writing. The pandemic intervened, but we had discussed the possibility of meeting up in Devon or Sussex. We also corresponded on the topic of becoming Irish: we shared a sense of dismay at various aspects of recent British history and the UK government.

In what transpired to be my last email to her (4 September 2021), I expressed my admiration for the interview in *la Repubblica* that had been reported that morning in *The Guardian*, and I sent her a quick fiction that I'd written in December 2019. I'd read this out at the annual Quick Fictions event at the University of Sussex the day before Boris Johnson's so-called landslide victory in the UK general election. (It was a 'landslide' for the Conservatives on the basis of their getting just 43.6% of the vote.) To Hilary, on 4 September 2021, I wrote:

> December 2019 feels a good while ago – and indeed the very brief piece I wrote (pasted below) felt spectacularly anachronistic within 24 hours of being written – but I send it here because it's about my mother (whom you sort of know) and it's so apropos what you have said about BJ.

And I duly pasted the text:

> *On the Eve of the UK General Election, 11 December 2019*
>
> We are living in uncertain times. But it is absolutely certain in my mind that if my mother were still alive, she would speak out against what George Monbiot calls the billionaire press. She would rail against its collusion with the Conservative Party and against all the machinations by which the British electorate have been, for forty years and more, twisted and lied to and fooled into believing in a deluded death-driven vision of the UK. She would take Boris Johnson by his mangey lifeless mane and dunk his head repeatedly in a barrel of Garden Bridge river-water for a public confession. I'm convinced of it. He would be stubborn, evasive, and resistant. And so, in response to his denials of the truth, my mother would be obliged to break over his head bottle after bottle, case after case, of Tignanello from his own sordid supply. She would do this like Bette Davis having a field day. Or like Hamlet, at last acting fast, heading across the North Sea, near the very end of the play. The most heartless, most mendacious British prime minister in history, with his slurry-bucket face of slurs and slurring lies, would be bang to rights, banged to rights. Until he finally produces what my mother wants from him, a brief and simple document: 'I confess, I confess! I am dangerous and unfit to govern. Offer my position to Greta Thunberg. We need to be moving on.'

Hilary's reply, written the same day (4 September 2021), began:

> Not so anachronistic – the hair of Boris gets more peculiar by the day. And he's still unfit for office.

And she went on to talk, in upbeat mode, about our shared interest in seeking Irish citizenship, and mentioned her friend Alison Light, who was also contemplating this move. Hilary's last words to me were about getting together in Ireland: 'It will be quite a party when we all meet up.' As with the descending sun machine, I still think of this as a party to come.

Index

(Note: This is not an index of the undermind. That is a project for the future. This index provides no references for the principal subjects, only for certain of their works – songs or albums by David Bowie, books or stories by Enid Blyton. The tethe implex would suppose the granphantasmata of Lola Onslow throughout.)

Index

Index

Index

Index

EU authorised representative for GPSR:
Easy Access System Europe, Mustamäe tee 50,
10621 Tallinn, Estonia
gpsr.requests@easproject.com

www.ingramcontent.com/pod-product-compliance
Lightning Source LLC
Chambersburg PA
CBHW041956050726
47507CB00032B/399

* 9 7 8 1 5 2 6 1 7 3 6 3 8 *